LAWRENCE DURRELL
and *The Alexandria Quartet*

UNIVERSITY OF OKLAHOMA PRESS : NORMAN

LAWRENCE DURRELL
and *The Alexandria Quartet*

ART FOR LOVE'S SAKE

BY ALAN WARREN FRIEDMAN

INTERNATIONAL STANDARD BOOK NUMBER: 0–8061–0871–1

LIBRARY OF CONGRESS CATALOG CARD NUMBER: 69–16728

FOR LAURIE—
who has borne this too

Acknowledgments

I WISH to offer my grateful thanks to the following people, all of whom offered valuable advice or assistance at various stages of manuscript preparation: David J. DeLaura, Richard M. Gollin, Elaine Hopkins, Bruce M. Johnson, Donald Petesch, William Howe Rueckert.

Parts of this study, in somewhat altered form, have appeared previously in *Modern Fiction Studies* and *Wisconsin Studies in Contemporary Literature*. They are reprinted here with grateful acknowledgment to *Modern Fiction Studies*, copyright 1967 by Purdue Research Foundation, Lafayette, Indiana, and The Regents of the University of Wisconsin, *Wisconsin Studies in Contemporary Literature*, the University of Wisconsin Press.

In addition, thanks are due to the following for their kind permission to quote from the works indicated:

Mary Graham Lund, "The Alexandrian Projection," *Antioch Review*, Vol. XXI, No. 2 (Summer, 1961).

The Twentieth Century Novel, by Joseph Warren Beach. Copyright, 1932, by The Century Co. Renewed, 1960, by Appleton-Century-Crofts, Inc. Reprinted by permission of Appleton-Century-Crofts, Division of Meredith Corporation.

Curtis Cate, "Lawrence Durrell," *Atlantic Monthly*, Vol. CCVIII (December, 1961).

The Rhetoric of Fiction, by Wayne C. Booth. Chicago and London, The University of Chicago Press, 1961.

Lawrence Durrell, by John Unterecker. New York and London, Columbia University Press, 1964.

David Higham Associates, Ltd.: (1) *Joseph Conrad: A Personal Remembrance*, by Ford Madox Ford. London, Duckworth, 1924 (2) *The English Novel*, by Walter Allen. Harmondsworth, Penguin Books, 1954.

Alexandria: A History and A Guide, by E. M. Forster. New York, Doubleday, 1961.

Lawrence Durrell: (1) *Zero and Asylum in the Snow: Two Excursions into Reality*. Berkeley, Circle Edition, 1947 (2) *A Landmark Gone*. Los Angeles, Reuben Pearson, 1949.

E. P. Dutton & Co., Inc. (as Lawrence Durrell's publishers in the United States): (1) *Acté* (2) *The Alexandria Quartet* (3) *Bitter Lemons* (4) *The Black Book* (5) *Collected Poems* (6) *An Irish Faustus* (7) *A Private Correspondence* (Lawrence Durrell's letters) (8) *Reflections on a Marine Venus* (9) *Sappho*.

Kenneth Young, "A Dialogue with Durrell," *Encounter*, Vol. XIII, No. 6 (December, 1959).

Faber and Faber, Ltd. (as Lawrence Durrell's British publishers): (1) *The Alexandria Quartet* (2) *Cities, Plains and People* ("Eight Aspects of Melissa") (3) *Collected Poems* (4) *Panic Spring* (by "Charles Norden") (5) *Prospero's Cell* (6) *Sappho*.

Acknowledgments

The Contemporary English Novel, by Frederick R. Karl. New York, Farrar, Straus & Giroux, 1962.

Conrad the Novelist, by Albert J. Guerard. Cambridge, Harvard University Press, 1958.

Lord Jim, by Joseph Conrad, edited by R. B. Heilman, Rinehart Editions. New York, Holt, Rinehart and Winston, 1963.

The Executors of the Percy Lubbock Estate: *The Craft of Fiction*, by Percy Lubbock. New York, Compass, 1962. Reprinted by permission of Jonathan Cape Ltd.

The Good Soldier, by Ford Madox Ford. Copyright, 1951, by Alfred A. Knopf, Inc.

Masters of Modern British Fiction, edited by George Wickes. New York, Macmillan, 1963. Copyright, 1963, by George Wickes.

New Bearings in English Poetry, by F. R. Leavis. Ann Arbor, University of Michigan Press, 1960.

Kenneth Rexroth, "The Footsteps of Horace," *Nation*, Vol. CLXXXIV (May 18, 1957).

A Private Correspondence (Henry Miller's letters). Copyright, 1962, 1963, by Lawrence Durrell and Henry Miller. Reprinted by permission of New Directions Publishing Corporation, New York.

University of Oklahoma Press: (1) Herbert Howarth, "Lawrence Durrell and Some Early Masters," *Books Abroad*, Vol. XXXVII, No. 1 (Winter, 1963) (2) *A Key to Modern British Poetry*, by Lawrence Durrell. Norman, University of Oklahoma Press, 1952. Copyright, 1952, by Peter Nevill Ltd.

Anatomy of Criticism, by Northrop Frye. New York, Atheneum, 1967. Reprinted by permission of Princeton University Press.

Swann's Way, by Marcel Proust, translated by C. K. Scott Moncrieff. New York, Random House, 1956. Copyright, 1928, 1956, by The Modern Library, Inc.

My Friend Lawrence Durrell: An Intimate Memoir on the Author of "The Alexandria Quartet," by Alfred Perlès. Middlesex, Scorpion Press, 1961

Axel's Castle: A Study of the Imaginative Literature of 1870–1930, by Edmund Wilson. London, Fontana Library, 1961. Reprinted by permission of Charles Scribner's Sons.

Howard L. Shainheit, "Who Wrote *Mountolive*? An Investigation of the Relativity-aesthetic of Lawrence Durrell's *The Alexandria Quartet*," unpublished honors thesis. University of Massachusetts, May, 1963.

Lawrence Durrell, "Acté or The Prisoners of Time," *Show*, Vol. I, No. 3 (December, 1961).

I am Jonathan Scrivener, by Claude Houghton (Oldfield). New York, Simon and Schuster, 1930.

The World of Lawrence Durrell, edited by Harry T. Moore. Carbondale, Southern Illinois University Press, 1962.

Mary Graham Lund, "Submerge for Reality: The New Novel Form of Lawrence Durrell," *Southwest Review*, Vol. XLIV, No. 3 (Summer, 1959).

Lawrence Durrell, "First Steps," *3 Arts Quarterly*, No. 2 (Summer, 1960).

Time Magazine: (1) "Theater Abroad: Marine Justine," Vol. LXXVIII (September 8, 1961) (2) "Theater Abroad: Goethe Go Home," Vol. LXXXIII (January 3, 1964). Courtesy *Time*; copyright, Time Inc., 1961, 1964.

Lawrence Durrell, by John A. Weigel. New York, Twayne Publishers, Inc., 1965.

The Craft of Fiction, by Percy Lubbock. New York, Com-

Acknowledgments

pass, 1962. Reprinted by permission of The Viking Press, Inc.

The Book of the It, by Georg Groddeck. Introduction by Lawrence Durrell. New York, Vintage Books, 1961. Reprinted by permission of Vision Press Ltd.

Books in My Baggage, by Lawrence Clark Powell. Cleveland and New York, World Publishing Company, 1960. Copyright, 1960, by Lawrence Clark Powell.

Finally, thanks are also due to the University of Texas Research Institute for providing a grant to cover the costs of manuscript preparation.

ALAN WARREN FRIEDMAN

September 15, 1969

Preface

WITH the publication of *The Alexandria Quartet* in the late 1950's, Lawrence Durrell, a prolific writer since the mid-1930's suddenly achieved both commercial success and serious critical consideration. Despite its anomalous nature, such Janus-faced attention is not really surprising; for the world of Durrell's writing is something various and new, rich yet firm, as soaring and mundane as mountains or cities. It is a heady brew of poetry and prose to be imbibed in great rapid bursts of taste—and one falls invariably into purple passages in attempting to convey its flavor. It is, at the same time, the substantial fare of a major craftsman.

Durrell takes his place—with Proust, the early Joyce and Lawrence, Henry Miller—within the tradition of artist as autobiographer, as transmuter of transient personal experience into the mold of permanence. His life has been a kaleidoscopic pattern of jobs and places, of being press officer, public relations official, editor, teacher, lecturer on British poetry, and in such unlikely places as Athens, Cairo, Alexandria, Rhodes, Argentina, Yugoslavia, Cyprus. And no place he has resided in or visited, no job he has performed, no person he has known, no idea he or someone near him has held, it would seem, fails to be both retained and transmitted through the products of his art.

Perhaps the central impetus in the work is Durrell's inherent sense of deracination and his concomitant need to belong somewhere. Indeed, he would seem to embody the very pattern of the rootless wanderer imbued with a highly developed sense of roots; for, like most placeless men, Durrell worships place—it inspires a sense of comforting wholeness, an enduring context that implies the underlying and permanent basis for the world's unending temporality. Regionalist novelists find permanence and stability in the people and continuing traditions of an area; Durrell, who superficially resembles them, has sought values outside the social structure, in the more externalized world he calls "landscape"—a collective noun encompassing ambience, atmosphere, essence, a way of life, all the innumerable forces impinging on the writer during his stay in a given place, as well as all his imaginatively felt and reconstructed reactions to them.

For Durrell, landscape embodies, parallels, even motivates and controls the intrinsic and extrinsic workings of his characters. Thus, their individuality seems often suffused, subordinated, to the *deus loci* who is the pantheistic deity of the place—as, on the largest scale, Alexandria dominates the various characters of the *Quartet*, for in it "Only the city is real." All of Durrell's major themes and motifs are expressed as interrelationships of character and place: alienation, noncommunication, a condition Durrell expresses in terms of illness, result when the individual clashes with a place of negative influence; if the dominance is overwhelming, the individual becomes will-less, passive, fails totally at art and love; if he manages to escape to a landscape fertile for him, he becomes cured, attains a new sense of selfhood usually ex-

xiv

pressed metaphorically as spiritual regeneration, begins to create (perhaps again, perhaps for the first time), and becomes capable of love.

But this overview somewhat simplifies and therefore distorts Durrell's complex achievement. For even a place essentially affirmative (for example, the Cyprus of *Bitter Lemons*, the Alexandria of the *Quartet*) may be destructive if its presence becomes too powerful, for landscape must only enrich, vitalize, aid; it must not be allowed omnipotence over the lives of its inhabitants. Thus, most Durrellean characters who endure and triumph come to recognize that flight or even periodic migration—though traditionally conceived in negative terms—is essential; with sadness, with regret, but with ultimate certainty, they leave even the best of places before its presence overwhelms totally. Flight, then, when undertaken for the right reason, becomes the supreme affirmative act; for, despite the ease of surrendering to a languorous landscape, such characters refuse to submit to its Circean clutches, and assert the independence, the integrity of the self, by seeking a place perhaps not so idyllic but more conducive to the rigors of creativity and the exigencies of realistic love.

Virtually all of Durrell's writing, then, is suffused with the pervasive and evanescent glow of place; yet place, though it affords him a unifying context for his apparently disparate body of writings, is not itself of paramount significance. It functions, rather, as central metaphor, as touchstone for the *Künstlerroman* treatment of the frustrated, isolated individual maturing into someone capable of meaningful human involvement. The process by which he achieves his fullest potential in both art and life (a process invariably expressed in terms of his relationship with place) occurs only through a total, active commitment to the creative process: "art for love's sake." Durrell's early fiction, poetry, verse plays, and island books all point toward the *Quartet*'s theme of hollow separateness and the individual's achieving fulfillment in love, if at all, through first achieving fulfillment in work, in art—and usually as a consequence of some violent and climactic breakthrough into the realm of volitional action. Only in the final moments of *Clea*, when the title character emerges from the water of the dead in which she was speared and entombed, is there release from the various forces inhibiting maturation, the evolution and realization of selfhood. Only at the *Quartet*'s end can Durrell's protagonist love fully and create as an artist—create, in effect, the *Quartet* itself.

Durrell, then, is neither haphazard nor arbitrary in his writing; he is a serious experimenter seeking the forms, the media, for best expressing the things that matter most for him. He will employ, as it serves his purposes, a lush and baroque style partaking of both prose and poetry; a rich pattern of ideas and ideas about ideas; a multidimensional universe and vision transcending the ordinary limitations of time; an aesthetic dependent for its values on private mythos (whose basic manifestation is eroticism) rather than on societal morality, on felt reality rather than on "objective" fact, on form at least as much as on content. These Durrell has evolved for himself and made uniquely his own; in varying forms and combinations they lie at the heart of virtually all he has written.

Still, we know of Durrell—and care about him—primarily because of the publication over a period of years (long enough to arouse suspenseful interest and short enough to sustain it) of the four interwoven books of the *Quartet*. In it, all dichotomies are not reconciled—for that is impossible and undesirable—but are brought into organic contact; and we learn that, though irreconcilable, they are not mutually exclusive. On the contrary, they interpenetrate, fusing and enriching one another. Thus, the *Quartet* is simultaneously promise and fulfillment, culmination and prophecy, a vast all-inclusive multiple genre bearing all the signs of an enduring and proliferating achievement. The force of its complex experience, compelling us with the color and intensity of a living confrontation, creates a world in which, perhaps for the first time, we can learn to become, in Durrell's words, our own contemporaries. This study, like the *Quartet* itself, is one means of beginning.

Chronology

February 27, 1912. Born Lawrence George Durrell, of Anglo-Irish parents, in the Himalayan area of India.

1923–35. In England. Attends school in Canterbury; fails to enter Cambridge (a fortunate thing, Henry Miller tells us); works at numerous odd jobs; begins writing.

1931. First book, *Quaint Fragment*.

1935. First novel, *Pied Piper of Lovers*. Marries Nancy Meyers.

1935–39. On Corfu with family: wife, mother, two brothers, sister. Writes *The Black Book* (published in Paris, 1938). Makes several visits to London and Paris. Stay on Corfu receives full-length treatment in *Prospero's Cell* (1945), his first island book.

September, 1937. Meets Henry Miller in Paris.

September, 1937–Easter, 1939. With Henry Miller, Alfred Perlès, and William Saroyan, edits and contributes to *The Booster-Delta*, a bilingual magazine published in Paris (seven numbers in all).

1939. Founding of *Poetry* (London), a little magazine

publishing his poetry, reviews, and letters for the next dozen years. Moves from Corfu to Athens; has visit from Miller.

1939–40. Teaches at Institute of English Studies in Athens and Kalamata.

June, 1940. Birth of daughter, Penelope Berengaria Durrell (Ping-kû). Durrell writes that after the first week he actually enjoyed "the nappies and the sun treatment and the fuss. . . . As good as having a new book out. Books grow in the same way and shed teeth and walk and sing" (*Corr*, p. 215).

April, 1941. In advance of the invading Germans, flees to Egypt via Crete.

1941–45. Foreign Press Service Officer in Cairo. With Robin Fedden, Terence Tiller, and Bernard Spencer (other exiled English writers), founds and edits *Personal Landscape*, a poetry magazine appearing in Cairo, 1942–45 (eight numbers in all).

1943. Separates from Nancy. "Nancy is in Jerusalem with the child. We have split up; just the war I guess" (*Corr*, p. 180; Christmas, 1943).

1944–45. Press Attaché in Alexandria. "I have my own office and almost no interference; so I can run things in the way I like. You [Miller] always used to laugh when I said I was an executive man, but I was right. My office hums like a top; and the people working for me LIKE it." Meets Eve (Gypsy)—to whom *Justine* is later dedicated—"a strange, smashing, dark-eyed woman . . . with every response right, every gesture, and the interior style of a real person . . ." (*Corr*, pp. 188–89; Spring, 1944).

June, 1945–March, 1947. On Rhodes, Director of Public Relations, Dodecanese Islands. Does much writing: *Cities, Plains and People* (poetry), *Cefalû* (a morality cast in the form of a naturalistic novel), most of *Sappho* (his first verse play), the early draft of *Reflections on a Marine Venus* (his second island book), and some short fiction.

February, 1947. Marries Eve.

March–November, 1947. In England, between assignments, trying to "make a little money from translations and various hack work." To his surprise, finds himself truly at home there. "England is really very pleasant, the easiest country in Europe to live in despite our groans. The Socialists have done a wonderful job on food distribution and price control. Though one is limited in everything, prices are lower than anywhere in Europe, and the distribution is equitable and just. People are hard up, but the old tag about the greatest benefit of the greatest number applies here more than anywhere else in the world. I am really very impressed and delighted. And civil liberties haven't suffered as in dictator countries" (*Corr*, p. 240).

1947–48. Director, British Council Institute, Córdoba, Argentina. Gives series of lectures later published as *A Key to Modern British Poetry* (1952).

1948. In England ("wonderful after Argentina"), unsuccessfully trying to live on his writing income.

July, 1949–December, 1952. Press Attaché, Belgrade, Yugoslavia. The stay is decidedly unpleasant. "Communism is something so much more horrible than you can imagine: systematic moral and spiritual corruption by every means at hand. 'The perversion of truth in the interests of expediency.' But when you see it at close quarters it makes your hair stand up on end. And the smug cooperation of the intellectuals is also terrifying! They are paid to shut up—and they have. The terrible *deadness* of everything is fantastic! It really is a menace, an intellectual disease" (*Corr*, p. 264; July, 1949).

1950. *Sappho: A Play in Verse.*

May, 1951. Birth of second daughter, Sappho-Jane.

1953–August, 1956. On Cyprus. Teaches at the Greek gymnasium; Director of Public Relations, government of Cyprus. Separates from Eve (Miller offers a kind of comfort: "Know how you must feel. . . . However . . . you will soon find that you are better off. . . . It will give you strength, courage, purpose, peace of mind. Take your time about finding another mate. Let her find you!" [*Corr*, p. 302]). Meets Claude (a French novelist born in Alexandria, "an Alexandrian Becky Sharp"). Writes *Justine*. Narrowly escapes death when civil war begins.

August, 1956–February, 1957. In England. Hurriedly completes *Bitter Lemons* (his third island book); sends his only typescript "without even reading it to Faber—so broke were we!" (quoted in Perlès, *Lawrence Durrell*, p. 34).

Since 1957. In Provence.

1957. Awarded Duff Cooper Prize (presented by Britain's Queen Mother) for *Bitter Lemons*.

1957. *Justine*.

1958. *Balthazar*.

1959. *Mountolive*. Visit from Miller.

1960. *Clea*; *Acté*; *Collected Poems* (from six earlier books, 1938–55).

1961. *Art and Outrage* (with Alfred Perlès and Henry Miller). Marries Claude in March.

1962. *The Alexandria Quartet* published as one volume.

1963. *A Private Correspondence* (with Henry Miller); edits *The Best of Henry Miller*.

1964. *An Irish Faustus*.

1968. *Tunc*.

Note

The following abbreviations are used in citing Durrell's works: TAQ: *The Alexandria Quartet* (the one-volume Faber and Faber edition, which includes J: *Justine*, B: *Balthazar*, M: *Mountolive*, C: *Clea*); Asylum: *Asylum in the Snow* which, along with *Zero*, was published with the subtitle *Two Excursions into Reality*); TBB: *The Black Book*; Key: *A Key to Modern British Poetry*; PS: *Panic Spring*; Corr: *A Private Correspondence* (with Henry Miller); S: *Sappho*; Cell: *Prospero's Cell: A Guide to the Landscape and Manners of the Island of Corcyra*; Venus: *Reflections on a Marine Venus: A Companion to the Landscape of Rhodes*; BL: *Bitter Lemons*.

Publication details of these and Durrell's other writings appear in the bibliography.

Contents

LAWRENCE DURRELL
and *The Alexandria Quartet*

I. The Evolving Lawrence Durrell

As for Joyce's first articles on Ibsen and Mangan, Lawrence's earliest poems, Hardy's essay on architecture and Jeffers' Flagons and Apples, it would have taken a clairvoyant to see greatness in these beginnings; and yet now it is possible to trace their authors' development logically back to them. (Lawrence Clark Powell, *Books in My Baggage*, p. 66.)

The heraldic universe is just this side of China, where it touches Ethiopia and the Dead Sea. (Lawrence Durrell, *Corr*, p. 66.)

Early Fiction

WITH the exception of *The Black Book* and the *Quartet*, Durrell dismisses all of his fiction as potboilers, pseudo literature ground out by an inexperienced adolescent or an impoverished would-be commercial writer. This self-criticism has some validity. The first two novels, *Pied Piper of Lovers* and *Panic Spring*, were neither financially nor artistically successful, although the latter is interesting for its languorous and Mediterranean exoticism in the manner of *South Wind*. *White Eagles over Serbia* is a fairly good juvenile adventure set in Yugoslavia. *The Dark Labyrinth*, as Durrell puts it, is "an extended morality . . . [cast in] that most exasperat-

3

ing of forms, the situations novel . . ." (*Corr*, p. 201). Each of the pale, dissatisfied tourists in *Labyrinth*, like Christian Marlowe, the protagonist of *Panic Spring*, makes both a literal and a psychological journey from England to the Mediterranean, and then enters the legendary Cretan labyrinth and achieves, as in all moralities, the fate implicit in his character. Most significantly, the descriptions of both landscape and the Cretan labyrinth offer a Mediterranean color and vividness tonally and symbolically contrasting with the bleakness and sterility of England, especially as the latter appears in the earlier, but much more important, *The Black Book*.

Durrell tells us he is especially attached to *The Black Book*

because in the writing of it I first heard the sound of my own voice, lame and halting perhaps, but nevertheless my very own. This is an experience no artist ever forgets. . . . *The Black Book* staked a slender claim for me and encouraged me to believe that I was perhaps a real writer and not just a word spinner of skill.[1]

Certainly it is not for a profundity of either plot or character that T. S. Eliot hailed *The Black Book* as "the first piece of work by a new English writer to give me any hope for the future of prose fiction." Both the story and those participating in it are slight and shadowy. The vitriolic narrator, who calls himself Lawrence Lucifer, is stereotyped, two-dimensional—flattened and narrowed by the pervasive "English Death." Much like the young Darley of the *Quartet*, he is deracinated and lost in a world he never made; a rebel without a cause; a young, sensitive member of the "modern" generation seeking values and coherence in a world essentially chaotic. More specifically, *The Black Book* fictionalizes a year Durrell spent in a London residential hotel in the early 1930's, a year of stagnation, of spiritual sterility, of marking time in a smug, dying England. Herbert Howarth has written:

[1] *TBB*, Preface, *xiii–xiv*.

4

The Evolving Lawrence Durrell

The sub-title to *The Black Book* in the original edition was . . . "A Chronicle of the English Death." It is an attempt to stir the pulse of England; by the violent over-statement of its argument to change England, to create her. "If art has any message," he writes in his *Key to Modern Poetry*, "it must be this: to remind us that we are dying without having lived."[2]

To varying degrees, all the characters partake of this negative existence; one, Horace "Death" Gregory, embodies it specifically and completely and, as the narrator's alter ego, represents those stultifying forces within both himself and his world which Lucifer must overcome to survive and grow. A *Bildungsroman, The Black Book* tells of Lucifer's spiritual journey from defeatism, fatalism, and nihilism (symbolized by the unrelieved dreariness of England's winter) to an affirmation of life, love, and creativity (symbolized by the warmth, color, and fertility of the Greek world he reaches at the end). Durrell's writing in *The Black Book*—the interweaving of naturalistic and poetic levels of narration, the experimental richness of language and style—anticipates that of the *Quartet*, for he attempts to break down language into something more fluid and less structured, a medium better able to transmit the sense of a timeless present embodying all time. Durrell's first significant attempt in this direction occurs in the love- and art-making chapter of *Panic Spring*.

One goes on, for no discoverable reason except this insane desire to make oneself real, to understand the splintered mirrors in oneself, and through oneself to reach out for that twin world, whose discovery is lost in a single second of two bodies in friction, heeling over like toy balloons whose strings have snapped, heading for the spaces among the planets. (P. 117.)

And he carries his experimentation much further in the

2 "Lawrence Durrell and Some Early Masters," 5–6.

surrealistic prose pieces he wrote at the same time as *The Black Book*. The most notable of these, *Zero* and *Asylum in the Snow*, probably Durrell's most abstract and abstruse writing, were published together with the perverse but appropriate subtitle: *Two Excursions into Reality*. Opening with a quotation "From the letters written by Nietzsche after he became insane," the work represents the ravings of an institutionalized madman whose search for lucidity in an opaque and confused world sets him apart from those about him.

Durrell's madman is not so insane that he fails to recognize that only the creative act, only learning to communicate, offers a possibility of release from the prisons within and without him. He strives to expand "the defined limit of language," to become "lucid, lucent, hallucid." In *Asylum*, he asserts that the oblique quality of his style is unplanned, not an end in itself, that "I am writing this with the most absolute precision, so do not be impatient" (p. 24). It becomes even clearer in *Asylum* than in *Zero* that the narrator's mental imbalance in some way symbolizes a failure of artistic expression. "I am a writer," he repeatedly proclaims.

Yesterday I said to the old man [the head of the asylum]: "It is getting towards Christmas. I have a confession to make. I am Lawrence Durrell, the writer, who wrote until one day the world came into terrible focus. I am the writer who never really wrote. Because the moment I became a real writer there was no partition of snow or minutes: and I had to come here for a long holiday from myself." (Pp. 24–25.)

Apparently, for this narrator who bears Durrell's name, the present moment and the ubiquitous snow became permanent and merged at the instant he considered himself a creator. The temporal flux has been dammed, and there exist only the vast Tibetan spaces of *Zero* and the snow-blanketed Christmas landscape *Asylum* shares with *The Black Book*. And the madman's (that is, the artist's) quest for communication with the strange, abstracted figures about him continues with small hope of success. "When I speak the words torment the doctors, because there is as yet no vocabulary, no glossary in the tongue I am using. It is a magnificent experiment, but I am lonely" (p. 33). Inevitably lonely, for to seek "an alphabet of essence" wins no sympathy. "I am excited by this writing," he declares; but "they say it is not good. They sweep it up like old snow and burn it, I remember, tomorrow. It is silly, but the old man is weary. Too much paper. Too much ink. He likes the bead work better, it is restful" (pp. 21–22).

For the man who craves above all to communicate, however, rest offers no solace, nor does the asylum keeper's patronizing of his suffering. "The old man said: 'Time the great healer.' But Time is the great separator. I cannot bear Time. There is too much time here among the snows" (p. 23). And thus *Asylum*, like *Zero*, employs a gargoyle-like surrealistic imagery as a vain attempt to find or create language that will permit time to become meaningful again, that will communicate, that will somehow bear the charged insight of the madman's vision.

Poems

Durrell's poems similarly pursue the chimera of language, that vaguely realized medium by definition inadequate to its message. But, through his heightened use of place, he seeks to impart fixity and corporality to the transitory and intangible. Thus, the impetus in the poetry—in fact the heart of all Durrellean imagery and design—is a passion for place that, as in a statement from a recent interview, attaches itself proteanlike to numerous different locales.

I think the Greek landscape [Durrell is quoted as saying] is absolutely saturated by intimations of the basic type of mind that grew up in it, and in Greece you feel the pagan world is very close. Where I live now, in the South of France, you feel something equally strong—you feel Nostradamus, the Provencal singers, the intense savagery, and a different sort of mysticism. In Dorset, where I was living last year, the Druids were pretty close, I thought.[3]

"Themes Heraldic" and "Deus Loci" (poems written fifteen years apart) express much of what Durrell is after here and elsewhere. "Themes Heraldic" (1936) is significant primarily for its title, Durrell's first imaginative expression of that atemporal state of being which bears relationship with the "Monuments of unaging intellect" in Yeats's "holy city of Byzantium." In a contemporaneous letter, Durrell writes:

In heraldry I seem to find that quality of magic and spatial existence which I want to tack on to art. Of course . . . one must make allowances for storing, parturition, experience and all that, involving time. But what I am trying to isolate is the exact moment of creation, in which the maker seems to exist heraldically. That is to say, time as a concept does not exist, but only as an attribute of matter—decay, growth, etc. In that sense then, it must be memoryless. I am afraid I cannot make this very clear even to myself until I examine all the terms and see precisely what they mean. But for myself I am beginning to inhabit this curious HERALDIC UNIVERSE when I write. If it seems a bit precocious of me to be trying to invent my own private element to swim about in, it can't be helped. (*Corr*, p. 23.)

"Themes Heraldic" is a tentative effort, lacking, no doubt deliberately, a tight sense of unity. As if laying a foundation for the construction of his future work, the poet tries out various possibilities: for themes ("Shall I renounce you for a new theme/Who are a warm green stone, green girl,/Warm in a white bone bed?"); for imagery ("How shall it be? Caught

[3] Kenneth Young, "A Dialogue with Durrell," 66–67.

in the sun's red loom,/Be woven to rock, to water, a new
manufacture./By the moon drawn, a green dolphin,/Up into
death sans fracture?"); for a central metaphor ("The paladin
of the body is rock,/Dark rock, the anonymous/Stark stone,
the prime ingot./This crystal of darkness is flesh./Call on
Him and the rock/Becomes flesh and the flesh/God. Rock
is His pseudonym."); for a basic attitude toward life and
landscape ("Even the amputated earth herself/Pours suicidal
tidal water,/Ebbs upwards, up along homeward elastic/On
the long tug wombward. Tides/Shine between your ribs, my
moon's/White suicidal sides."). For all the surrealistic obscurity of the poem, it is clear enough that Durrell is here
clearing paths for later exploration as well as for his subsequent entry into the "heraldic" realm of significant art.

"Deus Loci" is perhaps Durrell's most overt invocation of
"you O spirit of place." In a series of ten ten-line verse
paragraphs, the poem attempts to make explicit the romantic
pantheism underlying Durrell's thought and writing.

> All our religions founder, you
> remain, small sunburnt *deus loci*
> safe in your natal shrine,
> landscape of the precocious southern heart,
> continuously revived in passion's common
> tragic and yet incorrigible spring:
> in every special laughter overheard,
> your specimen is everything—
> accents of the little cackling god,
> part animal, part insect, and part bird.

The *deus loci* personifies the mythological spirit, joyously
Mediterranean, that simultaneously deified love and human-
ized the gods. More specifically, Durrell's earthly immortal
bears a striking resemblance to Bacchus, though the former
is a somewhat more restrained inspirer of vineyard revelry

and the religion of love. For the *deus loci* does not partake of Bacchus' maddened and uncontrollable frenzies; his root strength, unlike the classical deity's, lies not in an attitude or an emotion but in a people and a landscape. Thus, he inspirits such sober activities as the fisherman's setting forth and the forester's rising to "confront the morning star," and offers a comforting fellowship to those in mourning or afraid of the unknown. Yet most commonly, the poet suggests, the *deus loci* offers its presence through wine and love: paradoxically supplying the communion beverage; enriching the "small mid-day meal,/garlic and bread," of even the poorest peasant; setting in motion the joyful process—wine making, wine drinking, love-making—that leads to

> breath in kisses dropped
> under the fig's dark noonday lantern, yes,
> lovers like tenants of a wishing-well
> whose heartbeats labour though all time has stopped.

But in addition to being Bacchus and Eros, the *deus loci* is also Apollo in his role as god of healing—here ministering to the victims of that most common Durrellean ailment, the disease of love.

> Your panic fellowship is everywhere,
> not only in love's first great illness known,
> but in the exile of objects lost
> to context, broken hearts, spilt milk,
> oaths disregarded, laws forgotten . . .
> and further on, half hidden, the fatal letter
> in the cold fingers of some marble hand.

And in the final two stanzas, the poet reminds us of the crucial dual aspect godhood confers: simultaneous vast province ("beyond even the mind's dark spools") and intense immanence—which add up to the ambiguity of religious passion, with its concomitant sense of renewal, regeneration.

So today, after many years, we meet . . .
                —all [stale things]
refreshed again in you O spirit of place,
Presence long since divined, delayed, and waited for,
And here met face to face.

In "Deus Loci," perhaps better than anywhere else, Durrell personifies his powerful yet largely undefinable feeling for place, with its multifold associations of landscape, atmosphere, tone, religion, emotion, way of life, inspiration, and love. He does not entirely succeed in this poem, for precision sometimes yields to abstraction: "wherever the unknown has displaced the known/you encouraged in the fellowship of wine/ of love and husbandry. . . ." Nonetheless, such lapses are rare in "Deus Loci"; most of the images create no unwarranted obscurity, and the poem, with neither narrative nor dramatic structure, succeeds as only one of this kind could—as a lyrical evocation of a concept more felt than known and conveyed (if at all) by poetic implication, not circumscribing definition. And perhaps most important, it offers an archetypal treatment of place—that pervading, ever-recurring motif—that may serve as a paradigm not only for the bulk of Durrell's poetry but also for such works as *Sappho*, the island books, and the *Quartet*. In *Tunc*, though place remains tonally relevant, its function has been taken over by the "firm"—and the shift represents a significant loss.

Deriving their strength from these same concerns, A *Private Country* and *Cities, Plains and People* are his most interesting collections of poems as well as his best. The first lives in and through the Greece which is its central metaphor, its source of meaning and location; the second is a product of Durrell's crucial move from Greece to Egypt. Durrell's warm, fructifying "private country" is not simply a geographical setting but the inspiriting genius of the good life conjured up to the mind's eye by the name "Greece." "On Ithaca Standing" begins:

> Tread softly, for here you stand
> On miracle ground, boy,
> Here the cold spring lilts on sand.
> The temperature of the toad
> Swallowing under a stone whispers: 'Diamonds,
> Boy, diamonds, and juice of minerals!'
> Be a saint here, dig for foxes, and water,
> Mere water springs in the bones of the hands.

The very sense of Greece's aliveness warms the poet; its sounds blend into an ever-recurring refrain. It thus becomes a motto throughout his work, an archetypal image and setting: "Other men have their emblems, I this."

The Greek poems, though permeated by death and cessation, are unified by a single consolation, actually an affirmation, expressing itself in the landscape and arising from a sense of life's fullness. At times, as in "At Epidaurus," the poet wonders if he can live up to the landscape, can rise to the challenge implicit in its very existence.

> Here we are safe from everything but ourselves,
> The dying leaves and the reports of love.
> We, like the winter, are only visitors. . . .
>   The earth's flower
> Blows here original with every spring
> Shines in the rising of a man's age
> Into cold texts and precedents for time.

As in "At Corinth" and "To Argos," the poet, as yet alien to "This civilized valley," questions whether he or any modern non-Greek can regain the ancient spirit that was the fountainhead of Hellenic (and therefore all Western) vitality. "To Argos" doubts that "By the cold sound of English idioms" one can evoke the ghost of Greece past; "At Epidaurus," envisaging the coming war ("The somnambulists walk again in the north/With the long black rifles, to bring us answers."), expresses a fear that it will not be halted by the "useless inhabitants of the kind blue air," and certainly not by those, like the poet and his beloved, who have emigrated to Greece and found an elemental home there—but much too recently as yet to partake freely of its bounty.

Nonetheless, these poems do disclose the warm and vital breadth of Greek vistas. "At Corinth":

> The valley mist ennobles
> Lovers disarmed by negligence or weather. . . .
> Winter was never native here: nor is.
> Men, women, and the nightingales
> Are forms of spring.

They thus imply what other poems of *A Private Country* make overt: that here, despite the inevitability of death and war, may indeed be found the affirmation and meaning the poet seeks.

In the two 1937 Corcyrean lyrics "Carol on Corfu" and "Summer in Corfu," for instance, the poet takes cognizance of mortality, yet gives himself wholly to an eternality that seems to lie about him. He begins the first:

> I, per se I, I sing on,
> Let flesh falter, or let bone break
> Break, yet the salt of a poem holds on. . . .
> This is my medicine: trees speak and doves
> Talk, woods walk.

And because art and love have been created here and have found a responsive setting, they remain alive despite even the "empty weather" of a subsequently changed landscape.

"Letter to Seferis the Greek," perhaps the most successful

13

poem in the book and one of Durrell's finest lyric expressions, best epitomizes the process occurring in these poems, and also anticipates an extension of the process into several poems that treat a regenerative theme. For "Letter to Seferis" is a pure hymn of joy to "The magnificent and funny Greek" who created this alive land where "Something sang in the firmament."

> The stones of Athens in their pride
> Will remember, regret and often bless. . . .
> > > now surely
> Lover and loved exist again
> By a strange communion of darkness.

Though the poet warns us to "Consider how love betrays us," he emphasizes that Greece embodies Eros and thus calls to lovers everywhere to

> Remember the earth will roll
> Down her old grooves and spring
> Utter swallows again, utter swallows.

And the once alien poet who doubted the resuscitating powers of Greece now doubts no longer.

> I have no fear for the land.
> Her blue boundaries are
> Upon a curving sky of time,
> In a dark menstruum of water. . . .
> Soon it will be spring. Out of
> This huge magazine of flowers, the earth,
> We will enchant the house with roses,
> The girls with flowers in their teeth,
> The olives full of charm: and all of it
> Given: can one say that
> Any response is enough for those
> Who have a woman, an island and a tree?

The key phrase for the poet is "and all of it/Given," for as he elaborates his images of bounty and warm colors, the old insecurities fall away, and he recognizes with assurance that the immovable object of Greece remains greater than the irresistible force of time. With an effective twist to the traditional image of the inextinguishable flame, the poet analogically "proves" that "history with all her compromises/Cannot disturb the circuit made by this,/Alone in the house, a single candle burning/Upon a table in the whole of Greece." And, finally, the happiness of this small moment "here on a promontory" is not only perfect in itself but contains a prophetic promise.

> Nothing remains but Joy, the infant Joy
> (So quiet the mountain in its shield of snow,
> So unconcerned the faces of the birds),
> With the unsuspected world somewhere awake,
> Born of this darkness, our imperfect sight,
> The stirring seed of Nostradamus' rose.

"The infant Joy," a reincarnation of Greece's ancient spirit and an anticipation of the *Quartet*'s ultimate affirmation, prepares to inspirit the whole of "the unsuspected world," now stirring into wakefulness beyond the borders of Greece.

And finally, "Fangbrand: A Biography" depicts the implicit journey from alienation to identification and peace. Fangbrand comes to Mykonos not only a stranger but, of all things, a Christian missionary. At first,

> The island recognised him,
> Giving no welcome, lying
> Trembling among her Craters,

until, bifurcated by the totally divergent pressures of his religion and his environment, he begins to discover himself as he reacts to the landscape.

> At night the immediate
> Rubbing of the ocean on stones,

The headlands dim in her smoke
And always the awareness
Of self like a point, the quiver
As of a foetal heart asleep in him.

And then, that "foetal heart" at last beating, he feels himself "Marvelling for the first time/At the luminous island, the light."

Landscape had called to him and, as he answers, it becomes increasingly congenial and responsive. He finally discards all the inhibitions precluding meaningful existence. Even this early (1940), Durrell indicates both that the check is largely self-imposed and that, as Marlowe's Good Angel declares to Faustus in a somewhat different context, one may repent of earlier deviations so long as life remains.

Truth's metaphor is the needle.
The magnetic north of purpose
Striving against the true north
Of self: Fangbrand found it out,
The final dualism in very self,
An old man holding an asphodel.
He regarded himself in water . . .
'Self, you are still alive!'

The old man's conversion *from* traditional religion to Durrellean pantheism enables him to achieve not merely the major breakthrough *into* art but the supreme breakthrough *beyond* art and into life. "From now the famous ten-year/ Silence fell on him," a period so inordinately fruitful that, like the silence of most great religious teachers, it paradoxically produces nothing tangible for would-be disciples—no book, no "small/Paper of revelation left behind"—only a life of which one says, "Death interrupted nothing." And the ultimate beauty of Fangbrand's life, the poet concludes, is the pattern of potentiality it offers for all.

> So the riders of the darkness pass
> On their circuit; the luminous island
> Of the self trembles and waits,
> Waits for us all, my friends,
> Where the sea's big brush recolours
> The dying lives, and the unborn smiles.

Fangbrand's own "recoloured dying life" heralds the transformation each successful Durrellean protagonist undergoes
as he creates in his own image an internal deity of selfhood
(which becomes, metaphorically and externally, a *deus loci*).
Each must reject his own inhibiting other-directed equivalent
of Fangbrand's remote and sterile Christian deity; for, in the
heraldic universe, the *vita nuova* is predicated upon a simple
passion for being that either harmonizes with a previously
parasitic environment or impels one to some new setting
(usually Grecian), symbiotically attuned to humankind.

This last point Durrell dramatizes effectively in "Conon
in Exile," the final key poem from this book. Conon, an
artist-spokesman for several of Durrell's poems, has literally
employed art for love's sake, for his books have magnetized
many women to his bed. Yet to what ultimate purpose? "I
remember bodies, arms, faces," he says, "but I have forgotten
their names." At last, however, an old man in exile from the
daily business of the world, he recognizes the foolishness
inherent in merely flirting with art and life. The women he
sees now in a far different light.

> At last I understand
> They were only forms for my own ideas,
> With names and mouths and different voices.
> In them I lay with myself, my style of life,
> Knowing only coitus with the shadows,
> By our blue Aegean which forever
> Washes and pardons and brings us home.

And so at last he settles down to write his most important

work, "the immortal/*Of Love and Death*," already implicit in his new wisdom of self-understanding and the inspiriting blueness of Aegean quietude. Conon, then, in this final view we have of him, is in exile only from what one must of necessity abandon on entering Durrell's visionary realm of reality—his heraldic universe; in actuality, Conon for the first time has come home to the "Private Country" of himself.

Cities, Plains and People is Durrell's most complex collection of poems structurally, for it experiments with many forms he rarely employs elsewhere: the dramatic monologue, the fable or parable, a radio play, prose paragraphs, even telegraphese in "Pressmarked Urgent." Yet the experimentation effectively mirrors the uncertainties of dislocation and the consequent conflict and tension. Especially at first, the contrast between Greece and Egypt is intense, definitive—as between the two parts of "Two Poems in Basic English." The first, like *A Private Country*, gains sustenance from the fructifying, innocent landscape of Greece.

> These ships, these islands, these simple trees
> Are our rewards in substance, being poor.
> This earth a dictionary is
> To the root and growth of seeing,
> And to the servant heart a door.

The point, once again, is fundamental, "basic": Greece is consolation and reward, ubiquitous and anthropomorphic,

> An order and a music
> Like a writing on the skies
> Too private for the reason or the pen;
> Too simple even for the heart's surprise.

But in the second half, "Near El Alamein," Durrell uses the bloody battle of October, 1942, to symbolize both his and the world's transplantation into a dying landscape.

The Evolving Lawrence Durrell

> This rough field of sudden war—
> This sand going down to the sea, going down,
> Was made without the approval of love,
> By a general death in the desire for living. . . .
> Men walking here, thinking of houses,
> Gardens, or green mountains or beliefs. . . .

Thoughts of all the good things encompassed under the generic word "Greece," re-evoke what has been lost through war and exile. And this basic pattern—from Greece to Egypt, from peace to war, from life to death, from a landscape warm and comforting to one harsh and loveless—finds repeated and varied expression throughout much of *Cities, Plains and People* and Durrell's subsequent writings.

Consequently, in this collection Durrell's lyric voice prevails in only a few poems—"This Unimportant Morning," "The Pilot," "Water Music," "Delos"—for rarely is there occasion for a hymnal hailing of place. In the fine lyric, "This Unimportant Morning," the landscape is cloudless, untroubled.

> This unimportant morning
> Something goes singing where
> The capes turn over on their sides
> And the warm Adriatic rides
> Her blue and sun washing
> At the edge of the world and its brilliant cliffs.

And the inhabitants, the poet envisages, partake perfectly of their landscape, sharing its sense of springlike newness.

> Trees fume, cool, pour—and overflowing
> Unstretch the feathers of birds and shake
> Carpets from windows, brush with dew
> The up-and-doing: and young lovers now
> Their little resurrections make.

But though at times the poet of *Cities, Plains and People*

achieves an imaginative reconstruction of pristine joy, his focus is, rather, the fall from innocence, the resultant flight, and the quest for a new home somewhere "east of the garden of Eden." The entire degenerative process (climaxing in war, flight, and exile) unfolds most fully in the book's long title poem, beginning with the "perfect idleness" of childhood years in the heraldic realm of Tibet, where the boy the poet was—"immortal to my seventh year"—

> Saw the Himalayas like lambs there
> Stir their huge joints and lay
> Against his innocent thigh a stony thigh.

But mortality soon denied such a vision; making his descent into maturity, the poet had sought elsewhere for a congenial landscape. He entered "sad green" England, but "Here all as poets were pariahs." Despite its great poets, England remains "not a world as yet. Not a world." Next, Paris (city of youthful first love) proves delusive, for the rain "Surprises and humbles with its taste of elsewhere," and the poet heeds the call of Greece's "rocky island and the cypress-trees," the call of a landscape conducive to the mature art and love he discovers there. Greece, then, parallels but surpasses Tibetan innocence.

> Here worlds were confirmed in him. . . .
> And the rate of passion or tenderness
> In this island house is absolute.

All too soon, however, the poet discovers that "Art has limits and life limits/Within the nerves that support them." For "darkness comes to Europe" as the barbarians impose war and flight upon the poet now driven out of Eden, the poet who in his sudden pride took perfection too much for granted. The rest of the poem, consequently, he devotes to overcoming the natural sense of despair at the loss of "This personal landscape built/Within the Chinese circle's calm embrace." For his entry into the flawed world, he seeks consolation from all that Greece still embodies,

> For Prospero [that is, Corfu] remains the evergreen
> Cell by the margin of the sea and land,
> Who many cities, plains, and people saw
> Yet by his open door;

and from the faith that, despite man's incessant attempts to destroy all that the landscape bears for him,

> All cities, plains and people
> Reach upwards to the affirming sun,
> All that's vertical and shining,
> Lives well lived,
> Deeds perfectly done,
> Reach upwards to the royal pure
> Affirming sun.

Actually, "Cities, Plains and People" is not so simplistic as this sketchy outline might suggest; rather, the poet reveals a fluctuating response characterized perhaps as much by uncertainty and ambiguity—even despair—as by affirmation.

> There is nothing to hope for, my Brother.
> We have tried hoping for a future in the past.
> Nothing came out of that past
> But the reflected distortion. . . .

It is evident in fact that, though affirmation is Durrell's natural inclination, he recognizes that it must be achieved and that it cannot be meaningful if merely asserted against the pattern of failure inherent in much of reality.

The rest of the poems—tensely straining for their tentative affirmations—are re-creative, reintegrative. "Six Landscape Painters of Greece" reminds us that through art and landscape lies the way back. The sixth section, "On Alexander of Athens," is most revealing.

Alexander was in love with Athens. He was a glutton and exhausted both himself and his subject in his art. Thus when he had smelt a flower it was quite used up, and when he painted a mountain it felt that living on could only be a useless competition against Alexander's painting of it. Thus with him Athens ceased to exist, and we have been walking about inside his canvases ever since looking for a way back from art into life.

Such a passage opens enormous avenues for exploration, and its rich reverberations are felt in all of Durrell's subsequent serious writing. This indication of Athenian finiteness anticipates Durrell's post–*Quartet* comment regarding his choice of locale for that work.

When it came to choose my city, I (being a romantic) chose the most various and colorful I could remember; technical question. I had to have enough *color* to support four long volumes without boring. At first I started the book about Athens, then switched to Alexandria. There I had everything, different cultures, civilizations, religions, all together; so I could, if I was clever, keep my paint from drying until I had finished the whole canvas.[4]

In effect, Durrell suggests that in the *Quartet* he could not "go home again" to his Edenic Greece of early inspiration (though he tries once more in *Tunc*). But *Cities, Plains and People* already implies this shift of Durrell's artistic headquarters, for nearly all the poems of re-emergence, those striving to come to grips with the failures of the past and to achieve some fresh approach to the present and future, are set in Alexandria. Further, in miniature and preliminary form, these poems offer treatment similar to that of the major concerns of the much later *Quartet*. "Eight Aspects of Melissa," for instance, employs the key devices of the *Quartet* —mirrors, prisms, images, lake water—to reflect Durrell's

4 "Lawrence Durrell Answers a Few Questions," in Harry T. Moore (ed.), *The World of Lawrence Durrell*, 159.

early concern with multifaceted personality, love, landscape, and time; "Alexandria," one of Durrell's finest poems, foreshadows the deracination and isolation of Darley, the *Quartet*'s protagonist, when he feels art and love to be unattainable; and "Conon in Alexandria" offers a pivotal analysis of both the actual and potential of "this white city," the Hellenic capital of Egypt.

Taken collectively, these poems offer no single view of Alexandria, no simple consolation for the exiled, still Greek-oriented poet. But there is a discernible movement toward understanding and acceptance and away from a negative retreat into, or in opposition to, the self. Far more complex than Wallace Stevens' "Thirteen Ways of Looking at a Blackbird"—the poem it most suggests—"Eight Aspects" intertwines personality and landscape in an unstable, shifting relationship predicated upon truth's multiplicity. Paralleling her roles in the *Quartet*, Melissa successively embodies the liquid prism of Mareotis' salty depths and the "immense Darkness . . . of Egypt" that dominates the poet; she inspires artists and lovers seeking in the night, and comforts with sad tenderness those who search no longer; she whispers of hope through the "Waterbirds sailing upon the darkness/Of Mareotis" and through the "riders on a cloud/Whom kisses only can inform . . ."; and, finally, she wonders whether wisdom (Eve's undigested apple, dark Hungers in "the orchards of the mind") or "A Prospect of Children" can offer solace for mortality. Much like the *Quartet*, "Eight Aspects" employs an imagistic shorthand that is often obscure yet sensuously evocative.

> The mauve street is swallowed
> And the bats have begun to stitch slowly.
> At the stable-door the carpenter's three sons

> Bend over a bucket of burning shavings,
> Warming their inwardness and quite unearthly
> As the candle-marking time begins.

Both "Eight Aspects" and the *Quartet* remain open-ended, implying both that all aspects examined are equally significant and that an indeterminate number of additional aspects await the diligent seeker after "truth." Neither pretends to exhaust the many questions it raises, for each answer contains not only a multitude of new questions but also a proliferating chain of "truths."

"Conon in Alexandria" is perhaps the best of several poems of initiation, of the poet's psychological journey "Through many negatives to what I am." Through vivid imagery, it at first mocks Alexandria as, at best, a diluted version of Greece.

> Ash-heap of four cultures
> Bounded by Mareotis, a salt lake,
> On which the winter rain rings and whitens,
> In the waters, stiffens like eyes.

Exiled from Greece for four years already, the poet wonders when it will cease to haunt him.

> Steps go down to the port
> Beyond the Pharos. O my friends,
> Surely these nightly visitations
> Of islands in one's sleep must soon be over?

And the sense of frustration over all that has occurred to him is summarized in a single couplet—an imagistic poem in miniature—on the immense yet confining desert.

> A gown stained at the arm-pits by a woman's body.
> A letter unfinished because the ink gave out.

Yet squalid and inadequate as Alexandria seems to him, the poet finally comes to accept "this coast of torn-out lighthouses," this embodiment of all the negative qualities of exile, separation, loneliness (qualities it never entirely loses for him). For he announces at the end, "I have passed all this day in what they would call patience"; and patience—which Durrell elsewhere calls quietism and which is akin to Keats's "negative capability"—is perhaps the most fundamental prerequisite for a Durrellean artist. That Durrell's poetic persona has achieved it in Alexandria heralds Durrell's second distinct creative cycle; just as violent reaction against the English environment led him to an artistic and human development in Greece that culminates in the island books, so too his traumatic departure from Greece initiates a groping and tentative rapprochement with landscape that ultimately gains climactic expression in *The Alexandria Quartet*. And equally significant, as we shall see, is the eventual departure from Alexandria of many of *that* work's major characters.

Verse Plays

The quality of the verse plays contrasts sharply with that of the poems and fiction; where the latter reveal a generally increasing maturity and grasp of materials, the former manifest a regressive pattern. The more recent poetry and prose encompass a firmness of image and a vastness of scale generally lacking in the smaller, more tentative early attempts. The plays, however, diminish chronologically from the lush complexity of *Sappho,* to the fascinating but programmatic *Acté,* to the nearly sterile *Irish Faustus.*

The plays all hark back to Renaissance stagecraft in their use of dramatic verse, psychologically inevitable plotting, and contemporizing of history or legend. *Sappho* revitalizes and humanizes the long-vilified Greek poet; *Acté* portrays a beautiful slave princess who leads a doomed rebellion against Nero's misrule; *An Irish Faustus* gives a Durrellean twist to that hoary but inexhaustible fable. All have been performed, but with limited success. *Sappho*, for instance, ran for only twelve performances in Hamburg; *Acté*, for twenty-six.[5] Yet *Sappho* was hailed as "the outstanding offering" at the Edinburgh Festival of 1961, as a play containing "ample evidence that novelist Durrell could become a major English dramatist" in the modern verse play form pioneered by Eliot, Auden, and Frye. With regard to its theatricality, "The play was talky, structurally awkward, and failed to reach a natural climax. It was overloaded with subplots, and it did not capitalize on its most dramatic situations. It suffered from cloudy characterizations. But it was brilliant."[6]

At the play's heart is its title character; Sappho (not the sexual deviant of legend) reigns like an inspiriting Greek muse over the amorous, artistic, and spiritual life of Lesbos. Each of these three facets finds personification, directly or antithetically, in one of the play's major male figures. The antiamorous Kreon, Sappho's husband, is weak and indulgent, aging rapidly and greedy for the passing power money confers, a man "incapable of suffering from more than mild irritations" (S, p. 27). The even less attractive Pittakos, the military hero in the process of becoming tyrant, unconsciously parodies the aesthetic vision. A forerunner of *Acté*'s Nero, he tells Sappho, appalled at the direction of his career, that he would be an artist of reality, a reality manifesting itself most truly in the form of war.

> A bad medium, you might say, a bad medium.
> Yet from an indifferent soldier I have risen
> To something like an artist in my work. (P. 133.)

Swaggeringly self-confident, Pittakos learns too late of the bitterness inherent in the fulfillment of such desires as his.

[5] "Theater Abroad: Goethe Go Home," *Time*, January 3, 1964, p. 56.
[6] "Theater Abroad: Marine Justine," *Time*, September 8, 1961, p. 74.

Glutted with victory, he returns to reclaim the Sappho who had been his mistress before his rise to power: "You famous —I victorious. It is all, all/As I imagined it . . ." (p. 125). But Sappho not only mocks his smug self-assurance and sense of embodying divine righteousness but also ridicules his soldier's standard ("Never to question? Always to act?") and ultimately leads the forces which overcome and destroy him.

The third of the triad is Phaon, Pittakos' antithetical twin brother, who alone offers Sappho not meaningless physical contact but real kindredship of spirit. Phaon is in fact the paradigm of Durrellean affirmation, the form against which his fictional protagonists may be measured. In the best article to date on the plays, Lander MacClintock suggests Phaon's significance.

He had in childhood been a playmate of the youthful Sappho and, in young manhood, a poet. One day he discovered that he had leprosy and exiled himself upon a desert island. There, after seven long years of solitude, he had undergone a strange mystical experience; like Gide's Philoctète he had renounced the world and found himself in a higher reality. When Sappho and he now meet again after these years of separation, they find they share complete comprehension and a mutual point of view. Both are seeking reality, genuine individual freedom, are trying to be their true selves in all the possibilities of their being, she through love, he through renunciation; both despise the shams and cruelties of the world in which they find themselves; both hate violence and war as useless and futile. They are on the side of the angels.[7]

Phaon, then, is what the *Quartet*'s Pursewarden, Durrell's supreme creative embodiment, would like to be: an artist evolved beyond art, a figure whose life itself manifests the beauty and certitude lesser poets strive to imitate in their work. He is also a regenerative figure, healed of his disabling

[7] "Durrell's Plays," in Moore (ed.), *The World of Lawrence Durrell*, 67–68.

ailment, freed for love (a brief intimacy with Sappho that he terminates to thwart the constrictions of Lesbos) and for his intense solitary life amid a landscape that at first had been awesome and monumental in scale.

It was different [he tells Sappho] from anything you can imagine.
Solitude I knew, but never loneliness
As this was, in the midst of the Aegean.
It created strange new appetites in me,
That I had never known before: silence was one.
I lived in silence for whole months together
Letting the sea speak for me
And the wild crying of the gulls resound in me.
The taste of so much solitary beauty
Was something no one ever knew till now. (P. 49.)

But then the change, which in other Durrellean regenerative figures results from violence, occurred in Phaon through forced isolation and continuous inward-turning.

I will not say I was contented, no. For I had gone
Clean out beyond content, to a new state:
If you can imagine a repose that is
Positive, beautiful, determined as an act,
Without the lumber of the will to weigh it down. . . .
I sank so deep: past waking it would seem:
Into a clear profoundness like a pool
Where time became quite innocent of force,
Became simply a contemptible refracting medium
On which phenomena were printed.
The world became a flight of painted symbols.
I had the feeling I created for myself
A sort of refuge in the midst of change,
Like a small centre of healing in the midst
Of some great wound—for that is what the world is. (Pp. 50–51.)

And so, with this effective reversing of illness imagery, the newly whole Phaon, an egoist in the best sense of the word, entered Durrell's heraldic universe—a realm which is not so much a location as a state of mind (though Durrell usually expresses it metaphorically as a sense of place), a philosophical shift from becoming to being.

Paradoxically, it is not Phaon and Sappho but Pittakos, the supreme pragmatist, who rejects reality in denying the validity of ideas, in asserting man's essential hopelessness.

PITTAKOS: You cannot alter the nature of the world,
      Nor can Phaon.
SAPPHO: But we can, we can. And we are doing it. (P. 132.)

For, as Phaon explains, life on his "No-name" island— "married to an element/In which time seemed eternally to extend itself/Through every category, yet remain unchanging . . ." (p. 52)—embodies an existential significance unknown in Pittakos' childish war games and "bastard liberations."

> For Pittakos every advance is a retreat
> Upon himself, upon the burning questions
> Natural to a man as great as he is. . . .
> This is a work for children living in unreality. . . .
> Meanwhile we have a world upon our hands
> To make or unmake as our natures lead us. (P. 54.)

And thus Pittakos' actions, by this crucial reversal, prove not *man's* helplessness and alienation from landscape but only his own—for the very act of war becomes a violation of Attic virtue, a fatal failing of Aegean health. The fact that Phaon, though he shares his brother's fate (both are killed when Sappho's soldiers discover the tyrant hiding on Phaon's island), had created and lived *his* kind of life renders such an existence possible for other men—and thereby does truly alter the world.

Sappho is caught in-between. Her great love for Phaon fails

to hold him more than briefly; and, in ultimately adopting the alien standards of Pittakos, she shrinks the great poet and exciting woman she was to a mere instrument of distorting and destroying forces. At the end she is alone and desolated by success.

> So at last, after so very long,
> I have climbed up here
> On this icy peak of my indifference. (P. 183.)

Yet it is not simply that Sappho is doomed at the last; for, foreshadowing Justine, the very pattern of her existence is that of desire frustrated by fulfillment.

> When young I wanted to be loved: I am.
> Wanted to be famous and left idle: well, I am.
> Then to be rich: I am:
> Then to be happy: Well, I am—or am I?
> It is rather the failure in my *wanting*
> That troubles conscience more
> Than any certain lack in what I have. (P. 26.)

In Sappho, then, is the play's tragic essence; for only she is of ambiguous complexity, faces real decisions, changes meaningfully during the course of the play, attains monumental stature through loss and suffering—gains, that is, a nobility through anguish that partakes of the tragic.

She is also, finally, a "Marine Justine," and shares with the *femme fatale* of the *Quartet* her sensuality, exoticism, mythos, and multifaceted nature. Like Justine, Sappho embodies her setting, feels victimized by both a world profoundly sterile and boring and a mounting series of personal failings (a stutter, a congenital unhappiness, a closing in of years: "Do you think/Death for a woman is half as terrible/As one grey hair?" [p. 85]), and never escapes her loneliness.

But although both Sappho and Justine are artists in the

broad sense of the word, only the former is literally a poet—
and the crucial point about the play, as MacClintock puts it,
is that, above all, it

is a poem, a dramatic poem, to be sure, but primarily and essentially a *poem*, conceived as such, written as such. To separate the
form from the content is to distort both, since to the poet they are
one and the same; the expression and the thing expressed are
monolithic. One can relate the plot, analyze the play of emotions
and ideas, discuss their relation to contemporary and preceding
works, but all these matters are peripheral. The only way to get
its savor is to read the play, or better, to hear it recited. You must
allow the poet with his winged words to take you from sordid
reality into a world of beauty and fantasy.[8]

For *Sappho* lives primarily in its language and in the poetry
of its landscape—more vital for Durrell than the grayness of
Acté's Rome or *Faustus'* rain-sodden greenness—as in this
description of the death of a city.

It was spring weather and a sea of glass,
Quite green and vitreous, shining
Like a great transparent pane let into the sky.
We turned the headland, entered harbour.
I stood on deck in tears,
Taking the stillness softly on my cheek—
The basic taste of the Grecian airs.

No cigale sang, no tree moved, no wave ran.
Then as I stood, nearing the sea-shore,
The sea began to boil and softly, softly,
In many places all together,
By explosion from the ground there rose
Great clouds of brickdust, burning lime . . .

The hills appeared to lean into the sea
And all the papery houses too
Sank downwards into the earth,

8 "Durrell's Plays," 76–77.

Tucking their roofs in, bending up their walls,
And folding as they fell, like one who stoops
Into a doorway. There was no noise at first,
Only this silence and pure disappearance,
Houses being lowered, it seemed, softly into smoke.

A silence. A wave broke. Then another.

Now came the first prodigious shrieking—
All the noise the spectacle had left behind it,
Followed and caught it up. . . .

The waters of the bay boiled up,
And hissed along the blistering paint of the hull,
Like burning oil on mirrors,
In smoke and phosphorescent water. . . . (P. 157.)

This is the sort of thing Durrell does best—the single sharp stroke capturing setting and mood; the perfect foreshadowing touch ("No cigale sang, no tree moved, no wave ran."); the vivid kinesthesia of change achieved largely through personification; the acute sense of events forever happening in an eternal present (the houses leaning, sinking, stooping); the momentary silence; the masterful stroke of "pure disappearance" and "Houses being lowered . . . softly into smoke"; then the intensity of noise; and finally, a kind of extended transferred epithet in "the blistering paint of the hull" to suggest that only those on the ship remain to feel the monumental loss of the city.

The free verse, as MacClintock has noted, has

extraordinary litheness and flexibility. The variations in rhythm, in the length of the lines, the frequent introductions of colloquialisms and down-to-earth phraseology, prevent its ever becoming monotonous. . . . There are turns of phrase and figures of speech which stick in the mind like burrs because of their aptness and vividness.[9]

[9] *Ibid.*, 77.

And thus it is the clear, supple strength of Durrell's poetic voice—even more than the character of Phaon, the dramatic portrayal of man as simultaneous master and victim of the reality and landscape he inhabits, and the full-toned creation of Sappho herself—that makes Durrell's first play a successful aesthetic ordering of a rich complex of disparate raw materials.

Acté exists on a lower level of intensity than *Sappho*. Its characters, complexities, colors, and poetry are less incandescent, less animate. Where *Sappho* approaches tragedy, *Acté* or *The Prisoners of Time*, as Durrell says in "An Author's Note" to his second play, is melodrama, with star-crossed lovers doomed when duty makes them enemies. Yet of greater interest than the basic love-hate relationship between Acté, the rebellious Scythian princess, and Fabius, Nero's loyal but impassioned and compassionate general, is the relationship of art and life. Even more than in *Sappho*, all the characters are dominated by a sense of style, an intimation that, regardless of consequences, life cannot be amorphous but must, like art, conform to rules of regularity.

In this regard, it is Nero who plays the most complex of double roles. In himself, he is a fat and disheveled homosexual, a whining hypochondriac afraid of thunder, the dark, and the ghost of Agrippina. He goes to Acté, to be bullied by her, to be treated as the stupid child he is, and to be served a bowl of Scythian broth. As he enters for the first time, "he is anointing his eye with spittle. He wears a mask pushed onto the back of his head which, when he turns, gives the illusion of a second face which is exactly like his, only a livid and phosphorescent caricature" (p. 98).[10] The visual grotesque-

---

[10] As indicated in the Bibliography, the quotations from *Acté* are from the original version published in *Show*, rather than the later separate book publication. The latter has somewhat greater structural tautness and dramatic control, but it gains these at the expense of some of the more quotable lines.

ness sharply underscores the decadence of the Emperor and the Rome he personifies.

But Nero has a third face as well—that of a god of creation, "the archpoet of Rome!" Like many of James's and Hawthorne's protagonists, he is, in the words of Durrell's Note to the play, "tormented by the feeling that the world's pattern has a coherence and a meaning, if only it could be grasped." His obsessive desire is to become an artist of the beautiful, dominating life so as to make of it a work of art. At first, he tells Acté, he had emulated Augustus. "My laws were golden, I dispensed perfect justice,/I spread happiness and security everywhere." But nothing was changed.

> Things went on just as before;
> People were just as odious, fawning, stupid.
> Man was a slave. Despair struck me, utter despair,
> For life must be an art, otherwise it is not life.
> Do you see my dilemma? I had exhausted the path of good.
> Boredom, *boredom*, that was all it brought.
> Men felt no more, learned no more. Some other way
> Must be devised. Therefore, after much passionate
> Self-communing, I thought out another way
> Of fashioning the truth. It was all that was left me!
> . . . I decided I would build
> This other world for Rome or perish in the attempt! (P. 98.)

"This other world," predicated on violence and cruelty (the antithesis of what the lovers seek to embody), Nero *has* created; yet it too alters nothing, and the world and its inhabitants continue in their oblivious, *artless* ways.

The ironist Petronius Arbiter, Nero's chief adviser, functions as the play's aesthetician. At one point he tells Flavia, Fabius' vengeful wife:

> I feel you are wrong to hate so much.
> Not morally, you understand, but somehow artistically.
> There is an obscure connection between the act and wish

Which needs care in handling; one can damage oneself,
One can give a whole world blood poisoning. (P. 101.)

To the Emperor, an artist "losing his touch," he insists that
life has at last given him all the ingredients of art—Fabius
and Acté torn between love and duty.

And all you can think of is to have them both
Publicly impaled or chewed by mangy lions. Ach!
With your views on art, it's preposterous, preposterous! (P. 100.)

Petronius, who knows "that the artist/Must use life with
respect," is a harsh and mocking critic of Nero's aesthetics.

If you are going to revise life as you wish,
You must take the artist's way with it.
Why, it's a pure waste of a blind Queen,
It's a waste of a general of genius. A waste!
Besides if they are in love, that is another very
Important factor. Lovers have every right
To meet in a death embrace; to satisfy art, my duck,
Life must be satisfied first. . . .
It would be more subtle to let them both . . . well . . .
Tempt their own fate, particularly if they are lovers.
Nothing more thorny, nothing more dangerous than love! . . .
Listen, great artist; such people as your captives
Are so deliciously full of absolutes that it's a crime
To waste them on lions; they are simply aching
To die in the name of love or honor. Push the lever!
Throw them to destiny, but not to the gladiators.
And watch the fun, artist, watch the fun. Watch it!
That would be my way if I were writing them. (Pp. 100–101.)

Petronius convinces Nero that a true artist allows for
uncertainty in his work—for free will, chance, the unfore-
seeable—yet maintains control by building upon the predictable: human weakness. And so Acté is permitted to
escape back to Scythia and rebellion. Fabius is sent to oppose

and destroy her, while Petronius himself goes to "try and
trace their fate" before the fact so that, as Nero puts it,

We will have two forms of art to compare,
Reality and illusion, you in words and I in life.
So we will be the masters of life at last,
The heroes of the Roman destiny! . . .
I will do my part; it will be exciting to see
What happens on paper and in life. Eh? Life and art, the twins!
You are a marvel, Arbiter. If they *are* the same,
I shall know that life can be art after all.
What a relief that would be! (P. 101.)

But art and life, though inextricable, are not the same, and
both suffer from the attempt to equate them. Fabius and
Acté neither die together, as Petronius first intimated they
would, nor flee to exile, hardship, and glorious love—as he
actually wrote. Petronius, failing to anticipate, misconstrues
the character of Acté, who, refusing both the suicide and
flight Fabius proffers, reveals a complete transformation as a
result of sudden and total identification with place.

Beloved Fabius,
Something has altered in me—can you guess what?
Scythia! I am a Queen now, I crouch no longer
Under the whiplash of events; destiny guides a Queen.
Those mysterious imperatives I inherited
In the hour of my birth—I only understand them now.
An apple tree cannot bear roses. It is not in nature.
It is so wonderful to comprehend at last, such a relief.
Of course, the old heartbreak will be always there—
My love for you—and nothing changes that. Yet, yet,
I am stronger than myself, as strong as Scythia now. (P. 102.)

Like Sappho, Acté bears close resemblance to Justine—a
creature so much of Alexandria (in effect, equal to Alexandria
in the way that Cleopatra, a prototype Durrell often invokes,
was Egypt) as to appear capable of only the city's thoughts,

desires, and actions. Acté bears a similar exotic beauty, is described in terms equally appropriate to Justine ("Acté speaks with authority but impulsively, which suggests that she is both hot-headed and capricious as well as brave."), plots to make real *her* impossible idealistic dreams, and has also—until Fabius and perhaps after—been checked in love, having been raped when still a virgin. Further, both are destroyed (Justine deflated, Acté decapitated) when, having been drawn irrevocably to love, they fail to go all the way with it. Love, for Durrell, is a jealous and wrathful god, and the compelling demands of even a romantic, affirmative place must never come before it.

The play's final scene occurs in Petronius' villa. He is committing suicide—slowly and with great care, as one creates a work of art, and in accord with "a lifetime's reputation for measure and elegance"—because his wife has recently died and they had sworn not to outlive each other. Yet the scene, though thematically defensible, is dramatically inadequate, for Petronius has been only partly realized during the course of the play; even more important, he has had only a tangential relationship with the world of love. Acté and Fabius fail because they direct their aesthetic vision toward the external abstraction of duty rather than toward the love which was theirs to seize; but Petronius (the play's central commentator) fails because, like Nero, he employs his art as an end in itself and thus renders life sterile.

Consequently, one simply cannot believe that there is seriousness or meaning in Petronius' life, or suicide, or epigrammatic conclusion: "Life is so good when it is leading somewhere." He appears at the end not as an artist of life adding the perfecting touch with his final action but, rather, as an artistic and human failure employing the poetry and aesthetics of his would-be trade to delude himself and those about him. And here is the real danger in Durrell's style. Its dominant quality—a rich, reverberating ambiguity—fails tonally when, as with the infantile Nero's grandiloquence and Petronius' last speech, the speaker lacks the authority of substance. In *Acté*, Durrell's music, though harsh at times, accords as well with its subject and mood as any in the poems or other plays. Still, for the most part it rings hollow; themes and characters, interesting in themselves, fail to cohere, and the poetic machinery creaks as a consequence. The problem of how to make life a work of art, the tragic conflict of love and duty, the opposing claims of loyalty and rebellion—all are richly here, yet imposed upon, rather than intrinsic to, such characters as the one-dimensional Fabius, the timid-tyrannic Nero, the inadequate Petronius. Durrell's inspiration was excellent—most of the poetry is adequate or better—but the play's lack of effective follow-through and of a unifying focal point reduces a potential dramatic masterpiece to fascinating but static literature.

If *Acté* is a step or two below *Sappho*, then *An Irish Faustus* is a flight of stairs still further down. The disappointments of the play are many: the painful unevenness of the language and the poetry; the awkward break in the middle as the magic ring shifts in function from mere object to a symbol of Faustus' illusions; the ponderously heavy Gothic machinery; uncertainties of motivation and haphazardness of thematic development. In fact, the work fails so badly as drama that, according to *Time*, "Durrell himself was hooted from the stage at the end" of the Hamburg peformance.[11]

The moment of confrontation, the climax of the play, is the best thing in it. For Durrell dramatically reverses his inherited material: Mephisto vainly tries to tempt Faustus with the possibilities the ring offers for wealth, knowledge,

[11] "Theater Abroad: Goethe Go Home," *Time*, January 3, 1964, p. 56.

power, and Faustus rejects these as merely temporal. Resolved to destroy the ring, he drags a cowering, broken Mephisto with him into the blazing purgative fire of hell. Just before the descent, an already trembling Mephisto had done his best to dissuade Faustus.

MEPHISTO: O foolish dabbler in what you do not know.
FAUSTUS: I do not need to know. I imagine, therefore I am free.
How long it has taken me to understand that.
Shall I describe the journey we must take
Down to the slag heaps of nature's inmost processes,
The threshing floor of time and matter? (P. 64.)

And the descent into what a recent essay refers to as "the elemental darkness of a private Hades" (echoing Marlowe's Mephistopheles: "Why this is Hell, nor am I out of it.") frees Faustus from the shackling crutches "of time and matter." He emerges with his clothes burned to rags and his hair turned white but looking twenty years younger. Why? John Unterecker offers the following valuable comment.

Because more has been destroyed in those elemental flames than clothing, a ring, and a cross that Faustus had assumed would protect him against chthonic powers. Faustus' illusions have also been destroyed. He has been both purified and, to his surprise, educated. For experiencing first fear and then despair, he had in that throbbing world found himself at last suddenly transported beyond such private emotions to an acceptance of the design of things: "I found myself laughing./For the first time I knew I was in reality." And though Durrell's Faustus does not use the term *heraldic universe*, we who are adjusted to it in the rest of Durrell's work should have no difficulty in realizing that it is that universe which has opened up before him:

"I saw
The whole Universe, this great mine of forms
For what it is—simply a great hint. . . .
Yes, I saw it all so clearly for the first time from
There.

39

❀↑✳↩❀↑✳↩❀↑✳↩❀↑✳↩❀↑✳↩❀↑✳↩❀↑✳↩❀↑✳↩❀↑✳↩❀↑✳↩❀

I have never felt so happy, such relief.
It's as if my whole life had become a sort of vestige.
Somehow I must refresh it and renew it.
You know, I think I shall go on a long journey.
I want to see the world again through these new eyes."[12]

To put Faustus' experience into a broad, traditional context, one would do well to refer to Northrop Frye's discussion of epic where he writes, "To gain information about the future, or what is 'ahead' in terms of the lower cycle of life, it is normally necessary to descend to a lower world of the dead, as is done in the nekyia, or katabasis, in the eleventh book of the *Odyssey* and the sixth of the *Aeneid*."[13] Faustus returns enriched and transformed, having truly come in contact with reality for the first time, having "felt the very heart of process beating," and he now commits the act of affirmative flight that such characters as Phaon and Fabius had also attempted. But where Fabius failed utterly and Phaon brought with him seeds of destruction, Faustus departs unencumbered. His new life, self-contained but honest, brings him not to Sappho's "icy peak of . . . indifference" or to Petronius' "quiet valley/With its wintry vineyards and ghostly olive trees," where presumably death alone signifies reality, but to a secluded hemitage, where life and death are complementary, where his new sense of quietism evokes a concomitant response in the landscape.

Of course the world itself, as Durrell demonstrated in his first two plays, does not really change. There is nothing inherently stultifying about Faustus' environment at the beginning.

[12] *Lawrence Durrell*, 6, 34.
[13] *Anatomy of Criticism*, 321.

It is raining again [he says]—the eternal green rain of Ireland,
So softly, so purposefully, rain without end. (P. 11.)

And there is nothing invariably fructifying about the "snowy panorama of mountains and clouds" of the final scene (p. 84). Nonetheless, the world of Durrell's art *is* transformed when, as at the spiritually violent climaxes of *Panic Spring, The Dark Labyrinth, The Black Book,* the *Quartet,* and *Tunc,* sudden visionary insight sears away the blindness of self-delusion. And Faustus too, having achieved a new sense of self-dependence and inner quietude, inherits a landscape alive and anthropomorphic. Matthew, the old hermit, makes this explicit when he tells Faustus of his duties in the mountains, the duties Faustus has now adopted for himself.

> If duty is what you cannot help, then I have none;
> For I am helping everything by doing nothing. . . .
> I help the moon rise, the sun to set. I eat and drink. . . .
> I do absolutely nothing in a helpful sort of way.
> A little music, a little wine, and the spoils of solitude;
> An immortal trinity to live by and recreate.
> In fact, the recreation of time itself in the recreation
>   of man. (Pp. 88–89.)

The play concludes, then, with all conflicts resolved, all mundane worries left below the timber line, and the four card-players (Faustus and his companions) grown beyond art and desire and wholly at peace with themselves and their landscape. "The light slowly fades turning them into silhouettes. Outside the sky is bright and the snow-capped mountains glitter" (p. 92).

Durrell's heraldic universe—that condition of self-awareness and inner serenity treated metaphorically as a landscape responding and corresponding to the needs and proportions of men without dominating them—serves as a valid poetic equivalent of abstract affirmation. Characters either do or do not arrive there, and Durrell measures their success, and perhaps significance, accordingly. In each of the three plays, one major figure achieves the essential breakthrough. Their fates are different—Phaon is murdered, Petronius commits suicide, and Faustus, though self-exiled, stays alive to "help the moon rise, the sun to set"; yet for Durrell all embody equally the heraldic universe. For the reader, however, and despite the improvement in their fates from the earliest of the three to the latest, they portray a *decreasing* vitality and stature which seem to undercut the validity of Durrell's metaphorical realm. But this is simply to say that the poetic figure functions effectively only in a good work of art.

It might be useful, as a final comment, to suggest a reason for Durrell's steady decline as a dramatist. His line of development in the plays is really a surprising, perhaps even alien, one, for it runs counter to that of the poems and the fiction. The poems and the fiction emphasize that the process of transformation (or maturation), enabling a character either to begin to create as an artist or to feel he no longer needs to, parallels or heralds his being freed of checks on his ability to love. But love, around which Durrell constructs his finest edifices, increasingly dissipates its power in the plays. In them, we take Phaon's achievement most seriously, largely because of his brief but successful affair with Sappho, even though he feels constrained to abandon her when societal pressures threaten to reimpose standards he had done well to move beyond. The problems of *Acté* are greater than those of *Sappho* because of the dual focus of the former: the love affair of Acté and Fabius has dramatic significance, but it goes nowhere; Petronius attains the heraldic universe, but he has nothing meaningful to say of love. And *Irish Faustus*, with its protagonist a middle-aged pedagogue and Margaret a silly schoolgirl, is hollow at the core because, instead of love, the most impassioned expression in Durrell's best work of man's aliveness, he substitutes, in the final scene, the pallid comradeship of a staid old English club. And since no passion ever rears its unruly head *there*, no vision can long evade the stodgy death, confining and trite, that invariably lies in wait in an atmosphere and setting of such unresponsive, even antihuman, design.

Concomitantly, the key to the failure lies in the landscape and Durrell's declining sense of place in the plays. *Sappho* employs landscape in a way that might be termed classical Durrell. Lesbos, though essentially vital in nature, is landscape too pervasive and willful, and which one must flee to achieve meaningful existence; in contrast, the peaceful beauty of "No-name" conforms exactly to the needs of the rejuvenated Phaon and serves as objective correlative for the validity of his new life. Landscape thus plays a fundamental role in *Sappho*, one inextricable from its themes, characters, and poetry.

In *Acté*, to parallel Durrell's less certain control of his materials (especially his love theme), landscape plays a less organically central role. Rome is *any* seat of power; Scythia, *any* outlying, rebellious colony; and, most vague, the last scene in Petronius' country villa occurs simply "far from Rome." Finally, in *Irish Faustus*—where the heraldic universe is highly abstract and love impossible—landscape is virtually nonexistent. The few passing references to rain-sodden Ireland and the snow-capped peaks at the end do not alter the fact that *Irish Faustus* takes place anywhere and nowhere, and that the characters are in touch not with a real place but with only a projection of themselves. And the rule in Durrell is that to inhabit a negative or a too dominant landscape may ultimately stifle life, but to inhabit none at all, as is the case with Faustus and those about him, not only precludes even the *possibility* of life but invariably devitalizes the work containing them.

Island Books

If Durrell had written neither poetry nor fiction, he would never have become the literary phenomenon he has; yet for his island books alone he would command a position among contemporary writers. (In fact, some critics otherwise unsympathetic to Durrell's art find merit in only these books.) For this richly evocative prose most fully and most successfully exploits Durrell's love of place.

Prospero's Cell, like Gerald Durrell's superbly funny *My Family and Other Animals*, treats the years the Durrell family spent on Corfu; yet the two books are vastly dissimilar. Gerald Durrell, a child of ten when the family arrived on the island, writes mainly of his entomological escapades and of their effects—usually disastrous—on the rest of the Durrells. *Prospero's Cell*, on the other hand, makes scarcely any reference to the Durrell family—only Nancy (N.), Durrell's first wife, is at all important, and she does not appear in *My Family*—and, rather than focusing on one small corner of the island, it takes a broad view—both spatially and temporally—of this Greek world in miniature.

Much more than a travel book, *Prospero's Cell* is a conglomeration of literary genres. Much of it takes the form of an artist's journal covering the period from April 10, 1937, to January 1, 1941; yet the book's spontaneity is achieved only with time and distance, for Durrell did not write it until several years later in Alexandria.[14] Something of a history,

[14] In a letter written in 1944, he says, "I've done about half of a little historical book about Corfu; tried writing in the style of a diary—you know the French anecdotal novel type of things" (*Corr*, p. 188).

the book contains chapters with such titles as "The Island Saint" and "History and Conjecture," as well as a synoptic chronology, a brief bibliography, and a sketchy index. For the traveler, it contains vivid descriptions of the island and its people and a useful appendix, which includes, among other items, "Some Peasant Remedies in Common Use against Disease." And, finally, as its date and place of composition suggest, *Prospero's Cell* is a product of the creative imagination—a re-creation rather than simply a remembering. Its narrator (not simply Durrell, but Durrell as interpreted by Durrell) rejects the maps, tables, and statistics offered for inclusion by a helpful friend. "If I wrote a book about Corcyra," he says, "it would not be a history but a poem."[15]

In Lawrence Clark Powell's words, *Prospero's Cell* "is a Mediterranean prose-poem to rank with *Fountains in the Sand, Sea and Sardinia,* and *The Colossus of Maroussi.*"[16] Like its successors, Durrell's first island book employs many fictional techniques. For, in ways typical of his novels, Durrell here creates characters indeterminate and variable, yet of imposing stature; an aesthetic conflict concerning the various possibilities of interpreting and ordering reality;[17] a setting

15 As his next entry in his "journal," the narrator offers "Fragment from a novel about Corcyra which I began and destroyed [we are not told why]: 'She comes down through the cloud of almond-trees like a sentence of death, all dressed in white and leading her flock to the very gates of the underworld. Our hearts melt in us at the candour of her smile and the beauty of her walk. Soon she is to marry Niko, the fat moneylender, and become a stout shrew drudging out to olive-pickings on a lame donkey, smelling of garlic and animal droppings' " (*Cell*, pp. 20–21).

16 Introductory Note to *A Landmark Gone,* p. *i.* This pamphlet, privately printed for Powell, is a kind of précis, often word for word, of *Prospero's Cell.*

17 " 'Here we are,' " says the Count, [the character of greatest and freest imagination] . . ., "each of us collecting and arranging our common knowledge according to the form dictated to him by his temperament. In all cases it will not be the whole picture, though it will be the whole picture for you" (*Cell,* p. 107). And further down the same page, the Count is asked to

vast, pervasive, and alive; and, perhaps most interestingly, an "Epilogue in Alexandria" (where, after all, the book was written), offering the same kind of perspective shift as the Workpoints appended to the *Quartet* novels.

Durrell's intense awareness of place imposes a kind of unity on his otherwise disparate material—for he mixes his semiliterary journal with humorous anecdotes, aesthetic-philosophic discussions and meditations, more or less scholarly essays on selected aspects of the island, and the various apparatus already indicated. And the landscape and the atmosphere, like that of Greece in the poetry, serve as touchstones, as controlling metaphors, for Durrell not only writes of them with often lyric intensity but he also raises them—in a manner anticipating the Alexandria of the *Quartet*—to mythopoeic significance. "Other countries," he writes early in the book, "may offer you discoveries in manners or lore or landscape; Greece offers you something harder—the discovery of yourself" (*Cell*, p. 11). And because this has been true for Durrell, and because on Corfu the writing has gone well and life has been good, the "Epilogue in Alexandria" reads like the saddest of endings: the disillusionment following the loss of innocence.

In these summer twilights the city [Alexandria] lies in its jumble of pastel tones, faintly veined like an exhausted petal. . . . The last landmark on the edge of Africa. The battleships in their arrowed blackness turn slowly in the harbour. The loss of Greece has been an amputation. All Epictetus could not console one against it. (*Cell*, p. 131.)

---

describe the kind of book the narrator *will* write of Corfu. " 'It is difficult to say,' says the Count. 'A portrait inexact in detail, containing bright splinters of landscape, written out roughly, as if to get rid of something which was troubling the optic nerves.' " A comment which could serve as an accurate blurb for *Prospero's Cell*—and much of Durrell's other writings as well.

For with the coming of war and the loss of Greece, the demise of love has followed. "There is simply patience to be exercised. Patience and endurance and love. Some of us have vanished from the picture; some have had their love converted into black bile by the misery they have witnessed" (p. 132). And the final words of the book suggest the profundity of despair now gripping the world and its artists. A deracinated Durrell writes:

Seen through the transforming lens of memory, the past seemed so enchanted that even thought would be unworthy of it. We never speak of it, having escaped: the house in ruins, the little black cutter smashed. I think only that the shrine with the three black cypresses and the tiny rock-pool where we bathed must still be left. Visited by the lowland summer mists the trembling landscape must still lie throughout the long afternoons, glowing and altering like a Chinese water-colour where the light of the sky leaks in. But can all these hastily written pages ever recreate more than a fraction of it? (*Cell*, p. 133.)

The answer apparently is no—at least for Durrell the man—and his sense of inadequacy and hopeless frustration manifests itself in the failure of his marriage in Egypt during the war. As for Durrell the artist, he has succeeded better than he suggests, for *Prospero's Cell* is a richly evocative book, with its many well-portrayed incidents and characters serving as a check on the tendency toward vagueness and abstraction. The inaction of the book, though an accurate reflection of the languorousness of prewar Greece, is something of a weakness—perhaps the main one of the book. But such self-indulgence, though Durrell still gives way to it at times, becomes rarer in his more mature writings. A pattern of increasing intensity emerges in the island books: from casual prewar Corfu Durrell shifts to postwar Rhodes—with its desperate need of immediate action—of *Reflections on a*

47

Marine Venus, and then to the incipient civil-war Cypriot atmosphere of the tense and compelling *Bitter Lemons.*

If being cast out of Corfu represents a fall from innocence for Durrell and his Greek world, then the re-entry into Rhodes is an attempt at lifting the guilt that has descended. Or, to shift the metaphor to the one central to *Marine Venus* and to much of his other writings, Durrell seeks a cure for the spiritual diseases plaguing virtually all his characters— here made manifest by the war and its aftereffects. The narrator of *Marine Venus* writes of a people and a world ravaged by sickness and death, and he returns to his beloved Greece with great trepidation, as if going to visit an old, ailing friend who, he fears, may already be dead by the time he arrives. As he prepares to leave Alexandria "that spring afternoon of 1945," he thinks,

> Tomorrow I should see for myself whether the old Greek ambience had survived the war, whether it was still a reality based in the landscape and the people—or whether we had simply invented it for ourselves in the old days, living comfortably on foreign exchange, patronising reality with our fancies and making bad literature from them. (*Venus,* pp. 16–17.)

Durrell's own "disease" is "islomania," an ailment "as yet unclassified by medical science. . . . [A] rare but by no means unknown affliction of spirit," it causes its victims to "find islands somehow irresistible." And *Marine Venus,* Durrell adds, "is by intention a sort of anatomy of islomania" (*Venus,* pp. 15–16)—an examination of the complex interrelationship of stricken moth and compelling flame. For again Durrell does not offer simply a descriptive survey of his island, but rather a probing which is at once revelatory and exploratory, at once therapeutic and self-analytic, at once a finished work of art and one prematurely made public with the skeleton of its scaffolding still lying about.

48

The technique is one of planned formlessness, a deploying of the many pieces comprising the Rhodian mosaic, rather than a straightforward guide to the island or a continuous narrative of events occurring there. "If I have sacrificed form," Durrell writes in terms anticipating his technical concerns in the *Quartet*, "it is for something better, sifting into the material now some old notes from a forgotten scrapbook, now a letter: all the quotidian stuff which might give a common reader the feeling of life lived in a historic present" (*Venus*, p. 16). Like the Count in *Prospero's Cell*, Mills, an Englishman wholly a creature of Mediterranean Greece, tells Durrell the kind of portrait of the island he should write. " 'Not history or myth—but landscape and atmosphere somehow. "A companion" is the sort of idea. You ought to try for the landscape—and even these queer months of transition from desolation to normality' " (*Venus*, p. 36).

Mills himself aids greatly in this transition, for, like Fonvisin in *Panic Spring* and Balthazar and Amaril in the *Quartet*, he is a doctor endowed with remarkable curative power, who, in addition, personifies soundness of body and mind. "It would be difficult," Durrell remarks of Mills, "to think of anyone who seemed to be such a walking certificate for good health; it simply oozed from him, from his candid face, fresh complexion, sensitive fingers" (*Venus*, p. 34). In fact, Mills, like most exceptionally healthy people, takes illness as something of an affront, a misdeed perpetrated by the patient simply, or at least primarily, to get attention.

In his Introduction to Georg Groddeck's *Book of the It*, Durrell notes that Groddeck conceived of a man's physical condition (that uneasy mean between the two abstract extremes of total health and total illness) as the outward manifestation of the internal man. Thus, disease and illness are seen as expressions of a man's personal identity. To some-

49

one not totally committed to accepting his theory, Groddeck seems at times to carry it to absurd lengths—for instance, in asking an injured patient, "What was your idea in breaking your arm?"[18] Still, much of what Groddeck says can be accepted—we do, for example, tend to associate certain diseases with certain people, and see an appropriateness in *that* person's having *that* malady—especially with regard to the infirmities of literary characters. The blinding of Oedipus or of Gloucester, for instance, is clearly an objective correlative for spiritual blindness; the impotence of Jake Barnes or of Clifford Chatterley tells us something of the spiritual crippling caused by modern war and its aftermath, on the one hand, and by dehumanized technology, on the other. Disease or injury strikes, at one time or another, virtually every important character in Durrell's *Quartet*, and it invariably symbolizes some major aspect of the personality it strikes.

This relationship of disease and personality has little place in Durrell's earliest writings, although there are hints of it in *The Black Book* and *The Dark Labyrinth*. In *Marine Venus*, however, Mills serves to focus Durrell's increasing interest in the subject; and he is written of in terms anticipating the subsequent involvement with Groddeck.

His diagnosis of disease, [Durrell notes], seemed somehow to be a criticism, not of the functioning of one specific organ, but of the whole man. Like all born healers he had realised, without formulating the idea, that disease has its roots in a faulty metaphysic, in a way of life. And the patient who took him a cyst to lance or a wheezing lung to think about, was always disturbed by the deliberate careful scrutiny of those clear blue eyes. One felt slightly ashamed of being ill in the presence of Mills. It was as if, staring at you as you stood there, he were waiting for you to justify your illness, to deliver yourself in some way of the hidden causes of it. (*Venus*, p. 35.)

[18] Quoted by Durrell, Introduction, *The Book of the It*, viii.

Durrell's ailment, islomania, though it is not fatal, remains nonetheless uncured. In the epilogue to his second island book, he associates it with the permanent "wound" (obviously a consequence of love) he has received from his "Marine Venus." Durrell not only rediscovers "the old Greek ambience" but he helps to resuscitate it during his stay on Rhodes—both in his work while on the island and in this book—for he correctly notes that "by this writing," all his friends and all they have experienced on Rhodes are made forever a part "of this small green island" and of the "greater arc" which is all of Greece (*Venus*, pp. 183–84). But though Durrell, in his work and in his art, contributes to the rebuilding of a world and a way of life, he once again fails at love— and in the epilogue he is once more alone with the child, while E. (Eve), his second wife, is no longer "a familiar, a critic, a lover" (*Venus*, p. 16).

The poignancy of Eve's loss is, however, far less intense than that of Nancy's in *Prospero's Cell*, since the former receives scant treatment as a character. *Marine Venus*, like its predecessor, is richly evocative, containing several fine characterizations (especially that of Mills) and much good talk; but it represents something of a falling off, for it lacks the subjective immediacy of the first island book. The art is present, but not so artlessly deployed, and we get only intermittent glimpses of the artist's attempting to come to grips with the virtually intractable materials of both the creative process and his life, of both art and love. As a consequence, where *Prospero's Cell* seems of the very essence of Corfu (and of Durrell's persistent attempt to understand that essence in terms of himself), *Marine Venus*, though like all of Durrell's prose it contains vivid description and fine insights, is not so much *of* Rhodes as simply *about* it.

The last of Durrell's island books is by far his best, for it has all the virtues of the earlier ones and none of their failings —plus the fortuitous advantage of a significant plot. *Bitter Lemons* not only captures an atmosphere and a tone, a way of life and a people, but it details and examines the destruction of the Cypriot peace which culminates in the disastrous outbreak of civil war. The sense of place, then, is brilliantly and appropriately subordinated to the sense of the moment.

The book's apparatus is minimal (index, brief bibliography, poem entitled "Bitter Lemons"), for against the vibrancy of the here and the now, the intensity of the narrative, especially as Durrell counterpoints it against the usual Cypriot languor, additional trappings would be distractingly superfluous. For the same reason, the various concerns of Durrell as artist and as man seem almost incidental, irrelevant impediments to this monolithic flux, and are thus infrequent. And yet, simultaneously, *Bitter Lemons* is perhaps Durrell's most profoundly personal work, for it concerns nothing if not his physical and spiritual return to the Greek world, his own quest for the Hellenic warmth denied him during a chilling half decade in Yugoslavia.

Durrell arrives on Cyprus alone and alien, almost unable to believe in the continuing reality of the Greek world. "After five years of Serbia," he writes, "I had begun to doubt whether, in wanting to live in the Mediterranean at all, I was not guilty of some fearful aberration; indeed the whole of this adventure had begun to smell of improbability" (*BL*, p. 16). But after the initial moments of strangeness, the improbable once again becomes the familiar.

A vague and spiritless lethargy reigned. I was beginning to think that successive occupations had extirpated any trace whatsoever of the Greek genius when I was relieved by the sight of a bus with both back wheels missing, lying on its side against a house. It was just like home. Three old ladies were dismembering the conductor; the driver was doing one of those laughing and shrugging acts which drive travellers out of their minds all over the Levant; the village idiot was pumping up a tyre; the owners of the house against which the bus was leaning were hanging indignantly out of their drawing-room window and, with their heads inside the bus, were being rude to the point of nausea. Meanwhile, a trifle removed from the centre of the hubbub, and seated perilously on the leaning roof of the machine, with contorted face, perched an individual in a cloth cap who appeared to be remorselessly sawing the bus in half, starting at the top. Was this perhaps some obscure revenge, or a genuine attempt to make a helpful contribution? I shall never know. (*BL*, pp. 22–23.)

And within a week of his arrival, Durrell soon adds, "I had a dozen firm friends . . . " (*BL*, p. 29).

Yet reintegration, like the too quick urbanizing of the somnolent agrarian landscape of Cyprus, is an uncomfortable bifurcating process, for the ubiquitous slogan "ENOSIS AND ONLY ENOSIS" insistently reminds everyone on the island of the increasing intrusion of public affairs on what should normally be private intercourse. "This wonder of an Englishman who spoke indifferent but comprehensible Greek" (*BL*, p. 23), Durrell is readily accepted by the people he meets; and the Cypriots, clamoring for their "freedom" from the British, continue to proclaim their love for all the English, and especially for individual Englishmen like Durrell. Yet hatred ultimately proliferates beyond control and into impersonality, even to the point where Durrell himself is almost killed.

Actually, however, Durrell is not so much a passive victim of events as he would have us believe, for, though he attempts to dissociate himself from his compatriots, he becomes increasingly involved in the larger affairs of the island, thus automatically becoming a target for Cypriot anger and frustration. His original plan was to devote himself entirely to his own writing (and he does manage to write *Justine* while on Cyprus), but his funds dwindle and he accepts a commission "to write a series of articles on the issue [enosis] for an American Institute of International Relations Bulletin" (p. 121). Then he takes a job teaching English at the Nicosia gymnasium, where, as elsewhere, his British manner contrasts with Greek vivacity.

> To achieve silence was impossible—a soft but persistent susurrus like a slow puncture was the nearest one could get to this—and the normal was a growling wave of chatter which rose and fell like a sea. I tried, as an experiment, sending talkers out of the room one by one, in order to see at what stage the class became controllable. I was left at last with three students. As no corporal punishment was permitted in the school it was impossible to do more than gesticulate, foam, dance and threaten. . . . (*BL*, p. 129.)

Yet neither Durrell's essential Britishness nor his occasional condescension of tone when writing of the local inhabitants conceals his expansive philhellenism and an extroversion which overcome many potential barriers to friendship. Both in his tiny village of Bellapaix—where, with the help of seemingly all the local characters, he boisterously buys and revamps a small house—and at the school, Durrell establishes a contact of the most significant kind with the people about him, a contact whose permanency appears beyond question—until the acid of nationalism and terror begins to eat away all human bonds, and the air of even the most natural of moments becomes increasingly filled with the poison of uncontrolled political emotionalism. For instance, Durrell offhandedly writes of his female students, "They were uncomfortably united in one thing, besides Enosis, and that was a passionate, heart-rending determination to marry their English teacher" (*BL*, p. 130). And the dualism of thought and purpose that gradually overwhelms

the island enters the school and its students. "In these classes
... I encountered the same shifting wind of popular opinion
which hovered between anti-British intransigence and the old
ineradicable affection for the mythical Briton (the 'Philelef-
theros') the freedom-lover, who could not help but approve
of Enosis as an idea" (*BL*, p. 133).

But the British make little attempt to live up to such an
image, and the youths of the island succumb invariably to
hatred—for the cause is not only just in the main, it is also
pervasive, intense, monolithic. And only a few months later,
Durrell, inspecting a prison containing terrorists, comes upon
two former students of his: Joanides, a "fat ruffian . . . , a
natural comedian of such talent that I had been forced to
expel him at the beginning of almost every lesson," who
was arrested for carrying a grenade—" 'Ach! Mr. Durrell,' he
said, 'it was just a *little* bomb . . .' "; and Paul, ashamed because he had shown "cowardice" in failing to bomb a house
where small children were playing. Durrell's comment here
reveals the depths of his insight into the inner conflict of the
islanders, and his helplessness as well.

> Superb egotism of youth! He had been worried about his
> own inability to obey orders. It is, of course, not easy for youths
> raised in a Christian society, to turn themselves into terrorists
> overnight—and in a sense his problem was the problem of all the
> Cypriot Greeks. . . . "So you are sorry because you didn't kill two
> children?" I said. "What a twisted brain, what a twisted stick you
> must be as well as a fool!" He winced and his eyes flashed. "War is
> war," he said. I left him without another word. (*BL*, pp. 199–
> 201.)

But Durrell does endeavor to bridge the widening chasm,
for he has accepted the position of press adviser to the British
government—a job he held for years elsewhere—and attempts to establish communication between the conflicting

nationalities. Intellectually, he is himself guilty of colonial myopia, and he sympathizes with the British rulers, who "lived by the central colonial proposition which, as a conservative I fully understand, namely: 'If you have an Empire, you just can't give away bits of it as soon as asked.' I differed with them only in believing that in Cyprus we had an issue which could be honourably compounded. . ." (BL, pp. 158–59). Yet Durrell here underestimates his emotional commitment to the Cypriot character and cause, and he overestimates his capacity for self-blindness; he is, on the contrary, one of the few Englishmen to recognize relatively early in the crisis that EOKA's appeal was islandwide, that the potential blowup threatened not only domestic tranquility but also the whole structure of international relationships, and that to oppose vast force to the first tentative acts of terrorism would not only fail to cow the insurrectionists but would win them hordes of new recruits.

Durrell saw too that what failed for the British—perhaps above all—was their sense of timing. For one thing, as Durrell learns as soon as he begins his work for the government, the British totally lacked a Cypriot policy, with the impossible exception of maintaining the status quo at all costs. Policy subsequently develops only as feeble reaction to mounting pressures: a vague constitution plus partial censorship in response to a demand not for immediate and total independence, but merely for a promise of elections in the indeterminate future; a belated conference of the involved powers, doomed to failure because, during the period of British ostrichlike hiding, the originally quiescent Turks had gradually developed a no-compromise posture; and, too late to do any good, a new governor, one not inherently confused and incapable of seeing that the Cyprus problem was more European and international than it was colonial.

" 'Why,' said my friend, and this was to become an echo everywhere (even repeated by Makarios), 'did they not send us such a man a long time ago?' Why indeed!" Durrell is constrained to add (*BL*, p. 210).

On a different level, one perhaps of greater significance for the immediate purposes of this study, *Bitter Lemons* treats its subject in terms of literature, of an aesthetic. For one thing, in retrospect at least, Durrell recognizes the artistic unity of his writings on Corfu, Rhodes, and Cyprus. *Bitter Lemons*, he notes, "completes a trilogy of island books" (*BL*, p. 9). Beauty of landscape and natural setting, and Durrell's ability to re-create it in a stroke, intensifies progressively from book to book, from island to island.

The dawns and the sunsets in Cyprus are unforgettable—better even than those of Rhodes which I always believed were unique in their slow Tiberian magnificence. As I breasted the last rise where the road falls like a swallow towards Kyrenia I paused for a minute to watch the sun burst through the surface mists of the sea and splash the mountain behind me with light. . . . I would start to climb the range, the sun climbing with me, balcony by balcony, ridge by ridge; until as I breasted the last loop of the pass the whole Mesaoria would spread out under the soft buttery dawn-light, languid and green as a lover's wish; or else shimmer through a cobweb of mist like the mirage of a Chinese water-print. (*BL*, pp. 126–27.)

But such passages of pure description become increasingly rare in *Bitter Lemons*, for what proves to be an overwhelming rush of events pre-empts both the time and the vision; and if Cyprus prior to the outbreak of hostilities embodies art and beauty—in its landscape, its people, its ambience—then that tranquil perfection is desecrated by the philistinism of shortsightedness and hatred.

And the drama that takes place—the senseless tragedy most tragic in that, Durrell insists, "it need not have happened" (*BL*, p. 128)—assumes qualities and dimensions of classic proportions: the tragic blindness of the British; the wholesale wastage of property, lives, and a wonderfully vital way of life, perhaps best emblematized by the Cypriot youths, jailed as terrorists, who incongruously complain most about "the crowded conditions [that] prevented them from studying for their examinations" (*BL*, p. 201); the obscenity of terror that smashes "the slender chain of trust upon which all human relations are based" (*BL*, p. 215); and the hopeless, hollow despair that expresses the pity felt for both self and others—"I was, I realized, very tired after this two years' spell as a servant of the Crown; and I had achieved nothing. It was good to be leaving. . . . I felt bitterly ashamed of the neglect these people had endured—the poor Cyps" (*BL*, pp. 246, 250).

But the drama lacks catharsis, the purgative cleansing which permits a stable, if mundane, moral order at last to reassert itself. Cyprus the place remains; but, with the deaths of trust and Anglo-Greek amity, what hope can arise for the future? Durrell can find none.

The mythopoeic image of the Englishman which every Greek carried in his heart, and which was composed of so many fused and overlapping pictures—the poet, the lord, the quixotic and fearless defender of right, the just and freedom-loving Englishman —the image was at last thrown down and dashed into a thousand pieces, never again to be reassembled. (*BL*, p. 242.)

In the book's final episode, Durrell spends a day in the Cypriot hills with Panos, his oldest friend on the island. Except for the occasional appearance of troops, the day is idyllic: they picnic, they gather great bunches of wild flowers that fill the car; Durrell even abandons himself for a time to the cold calmness of the lagoon waters, and he makes perhaps his finest poetic image of the book: "A lizard lay asleep on the bamboo couch [in the hut by the water] looking like a Greek politician waiting for an opening" (*BL*, p. 236). But the effectiveness of the image lies not in its abstract cleverness but rather in its felt reality, in the unhappy fact of its appropriateness—at least from the British and Turkish viewpoints. The episode, then, is merely a lull, a brief respite between explosions; Durrell has already announced his imminent departure from the island, and Panos, presumably because of his intimacy with the Briton, was shot dead two days after the day in the hills. Durrell's final gesture—the discarding of all his daughter's mementos of Cyprus—is melodramatic but not inappropriate.

It would seem that Durrell has come full circle. *Prospero's Cell* began with an epigraph from *The Tempest*: " 'No tongue: all eyes: be silent' " (p. 11); and after *Bitter Lemons*, only silence is possible. The Cypriot-Greeks had mythologized the mainlanders, seeing them as "those paragons of democratic virtue. Their idea of Greece is of Paradise on earth—a paradise without defect" (*BL*, pp. 114–15). The Greeks, on their part, had envisaged a mythical Briton whose ideals were always noble and whose actions always effected those ideals. And Durrell, for all his inherent Britishness, had romanticized his Greek islanders and their home into embodiments of hospitality, vibrancy, vitality. Now the images, and the half-truths they depict, are shattered—not only on Cyprus and elsewhere but also within Durrell himself, for, in a revealing volte-face, he several times expresses a fear that Cyprus might be invaded from, of all places, Rhodes or Crete. Now only the other half of truth—with its ugly mask of brutality, stupidity, bitterness, and despair—is all that remains. These forces have been a powerful antidote, for they have finally cured Durrell of his deep-rooted islomania. But the cure is of course worse than the disease; no one but

Durrell has been writing books of this kind and quality in English in recent years, and it seems certain that he himself will write them no more. Thus, the price we pay for the *Quartet* and subsequent fiction is very large indeed.

The major point concerning Durrell's Greece should perhaps be underscored. It functions as complexly in his island books as it does in much of his poetry and as Alexandria does in the *Quartet*: as a pervasive motif and atmosphere, as a metaphorical control, and as a concrete manifestation of his often shadowy figures. Greece, and all that it includes as both concept and place, offers a kind of comforting unity, a sense of rootedness in a vast historical context which, for the most part, enables the implied poet of these works to look not only beyond good and evil but also beyond the logically expected optimism or pessimism and into the underlying aesthetic of events. Thus, Durrell the man despairs over Corcyrean loss, Rhodian desecration, Cypriot anarchy; but as an artist, he suffers far more for the larger significance of these events: the violation of the true and the beautiful. Yet here is the great consolation, for to violate a pattern is of course to imply it, and it is the permanence and strength of Durrell's Greek pattern, not the good or evil of daily events, that undergird and inspirit his island books and transport them from the transient province of travel reportage into the unaging realm of vision become art.

In the final analysis, the materials examined in this chapter demonstrate both the abundant variety of Durrellean forms and, simultaneously, the consistency of his concerns. The *Quartet*, as we shall see in the following chapters, represents no radical metamorphosis of Durrell's creative spirit. The scope has become vast, the writing finer, the characters more vital and complex, the themes more dramatic and immediate;

yet, for the most part, the pattern of the *Quartet* has not only long been forming in Durrell's mind but, writ small, has almost from the first found expression in the various forms of his writing.

II. *Justine* and
The Alexandrian Prism

I'm so glad I didn't read The Good Soldier *before writing* Justine *or I might never have finished her! This novel is an eye-opener with its brilliant organization and gathering momentum; it's fit to put beside the best of our time.* (Lawrence Durrell, quoted by Kenneth Young in "A Dialogue with Durrell," p. 65.)

> *I see no sin;*
> *The wrong is mixed. In tragic life, God wot,*
> *No villain need be! Passions spin the plot;*
> *We are betrayed by what is false within.*
> (George Meredith, *Modern Love.*)

*J*ustine, the first phase of Lawrence Durrell's four-part investigation of what he calls modern love, the Meredithian complex of human interrelationship, is a complete, if not entirely satisfactory, novel in itself. All the necessary ingredients—plot, setting, characterization, internal revelation, even a beginning, a middle, and an end—are present. Yet they are not so much made immovable parts of a fixed totality as they are organically interpenetrated—first some of one ingredient, then another, and yet a third, all touching though never coalescing—somewhat in the way that the various themes in the opening movement of a symphony are presented, elaborated, recalled, and expanded throughout the work. The artist works against time to create the sense of several themes existing simultaneously; as often as a theme reappears, those moments of initial presentation again become, to some degree, the present.

In music, an inescapably temporal art form, the problem of simultaneity remains essentially insoluble. Sounds occur in time and, in contrast to purely visual art, can never be completely abstracted from it. The novel too, according to Percy Lubbock, is

shadowy and fantasmal. . . . Nothing, no power, will keep a book steady and motionless before us, so that we may have time to examine its shape and design. As quickly as we read, it melts and shifts in the memory. . . . A cluster of impressions, some clear points emerging from a mist of uncertainty, this is all we can hope to possess, generally speaking, in the name of a book. . . . Since we can never speak of a book with our eye on the object, never handle a book—the real book, which is to the volume as the symphony is to the score—our phrases find nothing to check them, immediately and unmistakably, while they are formed. . . . Our critical faculty may be admirable; we may be thoroughly capable of judging a book justly, if only we could watch it at ease. But fine taste and keen perception are of no use to us if we cannot retain the image of the book; and the image escapes and evades us like a cloud.[1]

Yet surely the novel comes closest to approximating the mean between music's pure temporality and the spatial quality of painting. And the novel is perhaps the one form which offers the possibility for a marriage of space and time: the words are there on the page; we can point at and examine them; and, although they move through time as we read and are

[1] *The Craft of Fiction*, 1–3.

affected by the knowledge and emotion we receive from what follows them, we are always able to reapproach a moment of the novel's past as if it were again part of the present. Clearly, we cannot do the same if we are, say, listening to a piece of music.

According to Durrell, the first three parts of *The Alexandria Quartet* offer us repeated views of the same moments in time, a single set of circumstances continually returned to and re-examined in the light of subsequent data. "The first three parts," he writes, "are to be deployed spatially . . . and are not linked in a serial form. They interlap, interweave, in a purely spatial relation. Time is stayed. The fourth part alone will represent time and be a true sequel" (*B*, Note). And within each of the spatial elements, sequence will be determined as in a symphony, not by the force of chronological necessity but by the demands made by the creation upon its creator. As Darley says, "What I most need to do is to record experiences, not in the order in which they took place —for that is history—but in the order in which they first became significant for me" (*J*, p. 97). And reverberations of Proustian impressionism echo resoundingly in the shifting valleys and byways of Darley's Alexandria.

What is most immediately apparent, even within the limited confines of *Justine*, is the multiplicity of mutually qualifying voices, each of which, at one time or another, seems to speak with the force of privileged authenticity— especially on the ubiquitous subject of love. For love is all about us and all-encompassing, our one standard of good and evil in an otherwise amoral and valueless world; and since love is, without contradiction, something different for every viewer, it presents an endless potential for variations on a theme.

Love, then, runs the gamut of possibilities. It is Capodistria's rape of Justine, turning her first into a nymphomaniac and then, with his supposed death, into a "tubby little peasant" humbling herself by digging her "hard paws" into the adamant earth of a Palestine kibbutz; it is Arnauti who, having psychoanalyzed himself and Justine to the point of tragic self-destruction, learns too late that he has wasted what should simply have been enjoyed; it is Justine and Nessim, who seemed to Darley "to be the magnificent two-headed animal a marriage could be," and it is also Nessim's tragic awareness that the faultless satisfaction which Justine brought him "never touched her own happiness." It is Melissa, whose kindness, loyalty, and love are so vital that she willingly sleeps with the repugnant Capodistria to discharge Darley's debt to him; who would make of her life a work of art (Darley: "Her care for me was a goad, provoking me to give my life some sort of shape and style that might match the simplicity of hers" [*J*, p. 48]); and who, although ultimately incapable of living life, alone can reproduce it.[2] Then too, there is the love of Melissa and Nessim, which was born "as they stared at one another with a new understanding, recognizing each other as innocents. For a minute it was almost as if they had fallen in love with each other from sheer relief" (*J*, p. 162). Like an Adam and Eve untouched by even a potential for sin, they make beautiful love in the summer palace Nessim had built for Justine and then swim naked as day breaks on the creation of a new world. Yet they have been drawn together not by desire but by sympathy to share "their common hopelessness"—much as Darley and Melissa, having no tastes in common, had been united by

2 I discount here Justine's child, for it seems a further "check" from Justine's mysterious past rather than created life.

poverty, and Darley and Nessim were to be reunited by "a common fund of unhappiness" after the sudden disappearance of Justine.

Within the single-faceted viewpoint of *Justine*, it is the love affair of Darley and Justine which is most inexplicable, for each already possesses a love more beautiful and more complete than the one that is developing between them. It is not so much that Justine and Darley offer each other a real possibility for peace and satisfaction as that, for one reason or another, they are *necessarily* dissatisfied with whatever they already possess. Their sense of restless unbelonging isolates them, and they are driven relentlessly by a demon of destruction which overpowers the will and controls the body. Darley, even while making love to Justine, wishes only to die; Justine, with perhaps greater self-awareness, insists that "diseases are not interested in those who want to die."

Yet in much of Durrell's poetry, in *Panic Spring* and *The Dark Labyrinth*, in the surrealistic prose-poems and in *Acté*, disease or death claims those who have given up on life. In *The Black Book*, for instance, the very atmosphere of England is weighted with a dark cloud precipitating a rain of already stagnant water on its victims below. All are devitalized, fragmented, beyond cure, and "Death" Gregory pronounces a universal epitaph.

I am falling apart, the delicate zygon of my grain is opened. I am rusting, my knees are rusting, the fillings in my teeth, the plate in my jaw is rusting. If I were only Roman enough to own a sword we should see some fine conclusions to this malady. Alas! Are there only the dead *left* to bury the dead? It is the question not of the moment, but of all time. This is my eternal topic, I, Gregory Stylites, destroyed by the problem of personal action. (*TBB*, p. 201.)

The individual is essentially helpless too within the dark

labyrinthian confines of *Cefalû*; though each of the ensnared is plunged into the twilight depths of his own psyche, he himself can do little to implement the knowledge thus gained. The fate of each may be part of an over-all pattern, but it has little direct relationship to personal will.

Similarly in the *Quartet*, character becomes, in effect, anti-character: it does not so much impose itself upon its surroundings as it is imposed upon, and all the qualities normally associated with the traditional literary hero (valor, marked individuality, some form of superiority—above all, an ego determined to achieve an outlet in action) are either lacking or attributed to something other than individual characters —largely to the city of Alexandria. This denial of autonomy is made most explicit by Durrell in his Introduction to *The Book of the It* by Georg Groddeck, the German psychologist contemporary with Freud. The two, according to Durrell, were mutually influential, and the German was not simply a popularizer or disciple of Freud, "for Groddeck, while he accepts and employs much of the heavy equipment of the master, is separated forever from Freud by an entirely different conception of the constitution and functioning of the human psyche."[3] Groddeck's basic quarrel is with those who propound the notion of an autonomous, powerful ego, since he feels that they are unable to explain the mechanism controlling breathing, digestion, heart action, and the like. Groddeck sought a single entity, a unifying concept, a still point at which the parallel lines of voluntary and involuntary processes would meet—and he concluded that the concept of the individual, independent ego would not bear the weight. He posits, then, a "mysterious force" so powerful that it controls not only the involuntary bodily processes but also

[3] All the quotations in this paragraph and the next are from Durrell's Introduction to Groddeck, *vi–xix*.

the human will—and, in fact, all human creation as well. He says:

> The sum total of an individual human being, physical, mental, and spiritual, the organism with all its forces, and microcosmos, the universe which is a man, I conceive of as a self unknown and forever unknowable, and I call this the "It" as the most indefinite term available without either emotional or intellectual associations. The It-hypothesis I regard not as a truth—for what do any of us know about absolute truth?—but as a useful tool in work and life. . . .

We can never truly grasp this concept, he insists, never actually point to an It.

> The It is a way, not a thing, not a principle or a conceptual figment. . . . it is imagery, symbol, and the symbol cannot be spoken. It lives and *we are lived by it*. One can only use words that are indeterminate and vague . . . for any definite description destroys the symbol.

Simply, Groddeck sees the notion of the autonomous ego as, in individual terms, dangerously isolationist and disruptive. Just as every organ, every cell of the body in a sense has its own individuality, its separate " 'I' consciousness," which is produced by the It and which is a unit of the larger "I," so too the It-ego consciousness of an individual is, at least for Durrell, an inextricable part of a vast, symbolic whole, "a forever unknowable entity, whose shadows and functions we are." Thus, the multiple "consciousnesses" or personalities of each individual form facets subsumed within the single identity he presents to those about him. In a similar fashion, each human being represents an aspect of a larger totality; the It, then, becomes a kind of platonic form of which we all partake, a form which perhaps should be labeled, not beauty or truth or goodness, but humanness, a form which has as many manifestations on earth as there are people.

The relevance of this notion to the atmosphere, the *condition*, of *Justine* is crucial, for it serves as a metaphor for the all-pervasiveness of Alexandria, for the fact that the lives of Durrell's characters are all, in one way or another, interconnected with this unique Egyptian city whose people "have never been truly Egyptian."[4] Durrell attributes an It to the unknowable that is Alexandria; and its forces, conflicts, and will are greater, more "real," than its uncertain inhabitants. And one is reminded of the Laurentian symbol, which also partakes of fundamental mythic significance and which remains equally indivisible and undefinable. With reference to "entirely opposed accounts of the character of Ursula, in *The Rainbow*" by "two of his best critics, Stephen Potter and Horace Gregory," Walter Allen writes:

The difficulty is, of course, that we know, or think we know, so much about the psychology of men and women. . . . if there is anything to the findings of depth psychology, we must accept as legitimate the territory Lawrence chose for himself and expect future novelists to explore it further. Any such exploration must be through the symbol, since the unconscious, as unconscious, is by definition unknowable; or rather, is knowable only through the symbol. Lawrence is a master of the symbol in the psychological sense, as Jung has described it: "In so far as a symbol is a living thing, it is the expression of a thing not to be characterized in any other or better way. The symbol is alive in so far as it is pregnant with meaning."[5]

Durrell's intense sense of place, which caused him to reject his original Athenian setting for *Justine*, demanded of him a city "the most various and colorful I could remember; technical question. I had to have enough *color* to support

[4] E. M. Forster, *Alexandria: A History and A Guide*, 6.
[5] *The English Novel*, 362.

four long volumes without boring."[6] But the city, having been chosen, refuses to remain passive, and its massive presence, multiracial, multilingual, multisexual, demanded "of us [says Darley] nothing save the impossible—that we should be. Justine would say that we had been trapped in the projection of a will too powerful and too deliberate to be human—the gravitational field which Alexandria threw down about those it had chosen as its exemplars. . ." (*J*, p. 22). As Bonamy Dobrée has put it, "This story about the inhabitants of Alexandria is therefore a portrait of Alexandria, which 'lives' the characters."[7] Yet Durrell did not "conceive of the individual and the Alexandrian Its as existing in isolation from each other. They are interwoven and relative. . . . If one can transcend the personal—the fragmentary ego— then one can truly live, one can, we may say, join in the world's It-ness."[8] And Durrell, in his Introduction to Groddeck, suggests a way of moving beyond our isolation by becoming one of those rare spirits "who dares to replace [Descartes'] inexorable first proposition, with the words: 'I am, therefore I can love.' "

There is love, then, squeezed from this great "wine press" of Alexandria; but how are we to understand this love? Is it, as Georges Pombal believes, nothing but sheer animalism, two sad beasts looking for impossible fulfillment, a return to the wholeness of Hermetic philosophy, in the momentary coupling of their sweating bodies? For Alexandria *is* a city of the dirty-curtained brothel, "with its jabbing lights and flesh-

---

[6] "Lawrence Durrell Answers a Few Questions," in Moore (ed.), *The World of Lawrence Durrell*, 159.

[7] "Durrell's Alexandrian Series," in Moore (ed.), *The World of Lawrence Durrell*, 194.

[8] Howard L. Shainheit, "Who Wrote *Mountolive*? An Investigation of the Relativity-aesthetic of Lawrence Durrell's *The Alexandria Quartet*," 47–48.

wearing smells" compelling those who lie on its groaning beds "like the victims of some terrible accident, clumsily engaged, as if in some incoherent experimental fashion they were the first partners in the history of the human race to think out this peculiar means of communication" (*J*, p. 152). Yet Darley has already said: "This was presumably the identical undifferentiated act which Justine and I shared with the common world to which we belonged. How did it differ? How far had our feelings carried us from the truth of the simple, devoid beast-like act itself?" (*J*, p. 151).

Perhaps, as Darley suggests, these are unanswerable questions. But what, then, are we to make of Arnauti, who ultimately decides that love is the ability to accept and enjoy the beauty another has to offer, without the need to understand or possess completely? Arnauti's idea is not unlike the almost passive endurance Darley, having learned that "anything pressed too far becomes a sin" (*J*, p. 39), feels constrained to adopt at the end of the book. Possibly, as Justine insists, love is an expression not of the individual but of the It, or of Alexandria, which imposes its essence upon those within its web. In terms which make specific the relationship of the human and communal Its, Justine berates Darley for his feeble protestations against being victimized by the affair they are beginning. " 'You talk as if there was a choice. We are not strong or evil enough to exercise choice. All this is part of an experiment arranged by something else, the city perhaps, or another part of ourselves. How do I know?' " (*J*, p. 28).

Or perhaps it is Balthazar who speaks most authoritatively with the voice of the city. He has "the touch of a minor oracle," Darley tells us; he is a fellow student and close friend of Cavafy, the Greek whose poems articulate the It-ness of Alexandria, and he recognizes that "We are all hunting for rational reasons for believing in the absurd" (*J*, p. 79). Believing "that we are the work of an inferior deity, a Demiurge, who wrongly believed himself to be God" (*J*, p. 39), Balthazar thanks that God for making him a homosexual, for sparing him from "an undue interest in love. At least the invert escapes this fearful struggle to give oneself to another. Lying with one's own kind enjoying an experience, one can still keep free the part of one's mind which dwells in Plato, or gardening, or the differential calculus" (*J*, p. 82). Thus, Balthazar—according to Darley, one of the keys to the city— is best adapted to partake of the multiple possibilities life offers simultaneously. Yet Balthazar, having both literally and symbolically lost his watch key, is in a sense outside the flux of time—just as the sex of the homosexual he describes seems removed to an atemporal plane, one abstracted from intense human emotion. Balthazar thus appears an unlikely spokesman for those who must remain within time, those, like Pursewarden (according to Clea "a man *tortured beyond endurance by the lack of tenderness in the world*" [*J*, p. 194]), of whom the "lashings of sex" demand self-immolation. For, as we shall see with *Balthazar*—and even more so with *Mountolive*—the further one moves from subjectivity to objectivity, the greater becomes one's ability to judge disinterestedly, and yet the more insignificant and irrelevant become the resulting judgments.

Melissa, another of the voices of *Justine*, comes to embody the malaise of defeatism, the sense of *fin de siècle*, all too characteristic of Alexandria's victims of love. For, as Darley tells us, "I found Melissa, washed up like a half-drowned bird, on the dreary littorals of Alexandria, with her sex broken . . ." (*J*, p. 26). Her experience with Cohen, the old, gargoyle-like furrier, has been such that this gentlest of creatures can remain indifferent in her disgust for him and close her ears to his dying plea for compassion. Darley, though he overgeneralizes as usual, points the lesson to be learned from her attitude.

I realized then the truth about all love; that it is an absolute which takes all or forfeits all. . . . It terrified me to think that this old man, at such a point in his life, had been unable to conjure up an instant's tenderness by the memory of anything he had said or done: tenderness from one who was at heart the most tender and gentle of mortals. (*J*, p. 89.)

And, finally, there is Clea (whose rejection of the dying Narouz in *Mountolive* parallels Melissa's treatment of Cohen). If there is to be only one right view of love and life, Clea's may well be most profound, most meaningful, and perhaps even closest to that of Durrell himself. For Clea's love experience, her one and only love experience thus far, was pure beauty and perfectly achieved, and she is still living within its happiness. She is successful in her painting, "which she takes seriously, but not too seriously" (*J*, p. 108). She has no need of encumbering human ties, no desire to give herself to others, and no sense of inner failure because of this independence from love. Yet many people (Scobie, Balthazar, Melissa, Justine, Darley) are in some way dependent on her; and, for all her freedom from involvement, she is the one who most fully understands and appreciates her former lover. Clea says: "Justine cannot be justified or excused. She simply and magnificently *is*; we have to put up with her, like original sin. . . . Like all amoral people she verges on the Goddess" (*J*, p. 68). And Clea's understanding of love also seems most comprehensive and most relevant, for, as she says, love "is capable of appearing in an infinity of forms and attaching itself to an infinity of people. But it is limited in quantity, can be used up, become shop-worn and faded before it reaches its true object" (*J*, p. 109). Such is the case with Justine, apparently with Darley, and certainly with most of the minor characters—but definitely not with Clea. For as long as she is sustained and fulfilled by the love she has shared with Justine, Clea is satisfied and complete—and she can retain her independence and integrity even while sharing her bed with Darley. She knows that he has come to her flawed by the self-pitying masochism of his ego and that at the moment he has only negation, only a tarnishing of the beauty and love she knew with Justine, to give her. Thus narrowed, he is incapable of meaningful love, the kind that does more than seek mere momentary release through the physical act. And she is not for sale. Later, in the final book of the *Quartet*, Clea continues to recognize the advantages of detachment and individual freedom; but she no longer clings to the old images that die with the past, and she no longer shuns the bonds of new entanglement; unafraid, she offers her love to Darley.

And this is as it should be, for, as much as anyone, Clea, this "minor muse," serves as a touchstone of meaning and regeneration in a world essentially amoral and valueless. By the end of the *Quartet*, we shall see that it is her crucial role, as embodiment of a supremely viable, yet idealized, beauty and goodness in the two critical realms of love and art, that effectively denies Dobrée's judgment of Durrell's work.

What we feel that Mr. Durrell demands of us is a helpless, not a stoical acceptance of what at our most feeble we are, a submission without a protest to the idea that we are things lived by an It. . . . We must say of this striking experiment what Pursewarden said of Justine: "Justine and her city are alike in that they both have a strong flavour without having any real character."[9]

But again, the element of affirmation and orientation that is fundamental to Durrell's conception, and that Clea comes

9 "Durrell's Alexandrian Series," 203–204.

increasingly to represent, finds expression by the end of the *Quartet*.[10] That element necessarily rises, phoenixlike, out of the ashes of death and despair choking the fires of Alexandria. When Clea begins to paint with the artificial hand, when Darley is at last able to write, and when the two of them leave Alexandrian constrictions behind with the past, then the real character of Durrell's purpose manifests itself with a strength that finally counteracts the sense of submissiveness it has fought against throughout the *Quartet*.

Yet in the universe of *Justine*, the single, definitive viewpoint, even Clea's, is necessarily a contradiction in terms, and we should not *expect* a single-faceted viewpoint to perceive the entire prism. For, above all (and under all, and between all, and all about us) there is Alexandria—the world of lust and pure passion, of indifference and meaningful relationship, of sordidness and overwhelming beauty, of love in all its magnificent and endless forms, of love, as Darley implies in *Balthazar*, as complexity itself. "My 'love' for her, Melissa's 'love' for me, Nessim's 'love' for her, her 'love' for Pursewarden—there should be a whole vocabulary of adjectives with which to qualify the noun—for no two contained the same properties . . ." (B, p. 297). The one thing in common, of course, is that they are all, somehow, love, and that they are all conceived by Durrell within, as aspects of, and sustained by, the Alexandrian complex.

As all the pieces of this giant jigsaw puzzle of love fit themselves together, or are fitted together by a force essentially unknowable, we recognize again and again that the

10 Gerald Sykes, in "One Vote for the Sun," in Moore (ed.), *The World of Lawrence Durrell*, 147–48, insists that a sense of affirmation and rebirth is the dominant characteristic of *Justine* itself, and that we are, in effect, already in the sun of a new and vibrant aesthetic by the end of this book. But Sykes, as Moore indicates (*Ibid.*, p. *xviii*), is "a committed Durrellian," and he unfortunately overstates the case.

protagonist of *Justine* is not so much Justine or Darley, or
any of the other members of the "eternal quadrilateral" of
mutual, yet uncertain, need, as Alexandria itself, the prismatic world of love manifesting itself in various ways and in
numerous characters, which, as Durrell asserts in the Note
to *Justine*, is the only "real" thing in it. As Lionel Trilling
suggests, metaphorically Alexandria "is itself the protagonist
of the action, a being far more complex and interesting than
any of its inhabitants, having its own way and its own right,
its own life and its own secret will to which the life and will
of the individual are subordinate."[11] For the city, like its
human inhabitants elevated to higher power and synthesized
into a complex unity, has many sides and many voices; like
love, it is at one and the same time a night of beauty and
passionate tenderness with Justine or Melissa and a moment
of carnal lust in a filthy whorehouse; the city is "this eternally
tragic and ludicrous position of engagement"—without
which, as Darley discovers when, after losing Justine, he
leaves Alexandria for two numbing and dismal years in Upper
Egypt, nothing is meaningful. But this world of love, as
Darley insists, is a perverse one, never granting peace to its
seekers, never allowing the happiness of fulfillment. Darley,
though often not consciously aware of his own association
with Alexandria, recognizes its "strange equivocal power,"
and realizes that Justine, in her frenzied mania for unhappiness, is incapable of happiness in any ordinary sense of the
word. Whether due to Arnauti's check or a combination of
negative experiences (for example, the kidnapping of her
child), Justine's endless questing and questioning are both
inevitable and useless. Though founded on half-truth and a
generous dose of ignorance of complex motivation, Darley's
insight here is nonetheless sound. "How well I recognized

[11] "The *Quartet*: Two Reviews," 60.

her now as a child of the city, which decrees that its women shall be the voluptuaries not of pleasure but of pain, doomed to hunt for what they least dare to find!" (*J*, pp. 44–45). Once again there are seeming paradox and contradiction; once again realization raises more questions than it answers; and the single viewpoint is somehow too limited in scope and depth to envisage more than a minute aspect of a boundless whole.

Yet out of the muddied waters of paradox and ironic contradiction evolves the essential vitality of myth and poetry. These emerge when Durrell, echoing D. H. Lawrence's rejection of the "old stable ego of character" for *The Rainbow*,[12] discusses his break with the traditional form of the novel and its static view of human character. "A sort of rainbow I should say, which includes the whole range of the spectrum. I imagine that what we call personality may be an illusion, and in thinking of it as a stable thing we are trying to put a lid on a box with no sides."[13] He emphasizes that new forms of expression are necessary to replace the ones which he feels contemporary society has antiquated:

We have to break up the old pattern. That's what I've tried to do in this series—break up the personality and show its different facets. . . . I wanted to get away from this sterile realism and back to characters that aren't like life, but that are larger than life. Prototypes, if you want. . . .[14]

Thus, many of the characters have a mythlike aura about them, a depth and stature which further justify a multifaceted approach. We see this clearly in *Justine*. Justine herself is the goddess of love; Nessim and Melissa, in their

12 In a letter to Edward Garnett, quoted by Walter Allen, *The English Novel*, 361.
13 "The Kneller Tape (Hamburg)," in Moore (ed.), *The World of Lawrence Durrell*, 163.
14 Curtis Cate, "Lawrence Durrell," 69.

love, are not merely innocents but innocence itself; Balthazar and Clea are oracles of love; and Darley is man adrift—man, with neither faith nor hope, merely going through the motions of living. And what is true of the characters is again even more true of the city; Durrell's depiction of it "is not just an evocation, but a bodily conjuration of Alexandria—soft, sweet, corrupt and crazy. . . . It is a sanatorium with the luxury rooms full of uprooted, rotting infants and the corridors full of eyeless beggars exhibiting their sores."[15] The city, again, is more real than real, more the embodiment of love than love itself.

The poetic accomplishment—perhaps the most important of all—springs from the rhythmical quality of Durrell's writing; and, as in *Sappho* and the best of the poetry, it is the music of *Justine,* far more than the underlying rationale or belief or philosophical framework, which makes it come alive. It is evident that Durrell, perhaps even more in his novels than in his poetry, is primarily a poet. Most striking and vividly lyrical are many of the passages describing his female characters—Justine, for example: "In the warm bronze light her pale skin looks paler—the red eatable flowers growing in the cheeks where the light sinks and is held fast" (*J*, p. 114); and Clea: "Everything about her person is honey-gold and warm in tone . . . . she had been poured, while still warm, into the body of a young grace . . . into a body born without instincts or desires" (*J*, p. 107); and, best of all: "Melissa was a sad painting from a winter landscape contained by dark sky; a window-box with a few flowering geraniums lying forgotten on the window-sill of a cement-factory" (*J*, p. 46). In each case, the image is not only effectively visual but also appropriate to its subject—with Justine's statuesqueness highlighted by the playing of "warm bronze

[15] Kenneth Rexroth, "The Footsteps of Horace," 444.

light" on "her pale skin"; Clea's unfettered, animallike naturalness, by the implied notion of a casting not solidified into permanent form, but still liquid, at times evanescent; and Melissa's homely patience and love, by the pretty but common geraniums, ignored equally flowering and fading.

The complex and fragmented unity of the *Quartet* leads to questions of structure and technique even within the relative certainty of the single novel. In *Justine,* the quotations from Arnauti's *Moeurs,* the references to Pursewarden's *God Is a Humorist,* and the many citations from various diaries offer a basis for the broad groundwork of third-person omniscient narrative. Yet the use of the first person is necessary for Durrell's attempt to effect an intensive self-delving into the depths and reaches of the minds of Darley and the others. And the combination of the two methods adds to the total impression of layer upon layer of meaning and significance. Even in this, the first of the series, Durrell makes several specific allusions to his method. Early in the book, Darley remembers Justine "sitting before the multiple mirrors of the dressmaker's . . . and saying: 'Look! five different pictures of the same subject. Now if I wrote I would try for a multidimensional effect in character, a sort of prism-sightedness. Why should not people show more than one profile at a time?' " (*J,* p. 28). Proust of course tells us that they do, perhaps most graphically when he writes of Swann's revealing one face to Marcel's family and another to upper-class society.

Certainly the Swann who was a familiar figure in all the clubs of those days differed hugely from the Swann created in my great-aunt's mind. . . . But then, even in the most insignificant details of our daily life, none of us can be said to constitute a material whole, which is identical for everyone, and need only be turned up like a page in an account-book or the record of a will; our social personality is created by the thoughts of other people. Even the simple act which we describe as "seeing some one we know" is, to some extent, an intellectual process. We pack the physical outline of the creature we see with all the ideas we have already formed about him, and in the complete picture of him which we compose in our minds those ideas have certainly the principal place. In the end they come to fill out so completely the curve of his cheeks, to follow so exactly the line of his nose, they blend so harmoniously in the sound of his voice that these seem to be no more than a transparent envelope, so that each time we see the face or hear the voice it is our own ideas of him which we recognize and to which we listen.[16]

People, then, *are* like Justine before these mirrors; they do show more than one profile at a time, although each viewer is limited at any given moment to the single profile which his own perspective allows him to see. This is explicitly stated by Darley further on in *Justine*. "I realize that each person can only claim one aspect of our character as part of his knowledge. To every one we turn a different face of the prism" (*J*, p. 100)—which is a corollary to the fundamental *Quartet* notion that everyone interprets reality according to what he thinks he sees rather than what is "actually" there.

Each character in *Justine* is revealed through the image of himself he displays to those about him or, symbolically, by the relationship he maintains with the mirror world which inescapably reflects him. Our first contact with the mirror makes us suspect it of distortion, for what it reveals to Darley of Melissa's former lover, the bestial, pockmarked Cohen, is not ugly: "I caught a glimpse of him in one of the long mirrors, his head bowed as he stared into his wine-glass. Something about his attitude—the clumsy air of a trained seal grappling with human emotions—struck me, and I realized for the first time that he probably loved Melissa as much as I did" (*J*, p. 25). Actually, as both we and Darley learn later,

[16] *Swann's Way*, 25–26.

Cohen's love for Melissa is far greater than Darley's, and the mirror has not simply returned the appearance of reality presented to it but has made a subtle comment on it in reflecting the beautiful beneath Cohen's ugliness, and an even more subtle one by implying an ugliness beneath Darley's youthful masculine beauty.

Mirrors, then, though they may *seem* to distort, often reveal unsuspected facets of reality. Justine of course lives within the mirror, and Darley enters "her mirror-life" as Arnauti had. "The first words we spoke were spoken, symbolically enough, in the mirror" (*J*, p. 63). Often Justine is able to speak to others *only* through the mirror (most graphically illustrated when Arnauti holds a blotter to the mirror in order to read part of her letter to Balthazar); and it is only to the mirror that she reveals an aspect of herself Darley has never seen and perhaps could not admit exists—at least not until *Clea*. "Going to bed, she would catch sight of herself in the mirror on the first landing and say to her reflection: 'Tiresome pretentious hysterical Jewess that you are!'" (*J*, p. 35).

Nessim's mirror is a cup of bitter wine and spiders from which he has drunk.

Nessim questioned his reflection in the cheap mirror, puzzled by [a] whole new range of feeling and beliefs. . . . Under everything, however, aching like a poisoned tooth or finger, lay the quivering meaning of those eight words ["Your wife is no longer faithful to you"] which Melissa had lodged in him. In a dazed sort of way he recognized that Justine was dead to him. . . . (*J*, p. 167.)

And, as Darley tells us, Pursewarden too discovers death imaged in the glass on his wall; for,

in the very act of speaking . . . about religious ignorance he straightened himself and caught sight of his pale reflection in the mirror. The glass was raised to his lips, and now, turning his head he squirted out upon his own glittering reflection a mouthful of the drink. That remains clearly in my mind: a reflection liquefying in the mirror of that shabby, expensive room which seems now so appropriate a place for the scene [Pursewarden's suicide] which must have followed later that night. (*J*. p. 100.)

And even in death, Darley and the mirror cannot let Pursewarden be. "Nor, for the purposes of this writing, has he ceased to exist; he has simply stepped into the quicksilver of a mirror as we all must . . . " (*J*, p. 99).

Melissa's reflector, "a single poignant strip of cracked mirror" (*J*, p. 161), is characteristically sad, as, interestingly enough, are those of the more varied and complex Darley. Looking up boorishly from a marble table in a gruesomely lighted grocery he has entered in order to squander needed money on Italian olives, he first sees Justine, "leaning down at me from the mirror on three sides of the room" (*J*, p. 32); and, with no thought of the possibility that he has chosen merely a reflection, he enters into Justine's mirror world of love and pain, setting in motion a sequence *of* love and pain that soon touches and envelopes so many. Not until *Clea* do Darley's reflections reveal life and affirmation; at best, as in Mnemjian's barber shop, where "every morning Pombal lay down beside me in the mirrors" (*J*, p. 35), they are neutral in *Justine*, offering a brief respite from the bitter pursuits of pleasure. At worst, and perhaps more characteristically, Darley's mirrors are broken and ugly, and they offer no answers but the truth Darley has long refused to face. " 'I want to know what it really means,' I told myself in a mirror whose cracks had been pasted over with the trimmings of postage stamps" (*J*, p. 151). There is something sadly unsettling in Darley's thus questioning of first principles (about love, about life) by investigating—at first hand, but as voyeur— the earthly pose of brothel sex. Yet such immature seeking

necessarily precedes and makes possible the adolescent's subsequent entry into the special condition of self-understanding
and inner peace which Durrell calls the heraldic universe.

Durrell, though not yet Darley, is very much aware of the
difficulties such scenes create, and he has carefully prepared
us for them by separating himself to a certain extent from his
main character all along. Though it may be easy to be de-
ceived into accepting the opposite, Darley is not Durrell and,
as the Note to *Justine* makes clear, was never meant to be;
they are as different, and as similar, as James Joyce and Stephen Dedalus. There are various attempts at creating the
objectivity and author-character distance of an epic—the atmosphere of mythos and exoticism, the suspension of ordinary chronology, the beginning *in medias res*: "The sea is
high *again* today . . ." (*J*, p. 17—my emphasis). Darley, Durrell makes clear, is at this stage an essentially sterile figure, a
man who makes love "without passion, without attention."
" 'There are only three things to be done with a woman,' said
Clea once. 'You can love her, suffer for her, or turn her into
literature.' I was experiencing a failure in all these domains of
feeling" (*J*, p. 25). And this impotence of Darley's is all the
more a difficulty since, unlike the fatalism attached to Justine, Nessim, and Melissa, it lacks a clearly defined motivat-
ing impetus. Unless we posit a continuing reaction to the
"English death" of *The Black Book* or a supersensitive emotional response to the deracination, disorientation, and bank-
ruptcy that the young intellectual felt characterized the drift-
ing world of the 1930's, Darley's malaise is unaccountable,
yet nonetheless certain. Though he *seems* to speak with the
privileged voice of the author, though his validity as spokesman tends to lull us into an empathy with, and an easy acceptance of, his judgments, his position remains necessarily in-
secure. Again and again, although he remains a nonetheless

sympathetic character, he reveals great ignorance of both others and himself. He is untouched by Melissa's understandable though uncharacteristic bitterness toward him after she has discharged his debt to Capodistria; yet he cannot help being jealous of the capacity for strength and tenderness of even a dying Cohen. At the beginning of his affair with Justine, he speaks of "knowing how much she loved Nessim"; yet he never questions the obvious contradiction of this affair and what he simultaneously called the "ideal two-headed beast" created by the Hosnani marriage. Just as his suspicions of violence from Nessim at the duck hunt are completely inaccurate, so too (as we learn in *Mountolive*) is the understanding he here reveals of the great depths and strengths of the Copt's personality. "He thought and suffered a good deal but he lacked the resolution to dare . . ." (*J*, p. 30). For until the final pages of *Clea*, Darley's own indecisiveness contrasts sharply with Nessim's dynamic, though largely hidden, will to action.

Darley is quick to patronize and to judge (even to the point of worrying about hurting Nessim while making love to Justine and of mentally analyzing her "stupid side"); yet he appears foolish when his pose of "ironic tenderness and silence" sends Justine into "a towering rage." " 'You thought I simply wanted to make love? God! haven't we had enough of that?' " (*J*, p. 45). And after going to bed with Justine, Darley finds that Alexandria has become a different, a staler, city (for though he is helpless within this love, it is less of a beginning than an end), not to be renewed until the final book of the *Quartet*, and the mature, willed and creative, love he discovers and shares with Clea.

Both Durrell and Darley hold the theory of multifaceted personalities; yet, unlike Durrell (who, after all, wrote subsequent interpretations of the *Justine* events), Darley is as

yet incapable of understanding the nontheoretical applica-
tion of his hypothesis. At times, like Proust's Swann, he con-
tradictorily expects people to be unequivocal, monolithic,
readily comprehensible.

[Swann] knew quite well as a general truth, that human life is
full of contrasts, but in the case of any one human being he
imagined all that part of his or her life with which he was not
familiar as being identical with the part with which he was. He
imagined what was kept secret from him in the light of what was
revealed.[17]

Darley writes: "In the case of Justine . . . one could not help
distrusting her conclusions, since they were always changing,
were never at rest. She shed theories about herself like so
many petals" (*J*, p. 111)—a strange statement for one who
has professed a belief that all ideas are equally good, equally
valid. Justine is obviously groping among many "truths"—all
equally true—implicitly denying simplistic interpretations in
her search for self-understanding, as she did when she ob-
jected to Arnauti's endlessly probing attempts to discover
distinct cause and effect relationships. " 'You know I never
tell a story the same way twice. Does that mean that I am
lying?' " (*J*, p. 72). Darley, it seems, would have no answer
to such a question, yet Durrell implies one by the very fact of
his having written *Balthazar* and *Mountolive*.

Darley's views are often unsatisfactory in artistic matters
as well. For one thing, he is intensely jealous of Pursewarden,
whose ideas he does not entirely understand until the "Brother Ass" section of *Clea*. Second, he tells us at the beginning
of *Justine* that he is pleased with the censorship of man's art
and that he is undisturbed by the destruction of some of his
papers. And finally, as he summarizes it himself, he had failed
in his writing because "I lacked a belief in the true authen-

17 *Ibid.*, 516.

ticity of people in order to successfully portray them" (*J*, p. 159)—and he lapses into unfecund silence at the end. As he will have to learn—and ultimately does—if his quest for maturity is to succeed, the tendency to dogmatize people, to speak of them in the abstract, is inadequate because it prejudges, oversimplifies, dehumanizes. He needs to learn both that people and events do in actuality embody his relativistic theory and that there are often objectively verifiable data of which he alone has been unaware—that there are specific existential facts about, for instance, Justine and Nessim which he needs to learn—but that, even with full knowledge of all facts, we can never be certain that our understanding of people is complete. Although Darley's attitude may at times seem paradoxical, it nevertheless does imply the validity of his relativity thesis. And if Darley's reliability as a spokesman is thus uncomprehensive and incomplete, a second, perhaps more "objective," view of the events he has detailed so fully and so personally becomes not only possible but necessary.

III. *Balthazar* and The Enigmatic Pursuit of Love

It is only with the passions of others that we are ever really familiar, and what we come to find out about our own can be no more than what other people have shown us. Upon ourselves they react but indirectly, through our imagination, which substitutes for our actual, primary motives other, secondary motives, less stark and therefore more decent. (Marcel Proust, *Swann's Way*, pp. 183–84.)

The mirror sees the man as beautiful, the mirror loves the man; another mirror sees the man as frightful and hates him; and it is always the same being who produces the impressions. (Epigraph to *Balthazar*, from D. A. F. de Sade, *Justine*.)

*B*althazar is a reworking of *Justine*. With Darley continuing in his role as final commentator, Durrell's focal point is once again the love affair of Justine and Darley, and around it, variously related to it, revolve such now familiar characters as Nessim, Melissa, Balthazar, Clea, Pursewarden, Scobie. Many situations and events are either redramatized or rethought. Justine, for instance, is still the victim of Arnauti's "check" (though decreasingly so), of whatever unknown forces have removed and killed her child, and of the

ever pervasive Alexandria. As one commentator has noted, in
Balthazar

time is turned back, and the narrator relives his days in Alexandria: he sees that this loneliness was deeper than he knew; he
sees the underside of Justine's marriage to Nessim—Nessim's
spiritual impotence, Justine's terrible possessiveness. He sees that
to all her lovers she gave everything, knowing the value of nothing
—a woman tormented by the vagaries of her feelings, wounding
all those whom she loved; he sees Clea's beauty smothered in the
consuming shape of a sterile love; he sees Nessim's soul pushed
into a foxhole of shifting sands in the desert of his childhood
memories, suffering not only his, but his mother's trauma, and
his brother's wounds.[1]

Thus, events and characters of *Justine* become données for
Balthazar, and allusions are made to them not for their own
sake alone but because they are tacit premises for subsequent
thoughts and actions or because their "obvious" significance
comes to demand new interpretation. Therefore, Justine's
pre-*Quartet* heterosexuality (the rape, the affair with the
Swede, the marriage with Arnauti) is almost never explicit in
Balthazar; but her relationship with Clea, largely glossed over
in *Justine,* is explored at great lengths—significantly enlarging a previously minor facet of her personality.

Melissa's loyalty to Darley, her illness, her death, Nessim's
madness, the affair between Melissa and Nessim, the duck
shoot and Justine's subsequent running away—these are all
present in *Balthazar,* but, as it were, writ small. Other, minor,
elements of the *Justine* narrative assume a place in the fore-
ground in the second book: Nessim's manorial life with
Leila and Narouz; the events leading to the marriage of Nessim and Justine; the role of Pursewarden as both character
and spokesman. We are still concerned—in fact to a height-

---

[1] Mary Graham Lund, "Submerge for Reality: The New Novel Form of
Lawrence Durrell," 232.

ened degree—with such uncertainties and complexities as: the relationship of "objective" truth and an aesthetic of relativity, that of a narrative based on chronology (that is, the "despotism of time"[2]) and one based on various individual responses (in this case, primarily Balthazar's Interlinear, Pursewarden's epigrammatic utterances, and Clea's letter to Darley—in addition of course to Darley's remembrance of things past); the many roles of Alexandria; the multifaceted presentation of character and event and the need for continual readjustment of viewpoint on the part of those who would interpret them; the ever increasing variations on the themes of love and sex; and the dual emphasis on the creative act of the artist (Clea, Pursewarden, Darley, even Balthazar) and the concomitant maturing of Darley as human being, lover, and artist.

Even Balthazar's Interlinear, the dominant structural feature of the novel bearing his name, does not represent a technical break with *Justine,* for it is a logical extension of that novel's diaries, notes, *Moeurs,* and other interpretative paraphernalia. On the other hand, the Interlinear underscores the kaleidoscopic motif of variegated and shifting truth, for Balthazar, even while attempting to "correct" Darley's "erroneous" response to the incidents of *Justine,* denies any pretension to omniscience. With specific reference to the "fact" of Capodistria's death at the duck shoot climaxing *Justine,* Balthazar says: " 'Fact is unstable by its very nature. Narouz once said to me that he loved the desert because there "the wind blew out one's footsteps like candle-flames." So it seems to me does reality. How then can we hunt for the truth?' " (*B,* p. 278).

[2] B, p. 71. During Nessim's visit to the manor, Narouz has all the clocks stopped in order to make the time appear longer. Thus, man's "seeming" can be set in conflict with the instruments he has invented to measure aspects of his "being."

Yet Balthazar does not hesitate to suggest that such a thing as objective truth does actually exist and that his ability to perceive and interpret it is superior to Darley's. Having yet to see *Justine*, Balthazar nonetheless condemns what he assumes, not incorrectly, is Darley's subjective non-self-critical response to those happenings. Balthazar himself has been almost entirely an onlooker, and he feels he is therefore in a position to judge. He writes to Darley:

No doubt you are bringing us to judgement on paper in the manner of writers. I wish I could see the result. It must fall very far short of *truth*: I mean such truths as I could tell you about us all—even perhaps about yourself. Or the truths Clea could tell you. . . . I picture you, wise one, poring over *Moeurs*, the diaries of Justine, Nessim, etc., imagining that the truth is to be found in them. Wrong! Wrong! A diary is the last place to go if you wish to seek the truth about a person. Nobody dares to make the final confession to themselves on paper: or at least, not about love. (*B*, p. 211.)

In effect, he tells Darley that he—Balthazar—knows, though he may not always fully understand the significance of, the "real" motivation for Justine's giving herself to Darley and disappearing at the end, the "real" reasons for Pursewarden's enigmatic personality, the "real" explanation for the loss of his watch key, the "real" meaning of happiness, of love, of time, of reality. And, as Darley is the first to admit, Balthazar does not lie.

But does this necessarily mean that, instead, he tells the truth? Durrell's method forces us to ask whether anyone, even as perceptive, well-meaning, objective, and honest as Balthazar, can "tell the truth, the whole truth, and nothing but the truth." Is it even possible that one can approach awareness of, let alone communicate, the totality of a truth—since truth by its very nature is unstable—or is the following view of Pursewarden, who increasingly usurps the role of major spokesman in the *Quartet*, ultimately the only valid one? Darley, understandably troubled by the contradictory evidence of his own sensations as recorded in his *Justine* manuscript and what he has read in Balthazar's Interlinear, questions his very ability to know. "Did I really miss so much that was going on around me . . . ? Must I now rework my own experiences in order to come to the heart of the truth? 'Truth has no heart,' writes Pursewarden. 'Truth is a woman. That is why it is enigmatic' " (*B*, p. 340). But this statement is of course itself enigmatic, for, like almost all of Pursewarden's assertions, it is expressed with an ironic, almost self-disdaining, equivocation. For one thing, the pun on the word "heart" leaves Pursewarden with a means of evading intellectual responsibility if he should find anyone taking him too seriously.[3] And, second, the statement is of necessity only a partial truth, for it implies that no one can know a truth—not even the one being asserted here—in its entirety. Thus, if Pursewarden is the author's voice to any great extent here—and presumably he is—then Darley, though he is certainly at least partially serious, is simultaneously self-ironic and contradictory. Yet this should not be surprising, for such *seeming* inconsistency is, to a great degree, what the *Quartet* is all about. Durrell the poet, the evoker of romantically hazy and exotic setting, finds no place in the beautiful indefiniteness of Alexandria for infallible, Houyhnhnm-like characters— least of all as spokesmen—and he would insist that even in Pursewarden, perhaps the most didactic of his characters,

---

[3] Pursewarden uses this tactic not infrequently, especially with Justine. Once, when he had spent perhaps more time and effort than he intended explaining to her an apparently essential aspect of his relativity-aesthetic, she asked the wrong question. " 'Are you serious about all this?' " And he answered: " 'Not a bit' " (*B*, p. 307). The implication is that Justine asks a foolish question, seeking definitiveness where truth itself offers only ambiguity and multiplicity.

simplistic strictures must give way to unanswerables. "Yes, one has the right to raise philosophic problems in a novel without being able to answer them; indeed a good novel with good characters cannot avoid it. Human beings are really walking question marks, how's and why's and perhapses."[4]

Thus far have we come: Darley, an active participant in the *Justine* happenings, has been forced to acknowledge the inadequacy of his theorizing, though he is not entirely willing to surrender the "distorting mirrors" of his immediate emotional responses. Pursewarden, though we are still not fully aware of his central role as an involved character, seems to speak increasingly with the voice of authorial privilege and ironic detachment. And Balthazar, presumably a bystander, as close to an objective observer as we can have until the third-person "omniscience" of *Mountolive*, takes on the admittedly futile task of "correcting," of bringing closer to the "truth," the *Justine* manuscript. And he almost succeeds.

Yet of course in a sense he has been doomed to fail all along. True, he is more objective and less involved than Darley, but this implies, at most, that his vision is broader, more comprehensive, but not necessarily deeper. In effect, he too sees only a single facet of the prism. His stress is different but not necessarily truer, and perhaps he sees also with vision somewhat distorted—not, as in Darley's case, by the proximity of intense involvement, but by his self-deceptive and somewhat outmoded insistence on the objectivity (that is, the depersonalization) and the simplicity of facts once comprehended. It is with a sense of complete certainty, an unflinch-

---

[4] Lawrence Durrell, "The Kneller Tape (Hamburg)," in Moore (ed.), *The World of Lawrence Durrell*, 164. This notion, which implies that what man knows is essentially elusive, endlessly caught in an incessant stream of becoming, will be of special significance when we come to the "naturalistic" *Mountolive*. As we shall see, when Durrell wishes to present us with unequivocal "facts," he finds it necessary to employ an omniscient third person—a non-character—as narrator.

ing belief in his own ability to make absolute distinctions between truth and fiction, that Balthazar reveals the death of Justine's child (which is shown only in a vision—and not to Balthazar), solves the mystery of his missing watch key, pinpoints the hitherto hidden motivations of so many.

The shifts in emphasis from *Justine* to *Balthazar* suggest— and this is Balthazar's, not Durrell's, purpose—that, in reading the first novel, we had allowed our attention and emotional response to be drawn by matters so peripheral as to be almost irrelevant, but that now, in *Balthazar*, a proper focus has been achieved. Perhaps the most obvious instance of this is that Melissa, clearly the least complex of the sides of the *Justine* quadrilateral, diminishes in size from a major participant to a mere object of endless pity (Darley's, Balthazar's, Clea's, Amaril's), and we almost begin to doubt the wisdom of our earlier having expended so much sympathy upon her. And of course, as Melissa's role becomes minor, her outside involvements, her relationships with characters other than Darley and Nessim, become nonexistent. For example, Cohen, the scrofulous old furrier, vanishes like the Cheshire Cat in *Alice's Adventures in Wonderland*, except that, instead of a smile, he leaves behind four-fifths of his name (*OHEN*) soapily inscribed by Pursewarden on his mirror just before his suicide—and now "partly obliterated" by Nessim, who says, " 'There must be nothing for the Egyptian Police to find' " (*B*, p. 312). No one is simply allowed to die or to fade from the Alexandrian scene—for always more mystery is raised than solved, and only rarely is death not contingent and tentative.

As with Cohen, almost all the so-called minor characters are, in effect, traded in for new models, or are somehow forced to give way, as before an implacable wave, to a vitality *they* can no longer sustain. We see, for instance, that Cohen, rejected by the Melissa he had abused, died with the purity of his love for her intact. Melissa's death was almost an exact duplicate, except that she was discarded by the Darley to whom she had been, if anything, too faithful. Darley recalls that Amaril had examined her: "He described to me Melissa's condition adding only: 'It would help her very much if she could be loved a bit.' A remark which filled me with shame. It was that very night that I had borrowed the money from Justine to send her to a clinic in Palestine much against her own will" (*B*, p. 299). And there is hardly a more pathetic moment in the entire *Quartet* than when Melissa, unloved and dying, asks Clea, as a last request, to sleep with Darley out of friendship for her. But this pair of old and tired lovers, of perhaps too little complexity and perhaps too isolated by the very inexpressibility, for them, of their despair, are, as it were, replaced by a different pair: the strangely remote Leila, the Hosnani matriarch (who, according to Balthazar, had experienced, at the death of her husband fifteen years earlier, the same sort of nightmare and incipient madness that Nessim does after his loss of Justine), and Mountolive, the English ambassador and, seemingly, an interloper in the scheme of the already tangled *Quartet*. The far different love affair of Leila and Mountolive, we are to learn early in the third segment of this "Investigation of Modern Love," contained so much more promise and, consequently, ended perhaps less tragically but more dismally. At least Cohen and Melissa die when their roads come to sudden, and final, ends.

Mnemjian, the half-realized, misshapen dwarf, is literally exchanged, at the very moment of sexual climax, for Narouz, Nessim's harelipped, manorial brother who is intensely and (until he gives himself away) secretly in love with Clea. Darley is reminded by Balthazar's writing of his search, in a brothel, for an understanding of at least the physical position of love.

Now as I read these scenes in the Interlinear, my memory revives something which it had forgotten; memories of a dirty booth with a man and woman lying together in a bed and myself looking down at them, half-drunk, waiting my turn. I have described the whole scene in another place—only then I took the man to be Mnemjian. I now believe it was Narouz. (*B*, p. 326.)

For Capodistria, the depraved symbol of lust and degraded human emotion, we receive the amorous Amaril, the incorrigible romantic as gynecologist, an idealizer of women "in a city where a woman was, as provender, regarded as something like a plateful of mutton; a city where women cry out to be abused" (*B*, p. 298). Amaril, a man of great *tendresse*, has all his abstract desires consummated as virginal friendships—though "there is not a woman in Alexandria who is not proud to be seen out on his arm; there is not one who *if asked* (but he never asks) would not be glad to betray her husband or her lover for him" (*B*, p. 299)—until his fairytale-like romance with an ephemeral and masked (and, we learn later, noseless) young maiden during the amoral heights of the annual carnival.

The coarsely humorous and purely physical Pombal yields most of his role as court jester to that character of infinite sensibility and comically pathetic longings, Scobie.[5] Scobie

---

[5] Durrell underscores the interchangeability of the two. Pombal, after telling Darley of his misadventures with his destructively amorous mistress Sveva, exhibits a hat of "faded osprey feathers," a part of the "impenetrable disguise" with which he will escape further scrapes during the carnival. Darley comments: "He looked so funny with it on that I was forced to sit down and laugh. He reminded me of Scobie in his own absurd Dolly Varden . . . it is quite indescribable what this ridiculous creation did to his fat face. . . . As with Scobie, I was forced to plead: 'Take it off, for God's sake!' " (*B*, p. 336).

is perhaps the one figure whose character Darley still feels certain of. "He at least has the comprehensibility of a diagram—plain as a national anthem" (*B*, p. 221). Scobie, a policeman unaccountably made head of the Secret Service, has, as he puts it himself, " 'Tendencies,' " for in " 'female duds and my Dolly Varden,' " he seeks his involvements among the men of the city. Still, as he explains to Darley, he finds mitigating circumstances. It's " 'only . . . when the Influence comes over me. When I'm not fully Answerable, old man. . . . It's only sometimes when the Fleet's in" (*B*, pp. 231–32). And when he dies, fatally kicked by sailors he accosted while dressed in his "Tendency" clothes, his death, stupid and unnecessary (though perhaps inevitable) as it is, at least seems unequivocal and final. Yet even Scobie is not so easily pigeonholed and forgotten. It is clear that, regardless of any failings, he is warmly loved and even esteemed by many of the main characters in the *Quartet*; in addition, he is adored by the anonymous people of the city.

Here, everywhere, the cries of the open street greeted him and he responded radiantly.

> "*Y'alla, effendi, Skob*"
> "*Naharak said, ya Skob*"
> "*Allah salimak.*"

He would sigh and say "Dear people"; and "How I love the place you have no idea!" dodging a liquid-eyed camel as it humped down the narrow street threatening to knock us down with its bulging sumpters of *bercim,* the wild clover which is used as fodder.

> "May your prosperity increase"
> "By your leave, my mother"
> "May your day be blessed"
> "Favour me, O sheik."

Scobie walked here with the ease of a man who has come into his own estate, slowly, sumptuously, like an Arab. (*B*, p. 224.)

Balthazar's quick action makes of Scobie's ignominious death not the sordid scandal it might well have been but something noble or even more; and the splendid pomp and confusions of his funeral—" 'he was buried with full honours as an officer killed in the execution of his duty' "—elicits a not unfitting epitaph from Balthazar: " 'You would have thought he was a saint' " (*B*, p. 332). For, as we see in *Clea*, Scobie is indeed canonized as El Scob (a reincarnation of a local, long-forgotten saint, El Yacoub)—his bathtub, formerly a still producing fatal whiskey, now "being invoked to confer fertility upon the childless—and with success, too, if one could judge by the great number of offerings" (*C*, p. 715).

One further pair of characters, Arnauti and Pursewarden, have their roles reversed by the differently reflecting mirrors of *Justine* and *Balthazar*. The author of *Moeurs* has learned an important lesson from his marriage to Justine (that she was a woman to be loved or ignored but not analyzed), but presumably it is too little, too late, or both. In a sense, he is the reverse of Darley, who at least begins with the ability to love fully, learns (to paraphrase Plato) that an unexamined love is not worth having, and, by the end of the *Quartet*, achieves a kind of synthesis of love and art through his having gained understanding of the creative process. Arnauti is in effect rendered doubly impotent—both as lover and as artist—for what Durrell apparently sees as an unnatural alteration of the interdependence of body and mind. The rule in the *Quartet* is that to begin with a negative response to love (through either choice or incapacity) is to end in insignificance; to begin with a positive response (no matter what depths of inadequacy are reached subsequently) is to have at least a chance to achieve something of permanence, something worthy of affirmation.[6]

---

[6] It is Justine who formally exorcises Arnauti from the *Quartet*. " 'As for

And, in exchange for the shrunken figure of Arnauti, we receive the enigmatic Pursewarden who, though a suicide of seemingly minor importance in *Justine*, assumes a continually enlarging and crucial role as both character and spokesman throughout the tetralogy. In the first place, Balthazar offers Pursewarden as an explanation for much that was mysterious to Darley about the events of *Justine*: he was the "real" object of Justine's passion, and Darley was used simply "as a decoy in order to protect him from the jealousy of Nessim whom she had married" (*B*, p. 216); and it was his suicide, not any psychological disturbances resulting from Da Capo's supposed death, that led to Justine's sudden disappearance at the end of the first novel.[7] Second, there is hardly a matter of any significance in the entire *Quartet* upon which Pursewarden does not make an important pronouncement, either speaking directly or as quoted by someone else. Perhaps, as Henry Miller has said, Pursewarden is both an unbelievable and uninteresting character.[8] But Miller was reacting merely to

---

Arnauti, he nearly drove me mad with his inquisitions. What I lost as a wife I gained as a patient—his interest in what he called "my case" outweighed any love he might have had for me. . . . Much of it [*Moeurs*] is invented—mostly to satisfy his own vanity and get his own back on me for the way I wounded his pride in refusing to be "cured"—so-called. You can't put a soul into splints. If you say to a Frenchman, "I can't make love to you unless I imagine a palm-tree," he will go out and cut down the nearest palm-tree.'" Pursewarden adds that *Moeurs* is " 'all right, written by a born *lettre*, of course, and smells fashionably of armpits and *eau de javel*,'" and that Arnauti is " ' a "tiresome psychoanalytical turnkey with a belt full of rusty complexes" ' " (*B*, pp. 240, 287, 289).

[7] Darley now feels he understands why Pursewarden bequeathed him five hundred pounds to be spent on Melissa—"It was his guilt, I think, for what he knew Justine was doing to Melissa: in 'loving' me" (*B*, p. 236)—but neither he nor Balthazar as yet dares even to speculate on the motivation of perhaps the greatest mystery of the entire *Quartet*: Pursewarden's suicide.

[8] With reference to Pursewarden's interjections and notes, Miller writes: "This part—like an interpolation—seemed weakest to me, though containing much profound observation on art and life. . . . The humor didn't always come off, for me. To be frank, of all the characters in the quartet Pursewarden

Pursewarden's excessive verbiage and not analyzing his pivotal roles as theorist, artist, lover. In *Balthazar*, Pursewarden is an immensely interesting and important figure, perhaps more for the contrast his relationship with Justine offers to Darley's and for the joyful beauty and pathos of his wonderful sense of humor (which Miller underestimates, probably because he misses the pathos and sees only the comic) than for his sententiousness.[9]

Under Pursewarden's potent influence in *Balthazar*, Justine becomes a more dynamic character, less fuzzy around the psychomythological edges. She is no longer the monolithic sex goddess she often seemed in the first book, an emotional cripple inevitably irresistible, inevitably passionate, and inevitably bored (and often boring). Rarely does Pursewarden, unlike so many others, refer to Justine in the abstract (even then he is at most half-serious); on the few occasions when he does, he is forced almost immediately back to the human being he knows. Balthazar is speaking: " 'As for Justine,' said Pursewarden to me when he was drunk once,

is the least interesting to me. . . . I never get the conviction that he was the great writer you wish him to seem. I think he'd come off better . . . if you sliced down his remarks or observations. They get sententious and tedious and feeble sometimes. Too much persiflage. . . . What I mean, more precisely, is that one is not sure at times whether the author is taking his double-faced protagonist seriously or ironically." (*Corr,* p. 361.) Miller fails to realize that Pursewarden's double-facedness—as discussed more fully below—is both serious *and* ironic.

9 It is interesting to note in this connection that there can be no doubt that Pursewarden is on the side of the angels since he is supposedly something of a disciple of D. H. Lawrence. It may be that he is somewhat sententious in criticizing the master; yet the criticism itself could hardly be more wittily telling or apropos of the sort of thing so many critics find inadequate in such works as *Lady Chatterley's Lover.* "Lawrence had written: '*In you I feel a sort of profanity—almost a hate for the tender growing quick in things, the dark Gods. . . .*' He chuckled. He deeply loved Lawrence but had no hesitation in replying on a post-card: '*My dear DHL. This side idolatry—I am simply trying not to copy your habit of building a Taj Mahal around anything as simple as a good f——k*' " (*B,* p. 284).

'I regard her as a tiresome old sexual turnstile through which presumbably we must all pass—a somewhat vulpine Alexandrian Venus. By God, what a woman she would be if she were really natural and felt no guilt!' " (*B*, p. 285).

With him, Justine comes alive for the first time. For once she is capable of really laughing—"I mean in a way that was not mordant, not wounded" (*B*, p. 307)—when Pursewarden, in "his total ignorance of psychology," suggests she make the attempt (unknown to him, already made and politely rebuffed) to sleep with Da Capo "to lay the image" of her rape. In addition, she is capable of directing at him a fiery, if somewhat ludicrous, anger. "Coming back from Cairo they had several rows. 'As for your so-called illness—have you ever thought it might be just due to an inflamed self-pity?' She became so furious that she nearly drove the car off the road into a tree. 'Miserable Anglo-Saxon!' she cried, on the point of tears—'Bully!' " (*B*, p. 290). And she is able, again apparently for the first time, of being both rebuffed in her desires and of rising beyond to a love so profound that it encompasses a genuine and unself-conscious sense of humor. She forced herself past the rude and almost nude Pursewarden into his hotel room and, Balthazar continues:

"She sat down on the end of the bed and lit a cigarette, considering him, as one might a specimen. 'I am curious, after all your talk about self-possession and responsibility, to see just how Anglo-Saxon you are—unable to finish anything you start. Why do you look furtive?' This was a splendid line of attack. He smiled. 'I'm going to work today.'

" 'Then I'll come tomorrow.'

" 'I shall have the 'flu.'

" 'The day after.'

" 'I shall be going to the Zoo.'

" 'I shall come too.'

"Pursewarden was now extremely rude; she knew she had scored a victory and was delighted. She listened to his honeyed insults as she tapped the carpet with her foot. 'Very well' she said at last, 'we shall see.' (I am afraid you will have to make room in this for the essential comedy of human relations. You give it so little place.) The next day he put her out of his hotel-room by the neck, like a pet cat. The following day he woke and found the great car parked once more outside the hotel. 'Merd' he cried and just to spite her dressed and went to the Zoo. She followed him." (*B*, pp. 293–94.)

And, finally, it is Pursewarden who sees in Justine the woman she once was, the woman she might have been. He curses himself in the mirror for

"a self-indulgence which had brought him what most bored him— an intimate relationship. But in the sleeping face he too saw the childish inhabitant of Justine, the 'calcimined imprint of a fern in chalk.' He saw how she must have looked on the first night of love—hair torn and trailing over the pillow like a ruffled black dove, fingers like tendrils, warm mouth inhaling the airs of sleep; warm as a figure of pastry fresh from the oven. 'Oh damn!' he cried aloud." (*B*, p. 288.)

But love, as Clea has told us in *Justine*, is of limited quantity —and whatever potentially could have served as source of the love these two might have achieved together has been long depleted. " 'Odd, isn't it? He really *was* the right man for her in a sort of way; but then as you must know, it is a law of love that the so-called "right" person always comes too soon or too late,' " says Balthazar (*B*, p. 290). For Justine and Pursewarden, though we did not even suspect their relationship in *Justine* until *Balthazar*, it has been too late from the moment they first met.

The above contrasting of various sets of characters has been elaborated at some length to illustrate not only, as the second epigraph to this chapter indicates, that different mirrors (that is, different viewers) make different value judgments of the same characters and events (an obvious and superficial observation) but, more important, that once fairly rigid distinctions—between major and minor characters, between main plot and subplots, between a protagonist and those who interact with him—have been largely obliterated. *Justine* and *Balthazar* deal with essentially the same material, although *Justine* is temporally more inclusive (moving into the past through *Moeurs* and forward to the duck shoot and Justine in Palestine), and *Balthazar* moves spatially from Alexandria and the Alexandrian to the Hosnani manor. Yet the shift in main viewpoint from that of Darley to those of Balthazar and Pursewarden is accompanied, as we have seen, by a major alteration in the cast of characters, a new series of events surrounding the focal relationships, and an entirely different, and chronologically earlier, climactic action: the masked carnival and the murder of Toto de Brunel. And again, to underscore once more the fundamental change in attitude that has taken place between the two novels, it is in the aesthetic pronouncements of Pursewarden and, to a lesser degree, in those of Balthazar that the justification for the various shiftings is fully elaborated.

As to the basic notion of character, if an author may now have as many significant interpreters of a series of events as there are participants and witnesses, then "major" and "minor" cease to serve as valid distinctions. For instance, Melissa and Mountolive, though relatively uncomplicated characters, embody roles of shifting magnitude—and we recall Pursewarden's notion of dynamic personality, always different from one moment to the next, always different at the same moment from one observer to the next.

"We live" writes Pursewarden somewhere "lives based upon selected fictions. Our view of reality is conditioned by our position in space and time—not by our personalities as we like to think.

Thus every interpretation of reality is based upon a unique position. Two paces east or west and the whole picture is changed." . . .

And as for human characters, whether real or invented, there are no such animals. Each psyche is really an ant-hill of opposing predispositions. Personality as something with fixed attributes is an illusion—but a necessary illusion *if we are to love!* . . . "In the end," says Pursewarden, "everything will be found to be true of everybody. Saint and Villain are co-sharers." (*B*, p. 210.)

Thus, the situations and involvements posited for a Darley, a Justine, a Nessim, a Melissa are analogous to those that may equally be posited for an Amaril, a Sveva, a Scobie, a Leila. Though we may not dispense entirely with the concept of "minor" characters—for to do so would necessitate assuming that all have equal sensibilities, all respond in similarly complex and interesting ways—we may nonetheless see the concept as largely dated when every character is theoretically the independent fountainhead of actions progressively multiplying both in consequences and in the number of people upon whose lives they significantly impinge. Pursewarden's position may be extreme—" 'Reality, he believed, was always trying to copy the imagination of man, from which it derived' " (*B*, p. 286)—but the idea that life imitates art which he is echoing is simply a way of propounding an approach to both life and art that is as close as possible to being infinitely faceted, for there are in theory as many possible results of such imitation as the product of the number of people in the world and the number of conscious moments in their lives. Although in practice every novelist, every artist—in fact, every sentient being—must continually select and judge, the aesthetic theories propounded in *The Alexandria Quartet* imply that this is *the* modern artistic problem and one which the writer must attempt somehow to solve. Thus, " 'There are only as many realities as you care to imagine' writes Pursewarden" (*B*, p. 315), who attempts to come to viable terms with these realities by formulating a relativity-aesthetic for the novel, as he knew Einstein had done for the "real" world. Pushing the implications of the multifaceted approach to its logical extreme, we can see that any story might theoretically be told from the viewpoints—encompassing a vast spectrum between complete subjectivity and complete objectivity, though necessarily including neither extreme, since they are merely imaginative constructs—of all persons who in any way come in contact with it. If a given narrator has little direct involvement with the events he is relating and analyzing, like "Half-Rome," "The Other Half-Rome," and "Tertium Quid" in Browning's *The Ring and the Book*, he may very well simply shift the focus of his own and his readers' attention from the "objective" happenings to his personal reaction, to their relationship to his own life, and perhaps even to his "irrelevant" concerns with those people and incidents (that is, "minor" characters and "sub" plots) he sees centering on himself. In such a case, as in Conrad's *Lord Jim*, we become far less concerned with a specific and objectively definable plot than with its psychological manifestations and implications. And, as one obvious consequence, the climactic moment of a sequence of events would of necessity shift with different viewpoints, for each narrator of the happenings reaches *his* own point of no return, his own peak moment, beyond which all is denouement.[10]

Further, a single character, in living and then reliving the same occurrences, will, on the basis of what he has learned or experienced in the interim, very likely alter his primary judgment as to the climactic event. Thus, Darley, once Balthazar casts doubt on Da Capo's death and undercuts the very sig-

[10] See Chapter VI for an extensive analysis of the *Quartet* in terms of the relativity-aesthetic and impressionism.

nificance of his affair with Justine, comes to realize that the duck shoot and what he saw as its result—Justine's disappearance—were not so much climax as anticlimax. Yet Darley cannot accept the full implication of Balthazar's Interlinear—that the affair was over before it began, because it never had a chance—and, instead, seeks a climax which, though occurring prior to the duck shoot, is not so early as to antedate, and therefore implicitly deny any value to, his involvement with Justine. In addition, he seems suddenly to believe that he had achieved the kind of peace with her that Arnauti ultimately spoke of, for, when mentally with Justine again, he thinks of Pursewarden and then: "Yet what have I to complain of? Even this half-love filled my heart to overflowing. It is she, if anyone, who had cause for complaint. . . . I was happy sitting beside her, feeling the warmth of her hand as it lay in mine" (*B*, p. 368).

He chooses the carnival as his new climax for several reasons. First, he is puzzled by the fact that he had not even mentioned it before, and is concerned that he may subconsciously have been trying to hide something ("it is strange that I should not have mentioned it, even in passing" [*B*, p. 341]); second, it is an event of such intense color and atmosphere that it has remained vividly with him and, perhaps, assumed a far greater significance in his mind than the actual happenings warrant; and, third, he remains so emotionally involved with Justine, and therefore with what he sees as the threat to her from Nessim (though now it is more on Pursewarden's account than his own), that he selects the event he interprets—erroneously, Clea soon tells us—as climaxing the presumed plot of the jealous husband.[11] But even Toto's

[11] Darley specifically alludes to his lingering doubts on this point. "So much I wrote was based upon Justine's fears of Nessim—genuine fears, genuinely expressed. I have seen with my own eyes that cold speechless jealousy upon his face and seen the fear written on hers. Yet now Balthazar

murder is no climax for *Balthazar* in the sense of resolving mysteries.

Of the two climaxes and, similarly, of the conflicting interpretations offered in *Justine* and *Balthazar*, neither may be completely and finally rejected—or accepted. Even Balthazar, who retains an essentially traditional view of "objective" reality and would substitute it for subjective interpretation, realizes that the Interlinear does not so much supersede *Justine* as complement it. He himself offers us a vivid image for the slippery elusiveness of complex reality. " 'I love to feel events overlapping each other, crawling over one another like wet crabs in a basket' " (*B*, p. 293); and subsequently he provides a fairly specific and accurate technical analysis of the structure of the *Justine* manuscript he has read and of what he correctly foresees becoming the novel bearing his name.

"I suppose" (writes Balthazar) "that if you wished somehow to incorporate all that I am telling you into your own Justine manuscript now, you would find yourself with a curious sort of book— the story would be told, so to speak, in layers. . . . Not unlike Pursewarden's idea of a series of novels with 'sliding panels' as he called them. Or else, perhaps, like some medieval palimpsest where different sorts of truth are thrown down one upon the other, the one obliterating or perhaps supplementing another." (*B*, p. 338.)

And an earlier statement of Darley's should perhaps be juxtaposed here.

"Truth" said Balthazar to me once, blowing his nose in an old tennis sock, "Truth is what most contradicts itself in time."

And Pursewarden on another occasion, but not less memorably:

---

says that Nessim would never have done her harm. What am I to believe?" (*B*, p. 339). Of course Narouz's confession to Clea of the murder of Toto and attempted murder of Justine completely vindicates Nessim.   🖋

"If things were always what they seemed, how impoverished would be the imagination of man!" (*B*, p. 216.)

Thus, the two novels *Justine* and *Balthazar* do not negate each other, but, if the notion of the relativity-aesthetic has any validity whatsoever (and the trend of contemporary art and science suggests that it does), they exist together as prismatic equals—not hopelessly contradictory, but rather, and properly, mutually complementing, qualifying, and enriching.

Pursewarden, unlike Balthazar, is always profoundly aware of complexities and ambiguities, the ungraspable—as well as of the continuing need for a saving sense of humor and an ultimate affirmation of "joy unconfined."[12] For him, people are undefinable qualities, as unstable and illusory " 'as "matter" to the physicist when he is regarding it as a form of energy' " (*B*, p. 306). Consequently, in his writing, Pursewarden consistently denied that he was doing anything like offering definitive answers. Balthazar tells us that one novel of his contains a page with an asterisk

"which refers one to a page in the text which is mysteriously blank. Many people take this for a printer's error. But Pursewarden himself assured me that it was deliberate. 'I refer the reader to a blank page in order to throw him back upon his own resources—which is where every reader ultimately belongs.' " (*B*, p. 307.)

And it is this Tristram Shandyish "serious clowning," ironic and self-mocking, sincerely equivocal and wittily profound, which both Balthazar and Clea see as the basis of the laughter Pursewarden affirms as "perhaps the key" to the "new creature," the new kind of character, for which "we artists are hunting" (*B*, p. 381).

And Darley is destined to become such a character. As

---

12 After all, in the title of Pursewarden's trilogy, as well as in his attitude toward life, God *is* a Humorist.

much judged as judge in *Balthazar*, he has learned much since *Justine*, especially from Pursewarden. He is no longer so hampered by a single-minded and unequivocal view of events; he has become increasingly capable of allowing for varying, even contradictory, interpretations. While he has yet to achieve the ultimately necessary sense of humor and affirmation, he has nonetheless matured significantly. In *Justine*, Darley was primarily a participant, a rather simple, if sympathetic and occasionally perceptive, sensualist—his judgments based almost entirely on knowledge received solely through his senses, his scale of values often directly related to his immediate cravings. Even late in *Balthazar* he says, "Yes, who can help but love carnival when in it all debts are paid, all crimes expiated or committed, all illicit desires sated —without guilt or premeditation, without the penalties which conscience or society exact?" (*B*, p. 344). But of course there are always guilt and penalties, for what Darley had always found, what such characters of immediate and amoral sense perception necessarily find, were hollowness and sham—never the satisfaction and completeness he sought. Thus the validity of Pursewarden's playing on Darley's initials for the imposed nickname: Lineaments of Gratified Desire.

Yet Darley *has* changed for the better by the end of *Balthazar*, for the Interlinear has convinced him that another observer—nonmalevolent and at least equally honest—may well arrive at far different, and perhaps "more valid," conclusions with regard to the same set of circumstances. Darley has now learned to "doubt wisely"; he has moved outside the immediate flux of events, and, recollecting in at least partial tranquillity, is at last able to make critical judgments with a mind less dependent upon, less caught up in, the hasty rush of actions that endlessly alter even while he attempts to delineate and judge. In addition, having been evaluated and, as it were, weighed by another in *his* scale, and having consequently been forced to review and rethink all his own notions and judgments, Darley has learned the simple and elusive essential truth that things are often not what they seem—and that conflicting testimony may imply not the inadequacy of an observer but, on the contrary, his great perceptivity.

That Darley has not yet concluded his education is obvious when we recall the great stress this novel places on creative laughter, on a sense of total and unqualified affirmation (Pursewarden: " 'It is terrible to love life so much you can hardly breathe!' " [B, p. 293]), and on a dynamic and comprehensive view of the organic integration of life and art which, as Clea puts it, will harness the rhythms of time " 'and put them to our [the artist's] own use' " (B, p. 383).

"At first" writes Pursewarden "we seek to supplement the emptiness of our individuality through love, and for a brief moment enjoy the illusion of completeness. But it is only an illusion. For this strange creature, which we thought would join us to the body of the world, succeeds at last in separating us most thoroughly from it. Love joins and then divides. How else would we be growing?"

How else indeed? [adds Darley] But relieved to find myself once more partnerless I have already groped my way back to my dark corner where the empty chairs of the revellers stand like barren ears of corn. (B, p. 377.)

Metaphorically like Ruth among the alien corn (a scene the above image vividly recalls), Darley has made the difficult but necessary choice—if he is to become a full human being and artist—of seeking fresh creative soil among a still vital people. And, with Darley freed from the numbing silence of his two years in Upper Egypt, we begin to feel by the end of

Balthazar that he will eventually learn to speak fluently the new language through which, as Pursewarden emphasizes, the modern artist, the fully alive human being, must communicate.

Like *Justine*, *Balthazar* is vague about the future, for it too ends with Darley in a position of passive solitude. Perhaps it is only a larger reflection of events like *Mountolive*, one not imaged in the self-mirroring glass of a limited, single-faceted narrator, which can reveal whether this isloation is permanent or merely a momentary plateau before Darley's maturing progression resumes. Perhaps. At this juncture, one can only ask.

IV. *Mountolive* and The
Unreliable Narration of Facts

*This big novel is as tame and naturalistic in form as a Hardy;
yet it is the fulcrum of the quartet and the rationale of the thing.
With the fourth I can plunge back into the time-stream again
as per* Justine. (*Corr,* p. 327.)

The . . . central preoccupation of Conrad's technique [in Lord
Jim], *the heart of the impressionist aim, is to invite and control
the reader's identifications and so subject him to an intense rather
than passive experience. Marlow's human task is also the reader's:
to achieve a right human relationship with this questionable
younger brother* [Jim]. *Marlow must resist an excessive identification (which would mean abandoning his traditional ethic);
he must maintain a satisfactory balance of sympathy and judgment.* (Albert J. Guerard, *Conrad the Novelist,* p. 152.)

*To know the facts is one thing: to know the truth is another.
Facts are to truth what dates are to history—they record certain
events but they do not reveal the significance of those events.*
(Claude Houghton [Oldfield], *I Am Jonathan Scrivener,* p. 99.)

THE narrative form of *Mountolive,* especially as it appears
set in contrast to the first person of *Justine* and *Balthazar,*
seems to offer truth where the others offered opinion, objec-

tivity as a corrective to their subjectivity. Durrell attempts to explain it this way: "The subject-object relation is so important to relativity that I have tried to turn the novel through both subjective and objective modes. The third part, *Mountolive*, is a straight naturalistic novel in which the narrator of *Justine* and *Balthazar* becomes an object, i.e., a character" (*B*, Note). As this chapter attempts to demonstrate, however, it would be a mistake to equate Durrell's use of "subjective" with "false" or "inaccurate" and "objective" with "true" or "accurate," and consequently to read *Mountolive* as the "key" to the *Quartet* in the sense that a legend specifically and unequivocally explains all the symbolic shorthand contained in a map. The implied author of *Mountolive affords* us a third view of the *Justine-Balthazar* events; and the worth of that view must be considered in terms of its internal consistency and relationship to the whole and not, as would be all too easy and misleading, primarily with regard to an a priori evaluation of its "omniscient" technique. Only in this way can we avoid prejudging the adequacy of the *Mountolive* interpretation.

In its simplest terms, *Mountolive* is a story of almost gothic intrigue and violence, of mistrust and murder, of misplaced and thwarted love, of death and despair. Yet it is charged with the color and poetry of Alexandria. "It ripples with beautiful prose passages, and it has a gripping sense of mystery about it."[1] The entire book (and the Mountolive and Alexandria it depicts) is foreshadowed and embodied in the opening scene, the twilight fish drive on the Nile. The narrator speaks from within Mountolive's mind: "It was very beautiful, but it all stank so: yet to his surprise he found he rather enjoyed the rotting smells of the estuary" (*M*, p. 398). And this diplomatic "junior of exceptional promise" (*M*, p.

[1] Shainheit, "Who Wrote *Mountolive?*," 60.

397), this figure of great masculine beauty, will increasingly enjoy the "rotting smells" of mediocrity and negation produced by the artificiality he has chosen to substitute for what apparently could have been a brilliant and satisfying life. To this extent, Mountolive serves as a foil to Darley, for his story is a *Bildungsroman* with a difference: first, there are the maturation and success of the sensitive and apparently deserving adolescent (deserving despite the narrator's early reservation that, but for Leila, such things as painting and music "normally would have been outside the orbit of his interests" [M, p. 430]); but, second, there follows a spiritual decline when compromise and vacillation replace firmness and dedication as a way of life. Mountolive's stultifying embassy life in Russia gains him an ambassadorship and the long-delayed return to Egypt, but little else. "Surely now, he would at long last be free to *act?*" he imagines (M, p. 448); but "this engrossing delusion," as both Sir Louis (the retiring British ambassador to Russia) and the narrator correctly conceive it, reveals the paradoxical self-contradiction of Mountolive's attitude. One must consciously *choose* if one is to be free to act, and not merely hope that, like grace, such freedom will be visited upon one as an inevitable consequence of simply arriving at a desired status or geographical location. The inadequacy of Mountolive's attitude may be underscored by contrasting it with Darley's comparably stagnating exile in Upper Egypt and *his* finally achieving purgation of a similar false pride—as well as (by the end of *Clea*) the freedom and will required for independent action and creativity.[2]

2 According to the omniscient narrator, only one character is actually freed of restraints in *Mountolive*. Justine, seduced by Nessim's cause and the profundity of his commitment to it, appears no longer imprisoned by Arnauti's "check." "The secret they shared made her free to act" (M, p. 557). But see below.

The story of Mountolive of necessity involves an implied author with a firm knowledge of the surface facts of events— British policy, Coptic intrigue, Egyptian indolence, even solutions to the unsolved mysteries of the first two novels— and his presence is a telling comment on Mountolive's character as it simultaneously travels the paths of public success and private failure. The public success is obvious and is related in a straightforward, unambiguous manner: the talented but obscure junior embassy official, having served the requisite period of apprenticeship and exile, finally returns to his beloved Egypt in ambassadorial triumph. In Egypt, he arouses the envy of rival ambassadors for his extraordinary command of Arabic, for his intelligence, charm, and good looks, and for his unfailing sense of the proper and correct. Even when his opposition to the Coptic plot is frustrated, it is unquestionably because Egyptian bureaucracy and corruption are too powerful for any man to overcome. And Mountolive can even defend his intentions, for, when torn between duty to his country and responsibilities, on the one hand, and affection—first for Pursewarden and then for Nessim—on the other, he hesitates; in fact, despite his better judgment, he even sides with his friends until all possible doubt is resolved. It is true that his efforts to save Pursewarden and to destroy Nessim (which he never really wants to do) are equally unsuccessful; but such failures, the narrator tells us, are inescapable and not really a reflection of the individual, for all are ultimately limited by larger forces.

Nature is inherently ingovernable. They [Mountolive and Nessim] were soon to be drawn along ways not of their choosing. . . . They were both *bound* now [after Pursewarden's suicide], tied like bondsmen to the unrolling action which illustrated the personal predispositions of neither. They had embarked on a free exercise of the will only to find themselves shackled, bricked up by the historical process. And a single turn of the kaleidoscope had brought it about. (*M*, pp. 565–66.)

At this point—and indeed throughout *Mountolive*—impressionism yields to naturalism.

But if Mountolive is not to be condemned for his public or political acts, his decline as a man, as a spiritual and ethical being, is all the more blatant—in fact a graph of his life would approximate an elongated **X**, with the line rising from the left representing Mountolive's surface or public aspect; the line declining from the left, his concealed or private aspect. The point at which they irrevocably cross may be symbolized by Mountolive's double-faced vision as he returns to Egypt.

It was frightfully hot in the little cabin of the airplane. . . . His mixed elation and alarm translated itself into queasiness. Was he going to be airsick—and for the first time in his life? He hoped not. It would be awful to be sick into this impressive refurbished hat. . . . At any rate it became him. He was quite surprised to see how handsome he looked in a mirror. . . . He stepped forward tentatively to shake hands and realized that with the donning of his uniform everything had changed. A sudden loneliness smote him—for he realized that now, as an Ambassador, he must forever renounce the friendship of ordinary human beings in exchange for their *deference*. . . .

But the momentary spasm of loneliness passed in the joys of a new self-possession. There was nothing to do now but to exploit his charm to the full; to be handsome, to be capable, surely one had the right to enjoy the consciousness of these things without self-reproach? (*M*, pp. 496–97.)

The rhetorical question receives of course no explicit answer, but the supercilious tone of the passage and its use of such loaded words as "ordinary" produce an ironic distancing as the reader, though still largely sympathetic, begins to separate himself from an increasingly inadequate Mountolive.

At the outset of the book, Mountolive appears of proper youth and sensibility to commence the *Bildungsroman* quest for education and maturity. His love of Egypt, its warm, exotic sense of life, is strong. " 'Egypt' he said to himself as one might repeat the name of a woman. 'Egypt' " (*M*, p. 398). His affair with the older Leila—though obviously incapable of enduring—serves to initiate him into the rites of love and helps him to overcome his having been "educated not to wish to feel" (*M*, p. 403). Even his *gaffes* (for instance, his reference to Copts as Moslems, which understandably arouses the anger of Leila's husband) are more the failings of naïveté and inexperience than of prejudice or stupidity. And his difficult process of re-education appears well under way. "It was unpleasant to be forced to grow. It was thrilling to grow. He gravitated between fear and grotesque elation. . . . But he was not altogether a fool; he was learning the two most important lessons in life: to make love honestly and to reflect" (*M*, pp. 411–15).

Unfortunately, Mountolive is incapable of adequately applying these lessons to his life, and instead of growing through experience, he eventually becomes narrowed, inward-turning in the negative sense. Even his affair with Leila, like the "dark eyes of the woman" (*M*, p. 410), becomes uncomfortably equivocal as we learn not only that Leila, to Mountolive's astonishment, actually loves her dying husband but also that this strange and remote figure had encouraged her in this affair as a means of retaining that love. A pattern of uncertainty begins to develop in Mountolive's life, though it is easily minimized or ignored for a time. "At the outset his own feelings [toward Leila] somewhat confused him, but he was unused to introspection, unfamiliar so to speak with the entail of his own personality—in a word, as he was young he successfully dismissed them" (*M*, p. 410).

During the years that follow, Mountolive's life is increasingly molded by Leila's endless correspondence, for "in a way she set herself to make a man of him, using every feminine warmth, every candour" (M, p. 413), and she assumes her new role of pen pal–lover with elation, "for now at last she would be free to possess Mountolive as she wished—greedily in her mind" (M, p. 430). Her ardor during their separation—in fact, *because* of their separation—intensifies as she manipulates and exploits the lover she has created in her own image. She is thus able to possess him to a degree impossible during even their most intimate physical sharing of love. "In a few years she was able to confess: 'I feel somehow nearer to you today, on paper, than I did before we parted. Why is this?' But she knew only too well. Yet she added at once, for honesty's sake: 'Is this feeling a little unhealthy perhaps? To outsiders it might even seem a little pathetic or ludicrous. . .' " (M, p. 431). And indeed it does, especially since their separation has the opposite effect on Mountolive. He is incapable of holding her love firm and secure even in memory. "Leila appeared to be somehow fading, receding on the curvature of a world moving in time, detaching herself from his own memories of her. . . . His concentration was becoming dispersed" (M, p. 429). She manages to hold his interest and affection (though perhaps more from force of habit than anything else); in fact, whatever strength of personality he achieves is largely due to her. Yet, from Mountolive's point of view, she eventually ceases to maintain an independent existence, and becomes, in effect, an alter ego, a reliable and convenient sounding board. "He had come to depend on this friendship which still dictated, as a form, the words 'My dearest love' at the head of letters concerned solely with, say, art, or love (his love) or life (his life)" (M, p. 432).

As intimacy thus fades, it becomes apparent that their brief love affair was never strong enough to survive both separation and Leila's attempt to impose aesthetic standards upon it, to try to create an unaging monument to an attachment perfect only in retrospect. On paper, the lovers become somewhat abstract and sterile; although her letters are perhaps increasingly marvelous, and he, in response, teaches "himself to write well in English and French" (M, p. 430), they communicate less and less. He becomes her vicarious dabbler in European culture ("He informed himself in order to inform her" [M, p. 430]), without ever really enjoying the role; and she, the understanding (and never jealous) confidante for his several off-stage romances. Thus, when they finally do meet again, it is hardly strange that he feels a strong sense of unreality and does not recognize her at all. It is not simply that life and disease have left her ugly and petty "like some old Arab lady" (M, p. 619)—for her latest letters have in no way prepared either Mountolive or the reader for her *internal* depreciation—but that she has dramatically become a symbol of his own loss of innocence. "Leila had suddenly left him face to face with a reality which, he supposed, had always lain lurking behind the dusty tapestry of his romantic notions. In a sense, she had *been* Egypt, his own private Egypt of the mind; and now this old image had been husked, stripped bare" (M, p. 623). The lesson to be learned should be clear: the edifices of neither romance nor art can endure if constructed on a foundation of mirage and wishful imaginings. Their affair served many purposes (Hosnani kept his wife; Leila found a kind of release from enforced provinciality; Mountolive acquired some understanding of the people, traditions, and languages of Egypt), but a permanent approach to love was not among them. It would seem that only the appearance of love was ever present, that the appearance was deceptive, and that to cling to the appearance as to reality is simply to make the shock of awakening all the more damaging when it finally comes. And yet, we must continuously remind ourselves, this is only one interpretation.

At the end of *The Rhetoric of Fiction* (pp. 432–34), Wayne Booth includes "A Gallery of Unreliable Narrators and Reflectors." The list is admittedly noninclusive, for it arbitrarily cites only a single work of each author mentioned; nonetheless, it is significant that Durrell is included for *Mountolive*, his "key" to the entire *Quartet*. In this book, Durrell deliberately misleads us in many ways, perhaps the most significant of which is his narrator's presumably accurate knowledge of the solutions to factual mysteries. Justine's "diary," the basis for so much of Darley's and the reader's earlier interpretation of her character, becomes simply Arnauti's unused notes for *Moeurs*. Pursewarden's bequest of five hundred pounds to Darley for Melissa is the result not of a sense of responsibility because Justine used Darley (thereby abusing Melissa) to get at him (as Darley had assumed), but of his impulsive affection for Melissa's naturalness the night before his suicide. The traumatic moment when Darley and Justine are supposedly nearly discovered in bed by Nessim (who inexplicably turned away from the room at the last moment) becomes a mere case of mistaken identity, for the intruder was apparently not Nessim but Maskelyne, a British embassy official, prowling about for information concerning Nessim's intrigues. And it is the Coptic plot to help the Jews create Palestine, in defiant opposition to British-Arabic policy, that, according to the *Mountolive* narrator, primarily accounts for the marriage of

Justine and Nessim, Justine's promiscuity, Nessim's illness, Capodistria's feigned death, Justine's exile to a Palestine kibbutz.

In this novel, all love, all pain, seem subservient to the political struggle: it is most obvious in the marriage of Nessim and Justine: he wants the marriage to pave the way to his acceptance by the Jews in his plan to arm Palestine, yet hates himself for the necessity because he is in love with her. It did not ease the pain that Justine understood the ulterior motive. . . . It does not assuage his jealous agony to know that Justine's seductions of Darley and Pursewarden are necessary to the success of the plot.[3]

Yet the naïve, unreliable narrator would have us believe that all motives, all causes, are precise and unambiguous—and because his voice seems to assume the tone of authorial comment, the resulting irony is muted at times, and Durrell, like so many of his contemporaries, is censored for the sin of his narrator. As Booth rightly indicates, this is the danger inherent in the method. "The history of unreliable narrators from *Gargantua* to *Lolita* is in fact full of traps for the unsuspecting reader, some of them not particularly harmful but some of them crippling or even fatal."[4] Unlike, say, the barber in "Haircut" and Jason in *The Sound and the Fury*, "narrators whose every judgment is suspect,"[5] the implied author of *Mountolive* is far more complex. We have no reason to doubt the accuracy of his version of the Nessim-Maskelyne mix-up or of Capodistria's disappearance or even of Mountolive's psychological odyssey from excessive innocence to excessive experience. And, further, even the silences of the narrator often imply what seem to be valid interpretations—for instance, because no new explanation regarding

[3] Lund, "Submerge for Reality," 233.
[4] *The Rhetoric of Fiction*, 239.
[5] *Ibid.*, 274.

Justine's child is presented, we accept as accurate Narouz's vision as it has been reported by Balthazar.

On the other hand, the implied narrator has little interest in Durrell's "Investigation of Modern Love," Pursewarden's artistic theorizing, or Darley's maturation. Love has become either a matter of political convenience (Nessim and Justine, as well as Justine's extramarital affairs) or youthful romance that burns brightly but briefly (Mountolive and Leila) or something clandestine and dirty (Pursewarden and Liza). And the results differ only in degree: in the first instance, with the intrigue discovered and the basis of the love gone, hopelessness and separation; in the second, with innocence clung to long after innocence is dead, a too sudden confrontation and a monstrous ugliness;[6] in the third, the ultimate despair and negation of suicide. In fact, and this is probably what is most "wrong" with the book, *Mountolive* is a novel of virtually unrelieved agony and despair, culminating in an orgy of spiritual defeat, physical death, and a lamentation (over the death of Narouz) of almost classical Greek scope and intensity—all in direct conflict with the ultimate affirmation of *Clea* and the *Quartet* as a whole.[7]

Further, all such consequences are the inevitable products

[6] Even afterward, however, Mountolive remains incapable of facing the inevitable; instead, "he hit upon the idea of doing something he had never done since his youth: he would go out, and dine in the Arab quarter, humbly and simply . . ." (*M*, p. 623)—and secretively and anonymously. The attempt to re-create an idealized vision of the past before he became a great public figure seems successful at first. "He was on the way to recovering, to restoring the blurred image of an Egypt which the meeting with Leila had damaged or somehow stolen from him" (*M*, p. 626), but the terrifying scene in the house of child prostitutes strips him not only of many of his possessions but of his dignity and perhaps of some of his illusions as well.

[7] By "wrong," I do not mean to suggest anything about the novel's aesthetic or moral or dramatic significance, but simply that much of what it presents is fundamentally irreconcilable with the rest of the *Quartet*. In opposition to most critics who consider this matter, however, I maintain that Durrell has sound artistic reasons for creating this dichotomy.

of the narrator's persistent fatalism and his concomitant inability to find a viable, creative release from hopelessness. Mountolive's father, now an Indian fakir, has embedded the novel's motto "in a scholarly preface to a Pali text." " 'For those of us who stand upon the margins of the world, as yet unsolicited by any God, the only truth is that work itself is Love' " (M, p. 467).[8] Justine embodies this credo when she learns of Nessim's "work" and makes it and him her own. But for Mountolive, work is closer to hate and, though he encounters love (Leila and subsequent affairs) and art (the correspondence, halfhearted cultural forays at Leila's promptings, and—more for her sake than his own—amateur painting with Nessim), his increasingly ineffectual attempts to dominate events ("Surely now, he would at long last be free to act?") affects him physiologically. Finally, inevitably, "the unaccountable affliction with which he always celebrated his return home [to England]—a crushing earache which rapidly reduced him to a shivering pain-racked ghost of himself" (M, p. 469)—broadens its base of operation. "That night [after Pursewarden's suicide and Mountolive's consequent acceptance of Nessim as an enemy] he was visited by an excruciating attack of the earache. . . . This was the first time he had ever been attacked while he was outside of the stockade of his mother's security. . ." (M, pp. 546–47). Doubtless it was not to be the last.

Similarly, according to *Mountolive*'s narrator, the other major participants are also doomed to endless frustration and an ultimate incapacity to act at all. The Nessim of this novel is remarkably like his friend. At their first meeting, "Mount-

8 Durrell employs this notion most explicitly in *Tunc*: the protagonist, Felix Charlock, sells—and sells out—his work; love consequently becomes horrific for him. The rule in Durrell is that to deny the validity of one's work is to negate love.

olive instantly recognized in him a person of his own kind, a person whose life was a code. They responded to each other nervously, like a concord in music" (M, p. 409). Like Mountolive, Nessim seeks to achieve a rapprochement between his public image of patrician prosperity and his unsatisfactory private life. He comes much closer to success than Mountolive, for he truly and totally commits himself to the Coptic–Jewish cause and then unites this intensity with his great passion for Justine. He wins her when he offers her not simply the inevitable satiety of physical desire, but the first principles of his existence—his obsessions, his fears, his dreams. He wins her, in fact, only when he convinces her that he has made of his great task, the intrigue, something very like a work of art (a work that "itself is Love") and then asks her to participate in the creative process—to allow him, that is, to employ the "art" that the intrigue is for love's sake.

They come together in "a Faustian compact," a mutual sharing of souls, "their dark, passionate faces [glowing] in the soft light with a sort of holiness conferred by secrecy, by the appetites of a shared will, by desires joined at the waist" (M, pp. 554, 560). But Nessim, in this moment of intense and multileveled success (Justine's being a Jew will certainly aid the cause), forgets or chooses to forget the unpleasant.

The passion of their embraces came from *complicity,* from something deeper, more wicked, than the wayward temptings from the flesh or the mind. He had conquered her in offering a married life which was both a pretense and yet at the same time informed by a purpose which might lead them both to *death!* This was all that sex could mean to her now! How thrilling, sexually thrilling, was the expectation of their death! (M, p. 558.)

And when the pretending and the intriguing are ended, and discovery has led not to death but merely to temporary separation, their love seems totally unable to substitute for the old foundation of thrills and complicity the perhaps far deadlier dangers of anticlimax and dull, daily routine.

As for Justine and Darley, they are substantially reduced in scope and intensity within this narrative—to a point where they are virtually nonexistent as self-motivated, psychologically differentiated individuals. Justine, when she deploys her sexual prowess with the unflinching cunning of a military strategist sacrificing most of his forces to the exigencies of an over-all design, loses her aura of an abstract feminine mystique felicitously made flesh. No longer the patron saint of *femmes fatales* in *Mountolive*, she ceases in effect to be a woman at all when politics replaces sex as her essential distinguishing quality.

Pursewarden, still the artistic theorist, manages to offer some valid statements (many not unlike the crucial one of Mountolive's father) about life and art.

"The artist's work constitutes the only satisfactory relationship he can have with his fellowmen since he seeks his real friends among the dead and the unborn" (M, p. 439).

"One writes to recover a lost innocence!" (M, p. 475).

"People will realize one day that it is only the artist who can make things really *happen*; that is why society should be founded upon him" (M, p. 566).

The equivocality—even surface nonsense—of these statements heralds the essential Pursewardenesque note. The first suggests that the artist's isolation is both enforced and inadequate; the second, that the artist has experienced too much too quickly; and the third is quoted by the narrator as an ironic comment on the devitalizing effect of Pursewarden's suicide on the wills of Nessim and Mountolive. Occasionally Pursewarden acts as we would expect such a free spirit to act —most notably in the wonderfully staged scene in the middle of the night at Trafalgar Square when he waltzes Liza about under the watchful eyes of "Nelson Stylites," the astonished Mountolive, and a rather skeptical and very British bobby. Mountolive, as usual, plays the straight man.

"They are celebrating Blake's birthday" I explained in rather a shamefaced fashion, and the officer looked a shade more relieved as he followed them with an admiring eye. He coughed and said "Well, he can't be drunk to dance like that, can he? The things people get up to on their birthdays!" (*M*, p. 442.)

But such ambiguous statements and such moments of sheer exuberance are infrequent, for Pursewarden too has been metamorphosed into a political animal. And, despite his brief passion for Melissa and his hardly satisfactory writing ("the book which he was trying to complete [took shape] so slowly, painfully, in these hard-won secret moments stolen from an empty professional life" [*M*, p. 524]), *this* Pursewarden is conceived almost entirely as a rather unsuccessful junior attached to the Cultural Department of the British Foreign Service—the kind who, according to Mountolive's interpretation of their first meeting, " 'may have been a little intimidated by my rank...' " (*M*, p. 439).[9] Inevitably, Pursewarden's suicide is construed as the result of a cowardly incapacity to choose between duty (to a job he despised and a policy he condemned as blind and stupid) and affection not only for his friends but for their cause as well. This explanation may well be "true," but it is absurd, for the exigencies

---

[9] That Mountolive is creating a Pursewarden in his own highly subjective image should be obvious, for the actual poet reacts quite otherwise. "Poor David Mountolive! Pursewarden thought of him with compassion and affection. What a price the career diplomat had to pay for the fruits of power! ["Bitter fruits" Mountolive himself calls them all too soon.] 'His dreams must forever be awash with the memories of fatuities endured—deliberately endured in the name of what was most holy in the profession, namely the desire to please, the determination to captivate in order to influence. Well! It takes all sorts to unmake a world' " (*M*, p. 519).

of artistic consistency make it impossible for a poet, especially one of Pursewarden's uncompromising irony, even to hesitate (no less actually to commit suicide) over what, in his case, seems a clear-cut moral and aesthetic decision. Such a man *might* commit suicide because he "is riven with guilt from having committed incest" with his blind sister,[10] but it is nonsense to insist he would do so merely because he is confronted with a mortal attack on a posture of loyalty ("my country right or wrong") which he not only never maintained but would find ludicrous. And if such an explanation conforms to the facts, one can only shrug and say that the facts themselves are unreliable as a guide to truth.

Yet this interpretation of Pursewarden's character is not only the narrator's but Mountolive's as well. It is Mountolive who, embodying the loyalty he impressionistically projects onto Pursewarden, remains unable to understand the reasoning behind the Coptic plot, which he feels has so enfeebled him.

He sighed. What could any of them hope to gain from a successful Jewish insurrection? Mountolive believed too firmly in the English mystique to realize fully that anyone could have lost faith in it and the promise it might hold of future security, future stability. (*M*, p. 593.)

And it is Mountolive who now sees himself, as he had seen Pursewarden before him, hopelessly torn between duty and affection; in fact, throughout this book, it is Mountolive who has persistently sought, and found, superficial, "objectively" definable, single-faceted explanations for personalities, motivations, and actions we have been finding increasingly complex and internalized. One commentator has pointed out:

---

[10] George P. Elliott, "The Other Side of the Story," in Moore (ed.), *The World of Lawrence Durrell*, 92.

In his Notebook that comes at the center of *Balthazar*, Pursewarden answers, as it were, Mountolive's assumptions about the world and the way it runs: "We artists are not interested in policies but in values—this is our field of battle! If once we would loosen up, relax the terrible grip of the so-called Kingdom of Heaven which has made the earth such a blood-soaked place, we might rediscover in sex the key to a metaphysical search which is our *raison d'être* here below!"[11]

Perhaps, finally, we are in a position to confront the implicit question underlying much of this chapter.

Howard L. Shainheit poses the question in the title of his essay "Who Wrote *Mountolive*?" and he tries to answer it as follows:

This is a question, which, not unlike questions about motivation and character, can only be answered by the quite unsatisfactory "everybody and nobody." *Mountolive* . . . is the public view of the situation, is, supposedly, that common body of political knowledge. If it is considered otherwise, it has no rationale in the *Quartet*. . . .[12]

In a footnote, he adds:

Dr. Richard Haven suggests the following alternate theory: Whether "the truth" is presently known or not, most people (the public, so to speak) assume both that it exists and that it is knowable. The information in *Mountolive* might be considered as that set of ordering "facts" or "explanations" that are assumed to be existent. In this view it doesn't matter who is supposed to present the material, for the material is not yet publicly known, and, in fact, is largely unknowable by its nature (e.g., the conversations of Justine and Nessim).[13]

Actually, these two views are, in essence, indistinguishable, and, unable to arrive at any more satisfactory solution, Shain-

11 Frederick R. Karl, "Lawrence Durrell: Physical and Metaphysical Love," in *The Contemporary English Novel*, 59.
12 P. 64.
13 P. 72.

heit asserts: "that the novel might have been better off being written from a particular person's point of view is, it would appear, incontestable." And he offers "Mnemjian, the barber at the crossroads of the city's many political, social, economic, and personal paths [as] . . . the ideal person to relate the public aspect of the *Quartet*."[14]

In a sense, however, *Mountolive* is already "written from a particular person's point of view," that of its title character, in much the same way that *Great Expectations* is written from the point of view of its protagonist as he relives the events he narrates. There are differences of course; for if the narrator is indeed Mountolive, he always refers to himself in the third person; he never comments retrospectively; and, with regard to the surprisingly few incidents of which he can have no firsthand knowledge, he asserts, rather than speculates, on the basis of either information he has received indirectly or his predetermined view of those involved. All of this is consistent with Mountolive's character, which, unlike Pip's and despite all it has experienced, is essentially static. He retains the image of himself as a great public figure; he learns no moral lesson; and he remains certain that man is an uncomplicated creature who responds more or less predictably to any given stimulus.

Possibly Durrell did not consciously intend his narrator to be taken for an older but no wiser Mountolive; nonetheless,

---

[14] Pp. 64–65. Shainheit is understandably disturbed that the values offered in *Mountolive* are impersonal and therefore abstract. Earlier he wrote, "Whereas the fourth section of *The Sound and the Fury* is intended, it is obvious, to close the book and to point to certain values, *Mountolive* merely presents itself as a public account of the public side of the *Quartet* . . ." (p. 17). (Like Booth, he would have his author reveal strong moral standards which the reader can accept as a norm.) But Mnemjian is such a vaguely realized character that, unless his involvement in events were substantially increased, he could hardly espouse alternative standards of sufficient relevance to overcome the present objection.

this is precisely the kind of book we may assume such a man *would* write. Further, in addition to offering a possible explanation for the "inadequacies" of this book (the narrator's judgments, his unrelieved fatalism, the almost totally subordinate role of both love and art), such an interpretation also suggests that Durrell has enlarged the possible role of the unreliable narrator in fiction and, consequently, the demands placed on the reader of such fiction.[15]

For the most part, when previous writers presented a narrator (whether he was as relatively reliable as Marlow in *Lord Jim* or as relatively unreliable as Jason in *The Sound and the Fury* or anywhere in between), a reader could be reasonably secure in the knowledge that he would encounter exactly that degree of reliability he has been led to expect. (The critical controversy surrounding the governess in *The Turn of the Screw* is the exception, not the rule.) Durrell followed this practice in *Justine*, for Darley, though far more sympathetic than a narrator like Jason, is (at this point) hardly a more competent delineator of truth. *Balthazar* is more complex. Both narrators—Darley and Balthazar—seem to expect ultimate "truths" from the Interlinear; yet we learn that Balthazar's is simply another personal account; we recall that we have been repeatedly warned about the self-contradictory

15 Much additional evidence of narrator-Mountolive identity could be cited, but two further points should suffice: the climaxes of the first two books—the duck shoot and the carnival—receive only passing mention, since, from Mountolive's viewpoint, they are politically insignificant; Darley, objectively the protagonist of the *Quartet*, has almost no place in *Mountolive* because he has no political role. (See below.) Further, even the few incidents or attitudes in the book which may be cited in opposition to this interpretation (for instance, Pursewarden's condescending sympathy for Mountolive, quoted above in footnote 9) may be seen as Mountolive's honest, if inadequate, attempt to be fair and objective; in addition, however, it should be remembered that Pursewarden's attitude in this statement is remarkably similar to Mountolive's own self-judgment by the conclusion of the book.

nature of "truths"; and Darley, properly skeptical, is ultimately only partially convinced.

However, despite all the warnings we have received thus
far about the inherent impossibility of our or anyone's knowing *the* answer, we still come to *Mountolive* expecting just
that because, in contrast to *Justine* and *Balthazar*, it is written
in an "objective" form. What Durrell is implying though is,
first, that an author need not fulfill the expectation he has
aroused in his reader so long as he offers, as Durrell does, in-
controvertible evidence that such an expectation was an effectively arranged false lead; and, second, that an "objective"
narrator may well be in the *worst* position to reveal the
essence—and not merely the facts—of occurrences. Durrell's
multifaceted concept of reality and his relativity-aesthetic
necessitate both his giving a voice to the "objective" view of
events and his demonstrating that that view is, if anything,
less adequate than the more personal ones. Durrell's method
and structure throughout the *Quartet* confirm that a central
concern of his is

to suggest the difficulty of ever knowing (especially in love affairs)
what has actually happened and what people's motives really are;
the understanding that prevails at one moment is replaced or
modified by the understanding that comes with new information,
and the true explanation of an event virtually never comes at
the time of its occurrence. This does indeed have an aesthetic
effect in that it proposes a new kind of verisimilitude and, by
instructing the reader that he must be careful to accept no statement at its face value, involves him in the story in an especially
active way.[16]

And, as I have tried to indicate, this involvement becomes
increasingly active from one book of the *Quartet* to the next

[16] Trilling, "The *Quartet*: Two Reviews," in Moore (ed.), *The World
of Lawrence Durrell*, 56.

—for the appearance of certitude becomes stronger as actual truth becomes more elusive and uncertain.

It seems unnecessary to emphasize the significance of the fact that Darley, like Melissa in *Balthazar*, is mentioned in *Mountolive* only rarely and then condescendingly, as a mere object of universal pity. To Pursewarden, he is snobbish and parochial, dull and passionless, something of a dilettante with respect to both art and life; to Justine, he is no more than one of several "unobservant people [who] are beginning to notice" Nessim's failing health (*M*, p. 580); and to Mountolive, he is virtually nonexistent. Yet, as insignificant as he is made to appear, Darley manages to serve as a real, though barely discernible, source of light amid the gathering darkness of *Mountolive*. Pursewarden admits, albeit grudgingly, that this plodding, persistent schoolteacher "really *is* a good chap, and a sensitive one" (*M*, p. 482); and Melissa, instinctively and incisively understanding people, pays him the highest compliment while unwittingly prophesying Pursewarden's suicide. " 'Your life is dead, closed up. Not like Darley's. His is wide . . . very wide . . . open.' . . . She added with the tremendous unconscious force of veracity: 'He can still love' " (*M*, p. 531). No one else is so characterized in *Mountolive*, and no one else of major stature is ignored as fully. In offering *his* account, Mountolive would naturally tend to slight those, like Darley, who have played no part in the political machinations. From Mountolive's point of view, Darley's contact with those who have been involved would be, at most, peripheral; and, since the ambassador's views remain essentially unaltered by the events he has experienced, Darley himself remains peripheral, even irrelevant, during what passes as Mountolive's retrospective narration.

The difficulty with this approach to the book is, however, that the events seem carefully ordered, consciously and uncompromisingly, to portray Mountolive's spiritual decline and defeat; yet Mountolive never passes the judgment upon himself or reaches the self-understanding which presumably would be necessary if he himself is to be able to narrate his fall. Further, Mountolive, who is appalled when he suspects Pursewarden's and Liza's incest, might well be incapable of portraying them—especially together—this sympathetically; the expanded use of symbolism (in contrast with *Justine, Balthazar*, and *Clea*) is more appropriate to a strictly third-person narrative than to a first (where the tendency is to explain the personal significance of all potential symbols, thus stripping from them much of their possible ambiguity), and most of the symbol patterns (for example, the opening fish drive, Narouz and his whip, the Coptic ceremonies, the older Leila and her snake, Liza as a beautiful blind oracle) work against the actual narrative; and, finally, everything revealed by the *Mountolive* narrator has the ring of literal consistency—even that which Mountolive really has no business knowing—yet it is all ultimately inadequate. One should not, then, insist that it is literally the ambassador "Who Wrote *Mountolive*," for the following view is at least equally viable. It does not necessarily contradict the Mount-olive-as-narrator interpretation—since the evidence for both, and much of the interpretation of that evidence, is identical —but it is perhaps more comprehensive, more self-consistent, and, most important, simpler. Basically, it is proposed that what is offered as "truth" in *Mountolive* really *is* the truth— as literal and objective as any narrator can reveal it—but that truth abstracted from "felt reality" is neither beautiful, nor important, nor even very reliable. These lives *truly* were shaped to a great extent by the political events and forces enclosing and devitalizing them; yet, ultimately, who cares? Certainly not the artist (or the psychologist)—to whom such

truth is little more than an uninteresting footnote to the pro-
founder reality (the great volume) of felt experience; single
causes are complete and accurate as far as they go, but they
do not (and cannot) touch the essentials. Durrell's postro-
mantic fiction asserts, so to speak, that the reduced weight
allowed the individual within the subject-object scale (especially as societal forces—the objective end of the scale—gain
in strength, complexity, and number every day, and as subject
and object merge) creates a precarious disproportion, an
imbalance demanding the immediate use of counterweights
on behalf of the individual if the novel is not to become mere
historical reporting.

Thus, the naturalistic (or historical or objective) element
in *The Alexandria Quartet* is given an emphasis subordinate
to the romantic (or personal or subjective). Yet it is far from
ignored; Durrell not only devotes one-fourth of his space and
energies to it, but also comments (as in the epigraph to the
present chapter) that indeed *Mountolive* "is the fulcrum of
the quartet and the rationale of the thing"—which is not to
say, as many critics otherwise completely unsympathetic
to the *Quartet* imply, that *Mountolive* is its raison d'être or
Durrell's only worthwhile—even his only readable—accomplishment in fiction.[17]

On the contrary, *Mountolive* offers literal truth for what
it is worth (implicitly, about one-fourth of the total), as one

[17] To cite just one: Benjamin DeMott, having unequivocally condemned
the *Quartet* as "jammed with Gothic gimcracks," appallingly remote, the
work of a bad poet and second-rate thinker (a would-be innovator completely oblivious "to the whole line of investigation carried on by major
novelists since the beginning of this century"), manages to add: "To say
this much is not to deny that *Mountolive* is a readable novel with a brilliant
opening chapter, and that moments of power occur at intervals in all four
books, and that in conception the whole work raises extraordinary hopes . . ."
("Grading the Emanglons," pp. 457–64). But DeMott has misunderstood
either his own reaction to the *Quartet* or his argument against it, for his
conclusion hardly follows logically.

possible touchstone for the numerous individual time streams which flow past, above, and beyond it. And it is Durrell himself, in his role as the creator of the implied author of *Mountolive*, who takes objective truth seriously, accepts it as a fulcrum and a rationale—and denies that it is anything more. For while the naturalistic aspect must not be ignored, to dwell on it for too long, as has already been stressed in the above discussion on *Mountolive*, is to create a hopeless sense of fatalism (since individual intrigues and counteractions are incapable of influencing the public course of events), to subordinate totally the roles of both love and art (since they are largely outside the mainstream of historical events), and to deny the paramount value of felt reality. Thus, there can be no question that the mysteries apparently solved in *Mountolive* are truly solved; yet how pale, uninteresting—even foolish—such solutions appear beside the more subjective "truths" of *Justine* and *Balthazar*. (*Justine*, first sexually then politically motivated, is perhaps the outstanding illustration.) Public truth is acknowledged and respected (Durrell obviously and correctly feeling that the serious artist can do no less), and, for those who wish to read the *Quartet* in this way, it may be taken as the focus for such individual responses as the other three novels offer; for some readers, it may even be the criterion for judging the validity and significance of those responses.

For Durrell, however (and for most of his readers too, one suspects and hopes), the subjective response can never be invalidated regardless of its schism with objective truth, for nothing is ever quite this simple. The fact that Darley has responded to events in a certain way influences (aesthetically if not historically) those events. And if the response (say, Darley's initial certainty that Justine was in love with him) is sufficiently strong and convincing, and the "truth" (that

Justine was really using him and sex merely to ascertain the extent of his political information) contrastingly colorless and flat, then the juxtaposition of the two implies, so to speak, that any error is on the part of the latter. As Darley, at one of their last meetings, tells Justine, " 'I feel no resentment for the past. On the contrary I am full of gratitude because an experience which was perhaps banal in itself (even disgusting for you) was for me immeasurably enriching!' " (C, p. 693). For facts themselves seem to lie, to settle for something far less than total accuracy, when they insist upon substituting the pallid Justine of *Mountolive* for the far more interesting and dynamic one of *Moeurs*, *Justine*, and *Balthazar*. Thus, one of the crucial lessons *The Alexandria Quartet* teaches is that beauty lives in the eye of the beholder, that the tree falling in the forest is soundless without a listener, and that truth is devoid of validity and significance unless, and until, someone responds and interprets it through an aesthetically dynamic imagination.

V. *Clea* and The
Regenerative Affirmation of Art

The fourth part [Clea] *alone will represent time and be a true sequel.* (B, Note.)

You are uncomfortable about relativity? But my paper construct is only a toy, a shape, like a kaleidoscope made for the child of a friend. I hoped by this to restore action to the novel, for since Proust the novelist has become a ruminant where he isn't a mere pictographer. Stereoscopic narrative, stereophonic personality. It was just an idea. If you remember scenes or characters and can't quite remember which book they come in, it proves that the four are one work tightly woven, doesn't it? The joiner is the reader, the continuum is his private property. (Lawrence Durrell, "The Kneller Tape (Hamburg)," in Moore [ed.], *The World of Lawrence Durrell*, p. 163.)

DURRELL has predicated *Clea* as a necessary and final part of a sequence, not only a sequel in the sense of following the novels which have preceded it, but a continuation, an inevitable consequence, and a conclusion as well. *Justine* offered itself as hypothesis, the given to be examined and evaluated from a viewpoint of semidetachment (*Balthazar*) and then from one of total, though necessarily superficial, ob-

136

jectivity (*Mountolive*). Now, in *Clea,* the events of the first three novels are allowed to recede into the background of the relatively old and familiar, to decrease in intensity as happenings always do when they eventually assume their place within a broad temporal perspective. Granted sufficient time of course, one may finally look back at nearly any happening almost casually—without regret, without bitterness or hatred —perhaps with nostalgia or with the detachment of an artist.[1] One may even of course come to accept any past as a basis for building into the future.

Clea, in fact, is replete with the realization that the past is fixed and unalterable, that, once and for all, the flux of time has carried us forward from earlier concerns—forward beyond Justine's "check" (now cured by Pursewarden); beyond her child;[2] beyond the impossible love affairs of Justine and Darley, Pursewarden and Liza, Mountolive and Leila; beyond the Palestine plot; beyond Balthazar's cabal; beyond the negative influences of Arnauti, Capodistria, Narouz, Leila, Melissa. Significantly, Nessim's letter summoning Darley back to Alexandria contains the admonition, " 'Let the past remain a closed book for us all' " (*C,* p. 664). Finally and ultimately, one must—if one can—allow the dead to bury the dead, the living to get on with the business of living.

---

[1] One critic has oversimplified the *Quartet* into the following neat though not inaccurate formula. "As Justine had symbolized his [Darley's] education through passion, Balthazar through detachment, Mountolive through history, Clea now leads him to the most important phase of his career, for which all the rest was preparation, the practice of his own art" (Sykes, "One Vote for the Sun," in Moore (ed.), *The World of Lawrence Durrell,* 150).

[2] The child is mentioned only briefly by Pursewarden, who quotes Justine: " 'I found it, of course. Or rather Mnemjian did. In a brothel. It died from something, perhaps meningitis. Darley and Nessim came and dragged me away' " (*C,* p. 765). There are mysteries here—did the child, then, not drown? Was its fate common knowledge long ago?—but no longer anyone with interest enough to attempt solving them. Apparently belonging to a too remote past, they lack current relevance.

Yes, but the dead are everywhere. They cannot be so simply evaded. One feels them pressing their sad blind fingers in deprivation upon the panels of our secret lives, asking to be remembered and re-enacted once more in the life of the flesh—encamping among our heartbeats, invading our embraces. We carry in ourselves the biological trophies they bequeathed us by their failure to use up life—alignment of an eye, responsive curve of a nose; or in still more fugitive forms like someone's dead laugh, or a dimple which excites a long-buried smile. The simplest of these kisses we [Clea and Darley] exchanged had a pedigree of death. In them we once more befriended forgotten loves which struggled to be reborn. (*C*, p. 833.)

For, as Darley learns, though much of the past is dead and quiescent, even more of it retains at least potential vitality, and will not allow itself to be interred with the rest. Thus, the great task of *Clea* is not simply to assert the values which have emerged as viable and significant from the clash of antitheses in the *Quartet* (for such assertion, as the failings of Pursewarden's Notebook demonstrate, is invariably generalized, superficial, and abstract), but rather to dramatize convincingly the regenerative process as a result of which, in the end, the climactic affirmation about life and art may be made.

Certainly, *Clea* is a book concerned almost entirely with regeneration. Even the dead—or rather, those of its number who refuse to die with the past—are shorn of that which was harmful or inadequate about them in life, and reappear as totally benign influences. Perhaps the most clear-cut and important example of this is Scobie—the most vital of the *Quartet's* "minor" characters, a figure who, like Tiresias in *The Wasteland*, symbolizes affirmation and integration, and whose laughter, warmth, and humanity (but not his lethal whiskey or sexual aberrations) are resurrected in the all-fructifying El Scob. Melissa, at least for Darley, seems to fade and vanish altogether. "She had already sunk, pale star, below the horizon into the stillness of death . . ." (*C*, p. 661). "It was as if she had never existed, never inspired in me the pain and pity which (I had always told myself) would live on, transmitted into other forms perhaps—but live triumphantly on forever" (*C*, p. 681). But she is resurrected in the body of Clea, as we see when Darley describes the latter for the first time since his return to Alexandria.

She was sitting where once (that first day) Melissa had been sitting, gazing at a coffee cup with a wry reflective air of amusement, with her hands supporting her chin. The exact station in place and time where I had once found Melissa, and with such difficulty mustered enough courage at last to enter the place and speak to her. It gave me a strange sense of unreality to repeat this forgotten action at such a great remove of time, like unlocking a door which had remained closed and bolted for a generation. (*C*, p. 711.)

And this reincarnation is emphasized again when, after Clea's accident, Darley visits her at the hospital: "A sense of ghostly familiarity was growing upon me. In the past it was here that I had come to see Melissa. Clea must be lying in the same narrow iron bed in the corner by the wall." As if to make what has happened almost too explicit, Darley adds, " 'It would be just like real life to imitate art at this point' " (*C*, pp. 853–54).

Pursewarden, even more so after his suicide than before, is the dominant presence in the *Quartet*; yet his writings and theorizing become overexpository and nondramatic at times. The thirty pages in *Clea* supposedly extracted from his Notebook contain some uncomfortable infelicities—"Do you ask yourself what has turned me into nature's bashful little aphorist?" (*C*, p. 752)—and an enthusiastic excessiveness interlarded at times with plain bad writing.

The miracle of Pursewarden's Ideal Commonwealth! . . . One

fine day it will blossom: then the artist suddenly grows up and accepts the full responsibility for his origins in the people, and when *simultaneously* the people recognize his peculiar significance and value, and greet him as the unborn child in themselves, the infant Joy! . . . The new society—so different from anything we can imagine now—will be born around the small strict white temple of the Infant Joy! . . . But prepare, prepare! It is on the way. It is here, there, nowhere! (C, p. 761.)

The saving quality in this section is Pursewarden's fine comic wit, his refusal to take himself too seriously ("Please God, remember that even though I am an English poet I do not deserve to be eaten by rats. . . ." [C, p. 767]), as well as his skill in evoking people and setting, as, for instance, in his tale of the unnerving visit he and Justine made to a house of child prostitutes and of the "wonderful epic story" she told there.[3]

But, more crucially, Pursewarden here emphasizes the continuing Durrellean concern that the artist understand and fulfill his proper function. Like Phaon in *Sappho* and Petronius in *Acté*, Pursewarden echoes Otto Rank's thoughts on the subject, which Durrell quotes elsewhere.

The artistic individual has lived in art-creation instead of actual life, letting his work live or die on its own account, and has never wholly surrendered himself to life. In place of his own self the artist puts his objectified ego into his work, but though he does not save his subjective mortal ego from death, he yet withdraws himself from real life. And the creative type who can renounce this protection by arts and can devote his whole creative force to life and the formation of life will be the first representative of the new human type, and in return for this renunciation will enjoy, in personality-creation and expression, a greater happiness.[4]

[3] Pursewarden has a special talent for the gothic, a talent earlier and even more vividly displayed in the Sadean vampire story he tells during the murderous carnival in *Balthazar*.

[4] Quoted by Durrell, *Key*, 89.

Art for life's sake, then, is a central tenet of Durrell's regenerative theme, though he does not reject art as inadequate, but rather employs it as the proper means by which the "creative type" (Darley, most obviously, but the other characters at the end as well) enters the world of meaningful life.

The viability and relevance of both Pursewarden's intimate personal life and his artistic theories become hypotheses that *Clea* tests and, from one perspective, seems to reject. Pursewarden the man dies with Liza's suppression of the "total truth" (that is, *her* interpretation) regarding her brother—an act which prevents a resurrection of the "true" Pursewarden—and with her burning of his brilliant, we are told, but unpublishable letters.[5] As for Pursewarden the critic, not only does his notion of "a fourcard trick in the form of a novel" (*C*, p. 757) add nothing to what Durrell has already said in his Note to *Balthazar* and emphasized throughout the *Quartet* and elsewhere, but it *seems*, in the light of what happens at the end of *Clea*, erroneous and wrongheaded, an inadequate view of things which both Darley and Durrell appear to reject and condemn. It is incumbent upon the careful critic, however, to recognize the difference between hopeless contradiction and ironic paradox—a distinction crucial to much of Durrell's work already examined, and one I will consider most fully in my final chapter.

For the moment, though, we can see that Pursewarden remains alive not so much because of the words he has com-

[5] The truly sad thing about this act is that it will apparently deny Pursewarden the ultimate rank of major artist Darley and so many others insist he deserves. We never actually see any of the letters, but, though we may suspect Darley of exaggeration with regard to his first conclusion, we can accept the validity of his second. "I realised that there was nothing in the whole length and breadth of our literature with which to compare them! Whatever other masterpieces Pursewarden may have written, these letters outshone them all in their furious, unpremeditated brilliance and prolixity" (*C*, p. 790).

mitted to paper, and not even because he verbalizes the aesthetics of the *Quartet*, but rather for his great sense of irony
and the comic, for his unswerving commitment to artistic
creation, and for his Groddeck-like therapeutic powers, which
enable him to assist many of Durrell's Alexandrians to overcome various inadequacies and to approach, at least, a
previously unrealized potential. When Darley raises the apparently lifeless Clea from where she had been harpooned to
the bottom of their pool, Pursewardenesque touch of grotesque humor appears to lighten the gloom in Darley's mind.
"I heard the crash of Balthazar's teeth falling into the boat as
he jumped into the water beside me" (*C*, p. 850). Subsequently, it is from the horror hindering their love and art into
a new kind of completeness—into full artisthood (perhaps
Pursewarden's "Ideal Commonwealth")—that these two
long-submerged swimmers arise as they finally leave their so
heavily symbolic waters of the dead. And as Darley leaves
Clea for the last time in the *Quartet*—perhaps for the last
time ever, for not only reunion but a true fusing of their lives
seems inevitable upon their reunion in France—he thinks of
the madness that separated him from her and of an epigrammatic remark about the only possible healer of that madness.
"A phrase of Pursewarden's came into my mind as I softly
closed the door of the ward. 'The richest love is that which
submits to the arbitration of time' " (*C*, p. 856).

There is, as one Durrell commentator has noted, and as we
see in such works as *Panic Spring* and *Reflections on a Marine
Venus*, a "pronounced medical bias . . . in Durrell's nature,
in his reading, in his inventions and imagery."[6] The regeneration that characterizes *Clea* is actually a metaphor for the
curative process. Of the characters who survive to the end of
the *Quartet*, almost all have emerged—often through violent

---

[6] Herbert Howarth, "Lawrence Durrell and Some Early Masters," 10.

means—from some intense form of insanity or manic depression, usually manifesting itself as physical inadequacy.

Some of the shocking episodes of the *Quartet* terminate in acts of healing, without abdicating their fantasy, rather protracting it to greater extremes. The surgeon, in cooperation with the artist, will create a nose for Semira chosen with scrupulous care from all the noses history offers. The surgeon will replace Clea's hand, sacrificed to retrieve her from the shade of Narouz, with a new steel hand, competent, and more mature in its painting than the old.[7]

And so on. Once again Durrell has turned to Groddeck; for just as the "It" found expression in the mystery and pervasiveness of Alexandria and in characters who, in Lionel Trilling's phrase, "stand in a peculiar negative relation to the will,"[8] so too the creative, artistic nature of both disease and therapy is derived from *The Book of the It*—although, again, Durrell had anticipated his discovery of that work in his early writing.

In his Introduction to Groddeck's work, Durrell says that "while Freud speaks of cure, Groddeck is really talking of something else—liberation through self-knowledge; and his conception of disease is philosophical rather than rational." And Durrell employs nonmedical, nonrational, but nonetheless valid and effective, therapy for Nessim's madness, Darley's malaise, Clea's psychosis. Groddeck tells us that "Death is always voluntary; no one dies except he has desired death. . . ." And Pursewarden is a suicide, while others—Cohen, Melissa, Narouz, Leila—die at almost the very moment their frustrated love becomes self-destructively burdensome. Scobie is the single exception of significance, but he lives on at his saint's shrine and in the great ease with which almost

---

[7] *Ibid.*, 9–10.

[8] "The *Quartet*: Two Reviews," in Moore (ed.), *The World of Lawrence Durrell*, 57. Durrell himself has referred to his characters' "tendency 'to be dummies'" (quoted by Karl, "Physical and Metaphysical Love," in *The Contemporary English Novel*, 49).

everyone can imitate and evoke, and thus embody, the old pirate. Durrell writes, "The illness . . . bears the same relation to the patient as does his handwriting, his ability to write poetry, his ability to make money; creation, whether in a poem or a cancer, was still creation, for Groddeck. . . ."[9] And, since illness and health are like a pair of scales—sometimes a greater weight is on one pan, sometimes on the other, but neither is ever entirely empty—a complete schism between the creativity released by disease and that released by therapy is impossible.

Instances of this interdependence in the *Quartet* are numerous. Balthazar, as a doctor, is literally a healer. In addition, his Interlinear helps Darley to "see"; his hermetic cabal suggests the possibility of mystical-religious faith, even in intensely secular Alexandria; his seemingly healthy detachment from the vicissitudes of love is in striking contrast to the frenzied, diseased pursuits of so many others; and he offers us a Groddeck-like analysis of the inadequacies Darley displayed in *Justine*.

"You trust too much to what your subjects say about themselves— the accounts they give of their own actions and their meaning. You would never make a good doctor. Patients have to be found out—for they *always* lie. Not that they can help it, it is part of the defence-mechanism of the illness—just as your MS. betrays the defence-mechanism of the dream which does not wish to be invaded by reality!" (*B*, p. 311.)[10]

[9] Introduction to Groddeck, *ix–x*.

[10] The specific reference here is to Nessim's transcript of his madness, but the description applies as well to other of Darley's interpretations. It is clear that Balthazar has read Groddeck carefully, for Pursewarden later quotes a virtual paraphrase from Balthazar. " 'A good doctor, and in a special sense the psychologist, makes it quite deliberately, slightly harder for the patient to recover too easily. You do this to see if his psyche has any real bounce in it, for the secret of healing is in the patient and not the doctor' " (*C*, p. 763).

But Balthazar is also a destroyer of health, as we see in his frustrated ardor for a Greek actor and his consequent attempt at suicide, and in his crippling of Clea; yet the first is necessary if Balthazar is to have a part in the universal regenerative cycle of *Clea,* and the second, unwittingly, is the proper therapy for Clea's failures in both love and art.

Again, and with specific regard to the twin love-art theme of the *Quartet,* there is the crucial failure-success, destroying-healing of Pursewarden. In life, Durrell's theorist was, as Melissa bluntly announces, a man closed to love; his life had become " 'somewhat irresolute and shabby' " (*B*, p. 381), and he murders himself when his incestuous relationship with Liza, apparently the only love he has ever known, is terminated. As far as his art is concerned, Pursewarden too often "seems less the towering genius Durrell would have him to be, and his apothegms are often trivialities made to appear clever through verbal inversion."[11] Doubtless Durrell did not feel that Pursewarden was as much a failure as he seems to many readers, for references to his genius and great artistry are iterated often. Yet despite Darley's rave reviews of the letters, one feels a disappointment in being told rather than shown that Pursewarden wrote the sort of ultimate prose he sought. "In my art [Pursewarden says] I am free to be what I most desire to seem—someone who might bring resolution and harmony into the dying lives around me" (*B*, p. 381). Yet if we take art in its largest sense, and life as its

---

11 Karl, "Physical and Metaphysical Love," 51. Henry Miller, as already noted, objects to Pursewarden's sententiousness, his persiflage (*Corr*, p. 361). Trilling goes even further: "I find him [Pursewarden] a self-conscious bore, and in nothing is he so disappointing as in Darley's discovery that his bitterness is really tenderness" ("The *Quartet*: Two Reviews," p. 65). To a degree, all these comments are perceptive and valid; yet they gloss over the way Durrell's spokesman serves to inform and inspirit—despite Clea's attempt, in Hamlet's words, to "tell all"—the ironic, Pursewardenesque paradox of the *Quartet*'s concluding by beginning.

noblest creation, Pursewarden does largely succeed; he does help to provide an atmosphere conducive to resuscitation.

Pursewarden assumes the role of therapist: he makes of Liza, even at his own expense, a mature woman fully capable of loving; his humor and incisiveness cure Justine of her "check" and make possible her ultimate restoration; and Keats, like Darley and Clea, matures from "this shabby journalist" (as Liza calls him [C, p. 786]) into someone "we feel *will* become a writer"[12] now that he has learned for himself the significance and value of Pursewarden's sense of the ironic, of "Joy unconfined," of the enigma of truth. In addition, it is Pursewarden who asserts the therapeutic properties of art and offers its failures and its triumphs—both of which are purgative so long as the creative process has been intense —as a nostrum for mankind's ills, as a super-Hippocrates whose sure touch and great oath will somehow bring about his Ideal Commonwealth on earth.

I see art [Pursewarden writes in his Notebook] more and more clearly as a sort of manuring of the psyche. . . . Art, like a skilled masseur on a playing-field, is always standing by to help deal with casualties; and just as a masseur does, its ministrations ease up the tensions of the psyche's musculature. That is why it always goes for the sore places, its fingers pressing upon the knotted muscles, the tendon afflicted with cramp—the sins, perversions, displeasing points which we are reluctant to accept. Revealing them with its harsh kindness it unravels the tensions, relaxes the psyche. . . . These strange beliefs, Brother Ass [Darley], you will find lurking under my mordant humours, which may be described simply as a technique of therapy. (C, pp. 762–63.)

Even Narouz, who alive is characterized by a sadistic desire to take life (fish, bats—even people) largely as a consequence of his physical ugliness—which destroys for him the possibility of normal human intercourse—and his frustrated and frus-

12 Miller, *Corr*, 361–62.

trating love for Clea, becomes a catalytic force for positive change in this final novel. Alive, Narouz's strength and intensity are symbolized by the bull whip, which "is for him a way of imposing himself on the world, and [whose] cruelty is an expression of his desire to destroy those who will reject him. The whip becomes his power, his sensuality, his sadism. . . ."[13] He achieves paramount release in negation, destruction: his casually mentioned murder of a workman to avoid labor difficulties; the wonderfully vivid and terrifying slaughter of the bats (an episode whose raw savagery serves as an objective correlative for Narouz's usurpation of Nessim's rights of primogeniture); and his sudden and unexpected religious fanaticism, which, though perhaps an understandable consequence of the Coptic situation in Egypt, would become a rallying cry for a "holy war of religion" that would be suicidal for his people. Yet, in addition, this is a man whose brutality may be motivated by the highest of moral intentions (as in his Coptic commitment, perhaps even in his mistaken murder of Toto) or may be qualified by the humblest and purest devotion (as to his father or, in a different way, to Clea) or the sincerest of friendships (as during the early days with Mountolive). Further, this is a man who, though perhaps unwillingly, is sacrificed that his brother may live, who dies invoking the beloved whose name he has always held sacrosanct, and who receives in death the great and largely spontaneous public lamentation that concludes *Mountolive*. In death, moreover, this is a man whose beautiful island, now rediscovered, furnishes the backdrop for the most peaceful and satisfying moments of the entire *Quartet* and whose deadly spear gun operates on Clea like a surgeon's knife.

In the story Clea attributes to a tipsy Scobie, Narouz appears as a force of unqualified evil evoking the power of

13 Karl, "Physical and Metaphysical Love," 55.

black magic to destroy her. " 'There is a lake outside. He has made up his mind. He will try and drag you to him. You will be in a dark place, imprisoned, unable to resist him. Yes, there is one near at hand who might aid you if he could. But he will not be strong enough' " (*C*, p. 815). But this fore-shadowing of Clea's accident, though properly ominous and accurate enough in some details, really misses the point of that incident. Narouz's island is not a "dark place," but rather as idyllic a setting as any of Durrell's troubled lovers ever find. Clea's impalement at the bottom of the dark pool serves not as a means of permanent imprisonment but as a symbolic crucifixion ("Her right hand had been pierced and nailed to the wreck by the steel arrow" [*C*, p. 849]), a neces-sary sacrifice of a useless member in order to save the patient from the poison or madness or horror that threatens to engulf her. And it is symbolically appropriate that Narouz's spear gun be the instrument of excision since it was his mis-directed love, and Clea's unfeeling response to it, which brought on her disease and impaired her own ability to love. Feebly she had protested her indifference to Narouz's dying call to her. " 'What can I do, Nessim? He is nothing to me, never was, never will be. Oh, it is so *disgusting*—please do not make me come, Nessim. . . . Oh, Nessim, how disgusting that people should love without consent! . . . My flesh quails on my bones' " (*M*, p. 643). And despite the idyllic respite during the first half of *Clea*, the illness intensifies until Dar-ley, the "one near at hand," the feeble and pusillanimous schoolmaster, gives the lie to Scobie's black prophecy and proves himself "strong enough" to handle the gravest emer-gency. When they arise from Narouz's pool, Darley and Clea can no longer be endangered by any horror from the past.

Among the still living, regeneration is even more ubiqui-tous, and is often made blatant by the simultaneously symbolic and literal alteration of physical features—for instance, the marrying of artistic and medical skill to create a nose for Semira. Darley sheds his unmanly timidity only after discovering that he really did not need spectacles; Clea's ultimate artistic fulfillment is foreshadowed by the new laugh which, Darley remarks on his return to Alexandria, she had grown during his absence. Along with wisdom and confidence, Keats has acquired the body of a Greek god from the war and desert that are destructive of so many others. And Balthazar, having completely lost the detachment and self-assuredness that characterized his sexual life, cabalistic activities, and writing of the Interlinear, is literally almost totally destroyed in order that he may be reborn.

When Darley returns to Alexandria at the beginning of *Clea*, he finds Balthazar immeasurably aged, a near victim of suicide as a consequence of having fallen in love with a " 'small-spirited, dirty, venal and empty,' " but physically god-like, Greek actor. He had plunged to a depth of degradation, a despairing masochism, in which "I enjoyed being debased in a queer way, being whipped and scorned, reduced to a wreck! It was as if I wanted to swallow the world, to drain the sore of love until it healed' " (C, p. 704). Then, after his futile attempt at suicide, the slow healing process begins. Amaril's attention and assumed abusive treatment produce in Balthazar a purgative shame; afterward, " ' I submitted to Pierre Balbz who removed the teeth [whose threatened necessary removal had precipitated this crisis in the first place] and provided me with this set of glittering snappers— *art nouveau!*' " (C, p. 705). And with his new teeth, dark glasses, less conspicuous bandages on his hands, and a whole entourage of faithful friends, the rehabilitated Balthazar— his whitened hair left unaltered "to symbolise my return from the dead with a vanity chastened by experience"—makes his public reappearance. And, although it is due to his vanity that he subsequently allows Mnemjian to rub age and time from his hair, the effect of this dyeing is a dramatic symbol of his complete rejuvenation. "Indeed the change was remarkable. He was now, once more, the old Balthazar, with his sapient dark eyes turned ironically on the doings of the city" (C, p. 807)—once more the disinterested observer of the Interlinear, a healer, himself now cured, capable of wielding Narouz's deadly spear gun with the effect, if not the skill, of an expert surgeon operating with a finely honed scalpel.

Capodistria functions as Durrell's regenerative archetype, since, for Darley at least, he was dead from the end of *Justine* to the beginning of *Clea*; and the ironic marking on his empty grave reads, "Not Lost But Gone Before" (C, p. 807). Many of those seemingly lost or destroyed by the beginning or middle of *Clea* manage to find a path back from almost total defeat; yet often, as with Capodistria and his black magic experimentation, the process offers no simple ethical message but a "success" as morally ambiguous as life itself, or the city in which we have seen one form of it revealed, or the Justine who so comprehensively embodies both.

There was no question of true or false. Nymph? Goddess? Vampire? Yes, she was all of these, and none of them. She was, like every woman, everything that the mind of man (let us define "man" as a poet perpetually conspiring against himself)—that the mind of man wished to imagine. She was there forever, and she had never existed! Under all these masks there was only another woman, every woman, like a lay figure in a dressmaker's shop, waiting for the poet to clothe her, breathe life into her. (C, p. 694.)

Thus, all of what happens to the several characters is open to various and conflicting interpretations—according, of course, to the mythopoeic view of each interpreter. Liza and

Mountolive, for instance, apparently achieve an impressively profound love even though the deaths of Pursewarden and Leila were prerequisite. Yet Balthazar comments to Darley: " 'It seems to me that while . . . Liza Pursewarden was administering her death-warrant to her brother, Mountolive was giving the same backhander to Leila. So we pass the loving-cup about, the poisoned loving-cup!' " (*C*, p. 864).[14]

For Pombal too, recovery involves the destruction of others. Having for the first time in his life fallen totally, tenderly —even ascetically—in love with a woman (the pregnant wife of a front-line soldier), he is literally almost annihilated by her accidental and stupid death. Yet it is Pombal's love, far more than his reaction to its loss, which appears a sign of aberration. His meeting with Darley, when he first tells of this love, becomes a confession of great sins.

An expression of pain crossed his fat countenance and he groaned, pressing his hands between his knees as he uttered the word: "Fosca!" . . . He looked almost terrified. "I am in love with her." . . . And leaning forward with a look of despair on his countenance he lowered his voice . . . and the tears came into his eyes as he spoke the words: "You don't understand. *Je suis fidèle malgré moi.*" He gasped like a fish and repeated "*Malgré moi.* It has never happened before, *never.*" (*C*, p. 678.)

And it would appear that, once Pombal has succeeded in forgetting Fosca, it is never to happen again. Perhaps his reversion to his earlier, cavalier treatment of women as mere sex objects may be considered all to the good, for he divests himself of the tendency toward oversolemnity which char-

14 Balthazar's debunking echoes an equally bitter moment in the first novel. Darley, having been accosted by a truly profound love where it seemed least likely (in the dying Cohen), thinks of the lethal power of even those as gentle and innocent as Melissa. "Walking slowly home [from Cohen's hospital room] through the dark avenue . . . I remembered Justine saying harshly as she lay in bed: 'We use each other like axes to cut down the ones we really love' " (*J*, p. 94).

acterized his brief flirtation with love; yet his resurrected libertinage is as complex, morally and aesthetically, as the almost calculating passion of Liza and Mountolive.

Durrell's love ethic does not preach monogamy, but it does suggest that the maturing man, like Darley, generally outgrows his need for whores. Pombal, however, despite his lapse into fidelity, finds such restrictions alien to his nature; he does not leave Alexandria at the end because he perfectly embodies its amorality and, like the city, can pass from stage to stage of life without changing fundamentally. Clea, on almost the last page of the *Quartet*, waxes enthusiastic over Pombal's "recovery," seeing it as a "deeply encouraging thing" not because she believes mere sex to be better than love (her relationship with Darley demonstrates the opposite) but because she is wise enough to recognize and accept Pombal for what he is. No one value system, she implies, can work for all; and it is "deeply encouraging" when a creature of great energy like Pombal reaffirms an approach to life consistent with what seems most fundamentally himself.

In fact, the moral ambiguity characterizing Pombal's ultimate status is widely prevalent, for, as we have already noted, similar uncertainty, an apparently irreconcilable contradiction, qualifies the Liza-Mountolive relationship—and a great number of others as well. What, for instance, are we to make of Justine's latest substitute for love in her marriage —a passion based, as before, on pipe-dream intrigue ("something much bigger this time, international" [C, p. 876]) and on continued unlimited sexual conquest (Memlik, the corrupt but fiercely independent Egyptian official, has, improbably, become her most recent lap dog)? How too shall we think of Nessim? His case is even more open to multiple interpretations; although he has frequent moments throughout the *Quartet* when he appears completely lifeless, nonetheless, as Henry Miller puts it, "he has the qualities of a great and gentle monarch. . . . A royal personage, truly. . . . He moves with the dignity and felicity of a panther. His recovered happiness makes one's heart swell" (*Corr*, p. 364).

Yet that Nessim *is* in a state of "recovered happiness" at the end is open to question. His loss of an eye (and the consequent black patch so reminiscent of Capodistria) has produced not a cathartic purgation—as is the case with Clea and her hand—but a monumental and tragic sadness which serves as a kind of defense mechanism against Justine's shrewish temper tantrums. And, despite what Clea and Henry Miller tell us about Nessim's future, it is difficult to believe that either his conspiratorial efforts or his marriage will be any more successful than they have been in the past. His supposed rejuvenation ("'His appearance staggered me,'" Clea writes, "'he looked so much younger, and so elegant and self-possessed'" [*C*, p. 876]) can be viewed as mere summarizing exposition—Durrell apparently feeling that he has left loose ends lying about and that he must tie them together before they become hopelessly entangled—rather than as a dramatically significant last look at a character whom we might have expected to evolve in this way. But, again, the *Quartet* has repeatedly insisted, first, that personality is neither fixed nor predictable and, second, that while Clea offers a possible interpretation of events, neither hers nor anyone else's is definitive and binding.

The primary cause of our uncertainty concerning these various characters results perhaps from Durrell's thematic juxtaposing of love and sex.[15] There can be no quarrel with

---

[15] Unfortunately, there are critics who simply confuse the two. Carl Bode, for example, uses them interchangeably in his discussion of Durrell. "The central subject of the *Quartet* is sex, an 'investigation of modern love.' . . . The respect Durrell shows for all human coupling prevents the *Quartet* from being sensational and emphasized his conviction that the ultimate

his often repeated insistence that love is an indefinable, even mysterious, quality, that it manifests itself in a vast number of ways and forms, and that it is a uniquely significant and valuable foundation upon which two people may build a relationship. Often throughout the *Quartet* Durrell implies that sexual intercourse alone is only briefly satisfying; such presumably intense but ultimately loveless affairs as those between Darley and Melissa, Mountolive and Leila, even Justine and Clea, serve a function and are terminated. Those who receive nothing, or merely sex, in exchange for their love—Melissa (from Darley), Narouz (from Clea), Nessim (from Justine), Leila (from Mountolive)—lead lives characterized to a large degree by frustration and hollowness. Further, sexual contact is often sharply rejected when it is offered in terms that not only exclude love but would deny its existence—Nessim is disgusted and angered when Justine, whom he seeks to marry, tells him he may sleep with her if he wishes (M, p. 551); Clea allows Darley, stunned by the departure of Justine, to share her bed but not to make love to her (J, p. 181); Darley feels only indifference and disgust when Justine, their roles having been reversed, pleads with him "like an Arab mendicant, like some beggarwoman of the streets" for the privilege of merely lying naked beside him for a few hours (C, p. 698); and Pursewarden, all too aware of the immense humor of the situation, unhesitatingly refuses to satisfy the unhappy, frustrated Clea, who "burst in on him like a fireman into a burning building, startling

---

value of sex is what it can teach us about ourselves. Our only world is the world of self-exploration; love gives us the means" ("A Guide to Alexandria," in Moore (ed.), *The World of Lawrence Durrell*, 206–207). Mary Graham Lund writes with equal confusion: "It is obvious that men and women live to a certain extent in different subjective worlds, and equally obvious that sex is their best medium of understanding . . ." ("The Alexandrian Projection," p. 201).

him, and said with trembling lips: 'I have come to ask you to *dépuceler* me, please, because I cannot get any further with my work unless you do' " (*C*, p. 736).

Pursewarden tells us that love alone offers us a standard of values, that it is the "veritable nub and quiddity of this disordered world, and the only proper field for the deployment of our talents . . ." (*C*, p. 754). And love, like art, must be considered a therapeutic force, for, quite properly, "Durrell believes that sex, in its reality and in its highest manifestations, is a psychic and not merely a physical act. Men and women try to express themselves through each other, desiring a new spiritual revelation, conscious of intimations of undeveloped powers within or beyond them."[16] Yet even when love is present, actually or potentially, one receives no assurance that this is a real advantage; life itself, after all, offers no such guarantee. Darley's self-banishings from Alexandria (the "wine press of love")—to Upper Egypt, to his Greek island, and finally to France—suggest the hapless flight of a candle-encircling moth controlled by a positive phototropism it neither desires nor understands.

The narrator's view of love is that of Shelley: he sees with great compassion the scars of love, especially upon women, views the evils of love with anger and disgust, and makes his protagonist seek for himself assuagement of his terrible loneliness in a woman's love. "Like all egoists," the narrator confesses, "I cannot bear to live alone."[17]

And so Darley is drawn to Melissa, who proves inadequate, to Justine, who ultimately disgusts him (because she has used him? because she has wounded his vanity? because of her interminable promiscuity? because she is now so easily obtained? Durrell would doubtless assert that all of these—

16 Lund, "The Alexandrian Projection," 201.
17 Lund, "Submerge for Reality," 230.

and none—are true), and to Clea, whose "love for Darley seems idyllic at first, but it requires a horrible accident to bring her to terms with her art, perhaps eventually with her lover."[18] That is, we must assume that this final love relationship will achieve a permanent fruition—apparently in France, where each had planned to go regardless of the other—in order that Darley may assert his rather neat and perhaps simplistic art-love pattern:

Arnauti, Pursewarden, Darley—like Past, Present, and Future tense! And in my own life (the staunchless stream flowing from the wounded side of Time!) the three women who also arranged themselves as if to represent the moods of the great verb, Love: Melissa, Justine and Clea. (*C*, p. 792.)

But love is only partly responsible for the regeneration in *Clea*; only Justine and Nessim, Mountolive and Liza, and Darley and Clea remain paired at the end. The Hosnanis, as already indicated, continue to accept compromises in love; the ambassador and his wife are united as much by their having effectively destroyed previous love partners as by love itself. Only Darley and Clea, it would seem, have emerged virtually unscathed and deserving of a truly profound attachment. There is, for instance, something incalculably healthy and beautiful about their making love during a bombing attack, for this world-defying commitment to love serves as a supreme refutation of those busily destroying in the night outside. Darley, with his new sense of freedom in their mutual possession, speaks, like every youthful lover, of the city he no longer finds terrifying.

When you are in love with one of its inhabitants a city can become a world. A whole new geography of Alexandria was born through Clea, reviving old meanings, renewing ambiences half

---

[18] Lund, "The Alexandrian Projection," 200.

forgotten, laying down like a rich wash of colour a new history, a new biography to replace the old one. (*C*, p. 832.)

But Durrell offers alternatives to this image of romantic love. As we have already seen, the poison of Narouz's frustrated passion for Clea produces in her a malaise which destroys, at least temporarily, her capacity for this sort of innocence. In addition, Darley, having suddenly realized that Clea's "horror" has been her love for Amaril, reveals, unconsciously, a telling Groddeckean inadequacy in his relationship with Clea.

Between us we had never used this dreadful word [love]—this synonym for derangement or illness—and if I deliberately used it now it was to signify my recognition of the thing's autonomous nature. It was rather like saying "My poor child, you have got cancer!" (*C*, p. 855.)

Finally, there is something uncomfortable, ludicrous even, although necessary, in Darley's giving Clea artificial respiration, pumping her back to life "in this pitiful simulacrum of the sexual act—life saving, life-giving" (*C*, p. 851). The absurdity of what Darley does and says here lies in the juxtaposition and interdependence of aspects of an action that is both a sexual travesty and restorative of life—a juxtaposition which serves as a realistic, ironic comment on romantic love; yet, although the two are contradictory, they need not be mutually exclusive. Earlier, Darley had remarked:

"However near we would wish to be, so far exactly do we remain from each other" wrote Arnauti. It seemed to be no longer true of our *condition* [my emphasis]. Or was I simply deluding myself once more, refracting truth by the disorders inherent in my own vision? (*C*, p. 734.)

We cannot be any more certain than Darley that the subsequent French affair of these "regenerated" lovers will be firm and permanent; but then why should we be? Why, in fact, should we wish to be?

As with the theme of love, so too with the character of Clea—for her complexities of personality are also analogous to the whole multifaceted structure of the *Quartet*. As both literal and symbolic embodiment of rebirth, Clea is central to the regenerative process; and we recall that she has often revealed an impressive ability to impart vitality to those about her, to make them come alive as they have rarely, if ever, done: Justine in her Palestine kibbutz, Narouz just after his murder of Toto and on his death bed, Scobie at his shrine —to name just a few of the more obvious. Yet she herself is often stiff and wooden in contrast to the "real human being," the matured artist, she ultimately proclaims herself.

At times, she is too perfect in her role, too completely an embodiment of certain qualities and attitudes.

Her love for Darley, after he is done with Melissa and Justine, is noteworthy in that it turns out to be simple, natural, and a little dull. Perhaps one reason for Clea's lack of life is her absolute beauty; Pombal says that it would be easier for a man to make love to her if her face were covered.[19]

Pursewarden, who has already found the lovely Clea completely resistible—though he gallantly insisted, " 'My dear Clea . . . it would be anyone's dream to take you to bed . . .' " (C, p. 736)—sees her early one morning at the far end of a beach,

her marvellous hair swinging about her like a blonde Botticelli. I waved and she waved back, but showed no inclination to come and talk which made me grateful. . . . I thought for an instant of the lovely burnt coffee of her summer flesh, with the little hairs on her temples bleached to ash. I inhaled her metaphorically, like a whiff of roasting coffee, dreaming of the white thighs with those

[19] Carl Bode, "A Guide to Alexandria," 208–209.

small blue veins in them! Well, well . . . she would have been worth taking trouble over had she not been so beautiful. That brilliant glance exposed everything and forced me to take shelter from her.

One could hardly ask her to bandage them in order to be made love to! (*C*, p. 771.)

Clea is by no means less fully realized than other characters with whom we have less serious difficulties; nonetheless, it is Clea who is both meant to play the key role in the *Quartet*'s final novel and yet is denied—in what is probably Durrell's most grievous technical mistake—sufficient opportunity of elaborating her own viewpoint and, thus, of making us feel more sympathetic toward her and less uneasy about her uncertainties of character. Thus, with justification, one can maintain that Clea is

doggedly self-centered. Unfortunately, when Durrell tries to give characters will, he makes them selfish and solipsistic. Clea is Durrell's attempt to create a woman who is neither will-less like Melissa nor obsessed like Justine. . . . In Clea's characterization, nevertheless, there is much that is hackneyed. . . . She is given to hysterical gestures of emotion. . . . She is absurdly sentimental. . . . Two qualities Clea shares with the other characters are a failure to feel responsibility and an allegiance to her own sensations. . . . this lack of tension between a moral self and her desire for fulfillment gives her a curiously childish manner. . . . It is difficult to take Clea's feelings seriously after this episode [the affair with Amaril and her subsequent abortion]. Any action appears suitable if it advances her notion of maturity, if it has some effect upon her. Her ease in resolving all such feelings conveys the outlook of a selfish and expedient adolescent. Egocentric, vain, puffed by self-importance, she lives without wisdom.[20]

Although such criticism overstates the case against Clea, it is not inaccurate—at least from one point of view. For, as we have already seen, her indifference to moral considerations

[20] Karl, "Physical and Metaphysical Love," 52–53.

is evidenced when, at the end of the *Quartet*, she waxes enthusiastic over the perhaps ersatz loves of Pombal, Mountolive and Liza, and Justine and Nessim.

Based on our experience with the *roman-fleuve*, we expect that surely Clea, if anyone, is a reliable commentator, especially since her accident has supposedly purged her of her few failings and served, it would seem, to complete her as a human being. Yet the *Quartet* is not, was not meant to be, and could never become *that* kind of fiction, and Clea's impressionistic final evaluations of Mountolive's and Liza's "great stroke of luck," Pombal's "recovery," Justine's and Nessim's "break through at last" (*C*, pp. 875–76) remain tentative because single-faceted. Durrell indicates that everyone is entitled to his own opinion concerning the ultimate fate of such characters—for instance, Balthazar, also restored and at least as reliable as Clea, condemns the marriage of Liza and Mountolive as morally reprehensible—and the various responses must be weighed and evaluated before Durrell can be accused of evasion of authorial responsibility.

Durrell employs poetic equivocation as a matter of course. The two quotations at the beginning of the present chapter certainly suggest that Durrell wants it both ways, even with regard to his aesthetics: he is eager to advance his various theories, for he honestly and profoundly believes in them; yet he will resort to deliberate ambiguity rather than alienate those who understand that such notions are valuable only to the degree that they work in actual practice. He acknowledges that there are those who ignore or condemn his theories, who, with George P. Elliott, say:

When Durrell announces that *Justine, Balthazar,* and *Mountolive* are the space coordinate, I cock a wary eyebrow, for I (an English teacher) do not begin to understand the theory of relativity, and I doubt that Durrell (a *littérateur* in the foreign service) understands it either. When, in the prefatory note to *Balthazar*, he says concerning the whole *Quartet* that "the central topic of the book is an investigation of modern love," I groan, for I have no taste for sociology in my fiction, Kinseys in my psyche. When he names the first volume *Justine* and prefaces each of the four with a quotation from the Marquis de Sade, my heart sinks, for I have read in the monster and found him dull. Well, maybe Durrell has in fact accomplished the irrelevancies he threatened; I neither know nor care; but I am happy to report that he has also done something first-rate. He has written a good romantic novel.[21]

It is understandable that Durrell should have no quarrel with such critics for, though unconverted to his way of thinking about literature, they read and significantly enjoy his books.

Durrell's position in this matter is typical of his entire approach to his art, and one should not make the mistake of taking it as a compromise of integrity; in this case, for instance, intellectually to desire a wide, even a mass, audience, is far different from writing merely for the sake of gaining that audience. Similarly, within the fiction, Durrell's "equivocation"—his refusal to make a wholehearted commitment without leaving ample room and occasion for equally plausible interpretation that contradicts and therefore appears to undercut that commitment—has also been a matter of some concern. With regard to Pursewarden, Henry Miller—perhaps Durrell's most avid and unquestioning partisan—writes "that one is not sure at times whether the author is taking his double-face protagonist seriously or ironically" (*Corr*, p. 361). But surely the point is that Durrell takes "his double-face protagonist," as Pursewarden does himself, as both serious and ironic—as, that is, double-faced. Complex personality is not to be so easily circumscribed that

21 "The Other Side of the Story," in Moore (ed.), *The World of Lawrence Durrell*, 88–89.

the pinning on of a single label can define it. Only mutually contradictory and continually interchanging labels can be at all meaningful and valid.

If we take Darley, Durrell's adolescent become artist, as touchstone, then the *Quartet's* multifaceted aesthetic emerges with a great deal of clarity and force. Early in *Justine*, Darley had commented that "everything is susceptible of more than one explanation . . ." and that "all ideas seem equally good to me; the fact of their existence proves that someone is creating. Does it matter whether they are objectively right or wrong? They could never remain so for long" (*J*, pp. 69, 39).[22] On the other hand, Justine, despite all her talk about prism-sightedness before her dressmaker's multiple mirrors and her assertion that one may tell a story every which way without lying, now insists that objective truth does indeed matter a great deal; and it is she who tells an *Arabian Nights* type of love story in *Clea*. But, after living through and with one war, two cultures (Greek and Egyptian), three women, four novels, and Pursewarden's brilliant letters, Darley's climactic statement on art and the final lesson of his long education sounds like this.

It was only now . . . that I realized that poetic or transcendental knowledge somehow cancels out purely relative knowledge, and that his [Pursewarden's] black humours were simply ironies due to his enigmatic knowledge whose field of operation was above, beyond that of the relative fact-finding sort. There *was* no answer to the questions I had raised in very truth. He had been quite right. Blind as a mole, I had been digging about in the graveyard of relative fact piling up data, more information, and completely missing the mythopoeic reference which underlies fact. I had called this searching for truth! . . .

[22] With approval, Durrell has elsewhere written that "Groddeck believed that whatever was posited as fact could sooner or later be disproved . . ." (Georg Groddeck, *The Book of the It*, p. xv).

If two or more explanations of a single human action are as good as each other then what does action mean but an illusion—a gesture made against the misty backcloth of a reality made palpable by the delusive nature of human division merely? Had any novelist before Pursewarden considered this question? I think not. (*C*, pp. 791–92.)

Despite his highly dubious conclusion regarding Pursewarden's stature and originality, Darley does offer a significant and essentially simple resolution for all the *Quartet*'s apparent confusion: truth is relative, contradictory, endlessly discoverable from different viewpoints, and merely a reflection of Truth—which is absolute, mythopoeic, and unknowable. *Mountolive* remains unsatisfying because, while it offers a great deal of truth (that is, data concerning the *Justine-Balthazar* happenings), it lacks the Truth that transcends mere fact. Thus action, like personality, *is* illusory so long as it remains univocally bound in time and space; through art and through love, *Quartet* characters strive toward meaning and Truth.

To a degree, Darley's act of assuming full artisthood can be taken as rejection of the relatively aesthetic that has been of fundamental significance in Durrell's writing the *Quartet*.

One day I found myself writing down with trembling fingers the four words . . . with which every story-teller since the world began has staked his slender claim to the attention of his fellow-men. Words which presage simply the old story of an artist coming of age. I wrote: "Once upon a time. . . ." (*C*, p. 877.)

Darley may now write classical tales, sagas, or children's fairy adventures—that is, a straightforward or epiclike narration, such as the story which Justine told in the house of child prostitutes and which Pursewarden admired so much—but one cannot write the lush, baroque, sensuously evocative, and ambiguous *Alexandria Quartet* by beginning, "Once upon a time." What Darley has in effect announced is "that he is going to tell a story—really *tell* it as against representing it . . . ,"[23] or as against allowing it, like the *Quartet*, gradually and indirectly to tell itself by means of often contradictory diaries, journals, Interlinears, novels within novels, letters— as well as the "reminiscences, anecdotes, and imitations" with which, in *Clea*, "Durrell resurrects all the characters who have died. . . ."[24]

But Darley's "Once upon a time" serves the same function as Stephen's "Old father, old artificer, stand me now and ever in good stead," at the end of Joyce's *Portrait of the Artist*. Both figures have emerged not as identical with their authors but as artists in their own right. Durrell's various spokesmen have continuously offered such statements as this one by Pursewarden.

> When I was chided by Balthazar for being equivocal I replied, without a moment's conscious thought: "Words being what they are, people being what they are, perhaps it would be better always to say the opposite of what one means?" Afterwards, when I reflected on this view (which I did not know that I held) it seemed to me really eminently sage! (*C*, p. 757.)

Yet, as we have seen, equivocation is actually a metaphor for the multiplicity of both truths and ways to Truth. Durrell affirms life, then, by maintaining not confusion or chaos but the richness of complexity. And the emergence of Darley and Clea from the "misty backcloth of a reality made palpable by the delusive nature of human division merely" into the transcendent realms of art and life represents a consequent and ultimate affirmation not despite but because of the open-endedness of the *Quartet*. Durrell's work is no more definitive or conclusive than *Portrait of the Artist* or *Sons and Lovers*,

---

[23] Trilling, "The *Quartet*: Two Reviews," 64.
[24] George Wickes, *Masters of Modern British Fiction*, 540.

but no less so either. Like Stephen and Paul, Darley has successfully undergone the rites of initiation to maturity, and the future has become not fixed and glibly foreordained but —what is of far greater significance—complexly, uncertainly, and viably possible.

VI. A Key to Lawrence Durrell

Durrell has written me that almost all the ideas of the Quartet *are to be found there* [in A Key to Modern British Poetry] *in germ form.* (Carl Bode, "A Guide to Alexandria," in Moore [ed.], *The World of Lawrence Durrell*, p. 205.)

Where a problem is simple the ascertainment of each and every relevant fact narrows the field of inquiry. A solution is possible in the terms of mere knowledge. But where the problem is so profound that it enters the domain of Mystery, the emergence of each additional fact serves only to reveal the magnitude of the inquiry. The telescope did not enable man to solve the riddle of the stars. It illumined his ignorance by revealing the necessity for "thinking again the thoughts of God." (Claude Houghton [Oldfield], *I Am Jonathan Scrivener*, p. 274.)

I believe that a good critic should avoid the sin of a closed system: and if these lectures have the air of systematized arrangement it is because criticism demands an appearance of order in its method. Nevertheless they should be labeled "provisional hypotheses." I am anxious to avoid the dangers inherent in thinking along straight lines in a universe which science tells us is curved. (Key, pp. 6–7.)

A Key to Lawrence Durrell

A "Key" to Lawrence Durrell lies in his book of criticism *A Key to Modern British Poetry*. The bulk of the work treats the poetry of the 1890's and of the 1930's, individual poets such as Hopkins and Eliot, "movements" like the Georgians and the imagists; but its core is a comparative analysis of Tennyson's *Ulysses* and Eliot's *Gerontion*—and the resulting theoretical speculations. Durrell suggests that, discounting individual temperament, the visions of the two poems differ because a cultural shift occurred between 1840 and 1920. Consequent to the imposition of scientific investigation upon the veneer of unquestioning religious faith, man the heroic master of his earthly fate yields to man the victim. The movement of *Ulysses* is linear, unswervingly gathering its momentum until the apocalyptic affirmation of "To strive, to seek, to find and not to yield." In contrast, *Gerontion* is cyclical and ends where it began, at an intellectual impasse, loss of faith, negation—at "the exhausted subjectivity of the contemporary hero" (*Key*, pp. 13–14). "I would like to suggest," Durrell adds, "that a good deal of the despair in *Gerontion* comes of a realization that the world has gone off the rails" (*Key*, p. 19)—that old notions of human possibility, personality, values, validity, and time have been irreversibly altered by Darwin, Einstein, and Freud in the modern world of their creating. The rock foundation of certainty reveals itself as a base of restive sand blown by the winds of pluralism, relativity, subjectivity, the principle of indeterminacy.

Durrell's freewheeling, probing analysis continually leads him outside the arts and into such areas as anthropology, psychology, science, and mysticism, where, according to uncomfortable critics who cannot or refuse to follow, he has no business venturing.[1] Yet to dismiss out of hand, to assume

[1] See, for instance, George P. Elliot's comment, cited in Chapter V, pp. 160–61.

rather than prove that Durrell lacks the wherewithal for exploring in these areas, is circular and self-defeating, for it precludes, a priori, even the possibility that Durrell's approach is not haphazard or superficial.

Durrell's understanding of himself and what he seeks to accomplish is more incisive, more sensitive, than that of the precluders. He writes:

One dares not assert that poets and writers were consciously aware . . . of the gradual modifications of our thoughts about the universe or ourselves. Poetry is the raw material of sensibility, and the poet's job is to go on making poetry, not to think too much about why or wherefore. But poets belong to an age. They have ancestors and pedigrees like their poems. And they register the general drift of things by their work. (*Key*, p. 64.)

The modern artist, then, whether painter, musician, or writer, does not consciously become a student and exponent of, say, Einstein or Freud; but nonetheless his work necessarily and invariably reflects the revolution that has taken place in man's thinking about his universe and himself. All of man's concerns connect and fuse, impinging upon, and borrowing from, one another as a matter of course. And, as Durrell puts it,

literature is only one facet of the prism which we call culture. All the arts and sciences are simply different dialects of the same language, all contribute towards an attitude to life. What is this "culture"? I take this word to mean the sum, at any given time, of all the efforts man is making to interpret the universe about him. Ideas from the various departments of thought cross-fertilize each other, and it is sometimes a good idea to discuss one kind of thought in terms of another. (*Key*, pp. 1–2.)

Durrell rightly recognizes, then, the analogous nature of human activity and that when the poet speaks of relativity and space-time continuum and the principle of indeterminacy, it is irrelevant to ask whether he truly comprehends the technical significance of these terms. Durrell writes that in order to obtain a coherent view of the bewildering world of science Einstein formulated a theory which everybody has heard about and very few people understand. As far as we are concerned only two aspects of it interest us: its attitude to time, and its attitude to the subject-object relationship. (*Key*, p. 28.)

And, it should be added, these interest us not in the way they interested Einstein but only insofar as some artist, whether consciously or not, has employed them in some aesthetically satisfying form. F. R. Leavis maintains that "if the poetry and the intelligence of the age lose touch with each other, poetry will cease to matter much, and the age will be lacking in finer awareness"; and he goes on to cite Eliot's suggestion "that probably the modern's perception of rhythm has been affected by the internal combustion engine."[2] It would be difficult to justify criticism that condemns an artist for being alive in and to his time; Leavis of course would insist on the opposite—on the artist's being cognizant, in his work, of his temporal environment.

In both the *Quartet* and the *Key* (and less overtly in much of his other writing as well), Durrell stresses the theoretical basis for his approach to structure, personality, and aesthetics. Yet his fundamental concern—and it should be ours too—is not with theory per se, but with whether the creative product embodies it successfully. Our primary question should not be, "Does Durrell have the intellectual authority to speak of space-time or quanta?" but rather, "To the degree that his *work* speaks of them, does it do so meaningfully, decorously?"

Prior to Einstein and Freud, Browning's *The Ring and The Book*, with its several mutually contradictory voices, had taken cognizance of the gulf between "reality" and impressionism, or felt reality. Still, we are meant to value each of

2 *New Bearings in English Poetry*, 14, 24.

Browning's voices only to the degree that it incorporates and reflects an objective body of data. Meredith goes further in asserting the relativity of values when he has the highly wrought yet suddenly incisive speaker of *Modern Love* proclaim that "in tragic life . . . no villain need be." Such a notion implies that, as Lear learns, *all* are victims, none is guilty; and if consequences may be independent of human agents, then the concept of strict causality, of personal responsibility, becomes questionable. Ford Madox Ford offers us a touchstone when he writes, with specific reference to *Youth*, that

> Conrad was obsessed by the idea of a Destiny omnipresent behind things: of a Destiny that was august, blind inscrutable, just and above all passionless, that has decreed that the outside things, the sea, the sky, the earth, love, merchandising, the winds, shall make youth seem tenderly ridiculous. . . .[3]

In such a world, as in Meredith's and Durrell's, there are no villains, only burdened, suffering victims. And Ford's remark takes us back to Hardy's universe, where brooding presences (especially Egdon Heath) and unpredictable but powerful Chance impart a marionette quality to human creatures, and forward to Durrell's implacable and enigmatic Alexandria.

The crucial shift toward relativism is best reflected in the great novelists of this century—Conrad, Proust, Joyce, Ford, Faulkner, Woolf—all "impressionists" reacting in some degree against the limited "naturalists," who believed, according to Edmund Wilson, that "you had only to supply your characters with a specific environment and heredity and then watch their automatic reactions. . . ."[4] In art, impressionism developed as the attempt to capture and portray not objects in themselves but, rather, the play of light upon objects at a single instant isolated out of the flux of time. But impression-

[3] *Joseph Conrad: A Personal Remembrance*, 163.
[4] *Axel's Castle: A Study of the Imaginative Literature of 1870–1930*, 13.

ists felt something lacking in their approach, that they had somehow failed to "get at" the permanent nature, the form, of, say, a haystack. So they painted the haystack many times over, creating a series of stayed moments in the "life" of the haystack and the light moving upon it—something similar to the series of celluloid squares which, when flashed rapidly and consecutively on a screen, comprise a movie.

The cubists, though they conceived of themselves as reacting in violent opposition to the impressionists, actually employed an approach not unlike that of their predecessors but carried it several steps further. For one thing, they implied in their work that the concern with time was wrongheaded, that *of course* the observed object appears to alter from moment to moment, but that its essence, like a work of art or the other unaging monuments of man's intellect, remains fixed and unwavering. But they were also aware that objects, like events and people, have many sides, that they not only appear but actually are different both for every observer and for a single observer who shifts his position of observation. Their focus, then, became spatial, not temporal—for they sought to capture not the evanescent moment but the essence of an object by, first, abstracting it from the transience of time and, second, offering a composite which included, in theory at least, all possible angles of vision.

The crucial moment in the history of impressionism in the British novel occurs around the turn of the century, when its two inspiriting geniuses—Ford Madox Ford and Joseph Conrad—were agreeing that only novel writing was worth doing and that a new form for doing it was imperative.

We agreed [Ford writes] that the general effect of a novel must be the general effect that life makes on mankind. A novel must therefore not be a narration, a report. . . . We accepted without much protest the stigma: "Impressionists" that was thrown at us. In those days Impressionists were still considered to be bad people. . . . But we accepted the name because . . . we saw that life did not narrate, but made impressions on our brain. We in turn, if we wished to produce on you an effect of life, must not narrate but render . . . impressions.[5]

The most interesting book in the impressionist tradition may well be Ford's *Personal Remembrance* of Conrad, for it not only contains much of the important early talk regarding impressionism but it is itself, according to Ford, an impressionist novel. In a way that vastly enriches the notion of impressionism, Ford writes in his Preface that his *Remembrance*

is conducted exactly along the lines laid down by us, both for the novel which is biography and for the biography which is a novel. It is the rendering of an affair intended first of all to make you see the subject in his scenery. It contains no documentation at all; for it no dates have been looked up, even all the quotations but two have been left unverified, coming from the writer's memory. It is the writer's impression of a writer who avowed himself impressionist. Where the writer's memory has proved to be at fault over a detail afterwards out of curiosity looked up, the writer has allowed the fault to remain on the page; but as to the truth of the impression as a whole the writer believes that no man would care—or dare—to impugn it. (P. 6.)

Regardless of whether Ford is right—or whether, on the other hand, he is merely attempting to avoid responsibility for his "facts"—it is another book of his, *The Good Soldier*, which, along with Conrad's *Lord Jim*, ranks as probably the greatest achievement of pure impressionism. Of course these two novels are not masterpieces *because* they epitomize a living tradition; if anything, the tradition continues to live because of what Ford and Conrad have achieved within it. In both instances—and here intimations of Durrell's *Quartet* become pronounced—the novelist sets in motion a limited

[5] *Joseph Conrad: A Personal Remembrance*, 182–84.

narrator who attempts to gain total understanding of a finite and circumscribed sequence of events. Yet the hard core of truth remains forever elusive, for everything that occurs—in all three works—is capable of, and receives, a variety of mutually contradictory interpretations. After all, "To know the facts is one thing: to know the truth is another. Facts are to truth what dates are to history—they record certain events but they do not reveal the significance of those events."[6]

Early in *Lord Jim*, before Marlow has taken over the narration, Conrad's "objective" narrator anticipates him in his outrage over the trial proceedings. "They wanted facts. Facts! They demanded facts from him, as if facts could explain anything!" (p. 23). As in the *Quartet*, the more "facts" we learn, the less significant they seem; it is not despite but because *Mountolive tells* us the most, offers the most in the way of objective, external truth, that it has least to say about truth itself, about the essence of reality that is captured, if anywhere, in the heart and mind of the interpreter. Dowell, the narrator of Ford's *The Good Soldier*, asks the rock-fundamental thematic question for all impressionists—"If for nine years I have possessed a goodly apple that is rotten at the core and discover its rottenness only in nine years and six months less four days, isn't it true to say that for nine years I possessed a goodly apple?" (p. 7)—one that can be answered only by the strict naturalists. For the impressionist, who must juxtapose the moment of discovering rottenness with the continuing reality of what has preceded it, the question admits of no answer. The great achievement of the impressionists, however, is that their work asks such questions.

If we take "impressionism" as the generic term, the precipitating movement in literature as in painting, then "stream of consciousness" may be considered analogous to "cubism."

[6] Claude Houghton (Oldfield), *I Am Jonathan Scrivener*, 99.

173

Both are intensifications of impressionistic technique, slicing through time to achieve an impression of time that is timeless. In his *Key*, Durrell cites Gide's attack on the naturalistic school's slice-of-life approach.

"The mistake," he adds, through one of his characters, "the mistake that school made was always to cut its slice in the same direction, always lengthwise, in the direction of time. Why not cut it up and down? Or across? As for me, I don't want to cut it at all. You see what I mean. I want to put everything into my novel and not snip off my material either here or there." That would stand as a very good working credo for the stream-of-consciousness novel." (*Key*, p. 26.)

Even in their pure forms—and they usually exist together —impressionism and stream of consciousness suggest differences of emphasis, not mutual exclusion. The former employs a dual focus, as narrators like Dowell, Marlow, and Darley probe the depths of their own understanding in an attempt to reconcile it with the inpourings of an external reality that contradicts and undercuts it. We are always most concerned with felt reality, with the impression experience makes upon the interpreting consciousness, but there can never be any doubt—as *Mountolive* most clearly demonstrates—that the external realm of events not only exists but also has a coherence all its own.

Stream of consciousness is more monolithic in its fixing upon the "stream" or flow—not of time (for that is the conventional chronological approach) but "Of Time and the River," of "All-Time" or *la durée*—within the I-consciousness. In Proust, Richardson, Joyce, and Woolf, external events scarcely matter at all; indeed, there are times when we wonder whether they even exist. Although both *Stephen Hero* and *Portrait of the Artist* employ a limited third-person point of view, a significant difference between them, as Walter Allen indicates, is that while the earlier Stephen is the central character,

> he is merely one among many, all of whom are present objectively, that is, for the time they are present on the page they have as much validity as Stephen himself. . . . in the *Portrait* there is really only one character, Stephen himself, and the whole action takes place in his consciousness. Indeed, his consciousness *is* the novel; the other characters . . . are "there" only insofar as they impinge upon his mind. Whatever reality they have they have through Stephen.[7]

Plot, action, even character—all the old touchstones of technique—yield to pure flow or duration in Woolf and Richardson, to mood and suggestiveness in Katherine Mansfield, to mythos and cosmic rhythms in Joyce and Lawrence, and to a poetic expansion of sensibility in all.[8]

Durrell's best writing, especially the *Quartet* and the *Key*, reveal that he is conscious heir to the dual tradition of Ford-Conrad impressionism and Proust-Joyce stream of consciousness, and perhaps the most significant contemporary practitioner of experimentalism in the novel. It is noteworthy that Walter Allen, in what is meant as a deprecating comment on the *Quartet*, suggests its kinship with Proust and Joyce, among the earlier writers, and then with only

> Joyce Cary's *Herself Surprised–The Horse's Mouth–To Be a Pilgrim* triptych, to which Pursewarden's notion, "We live lives based on selected fictions," is not by any means foreign, and where . . . to see the action as a whole we have to hold all three novels in mind simultaneously, [and with] C. P. Snow's *Strangers and Brothers*, where there are, so to speak, simultaneous actions proceeding in the various parts of the sequence.[9]

[7] *The Modern Novel in Britain and the United States*, 4.
[8] See William York Tindall, "The Stream of Consciousness," in *Forces in Modern British Literature*, 1885–1956, 187–211.
[9] *The Modern Novel* . . . ., 285.

Yet even a cursory reading reveals that neither of these sequences demands or risks as much as the *Quartet*; nowhere, except in the Blake- and Joyce- inspired *Horse's Mouth*, do they reverberate with that richness of complexity, that sense of the old constrictions of technique and language being blasted which is the hallmark of the modern experimental novel since Conrad.

Each of the books of the *Quartet*, like the sections of *The Sound and the Fury*, is an impressionistic rendering of an overlapping complex of events. But "whereas the fourth section of *The Sound and the Fury* is intended . . . to close the book and to point to certain values, *Mountolive* merely presents itself as a public account of the public side of the *Quartet*. . . ."[10] Durrell's narrative focus, taken in order from *Justine* to *Clea*, embodies a pattern of immense significance: first, Darley's totally involved view; second, Balthazar's somewhat removed reaction to the first; third, a totally detached "objective" account; and fourth, a reconsideration several years removed from the fact. If Durrell truly intended to "get at" what in actuality happened, he has gone about it in a peculiar way; the interpretations are increasingly disinterested and certain of facts yet, simultaneously and consequently, decreasingly able to speak significantly of the events and to animate them. In fact, as truth, in the narrow sense, takes shape in the temporal sphere, it assumes an antagonism toward the initial impressionistic responses which it contradicts. But it cannot successfully negate or dislodge from us *our* impression that somehow Darley's pristine reaction is nearer to Truth, which resides more in appearance (felt reality or impression) than in reality itself. It is not Darley, then, but the superficial "facts of reality" which become the most unreliable narrator of Durrell's *Quartet* and thereby

[10] Shainheit, "Who Wrote *Mountolive*?" 17.

tend to negate only themselves. Ultimately, if we are at all sympathetically attuned, we cease trying to sort out a truth which, according to Balthazar, "is what most contradicts itself in time" (*B*, p. 216), and we recognize the irrelevance (the virtual nonexistence even) of external reality. For it turns out that, in terms of the distinction made above, Durrell has written not an impressionist novel (although the viewpoint of each of the four parts is impressionistic) but a stream-of-consciousness novel, a multifaceted, cubistic abstraction from time and circumstance. "Durrell maintains both that if there were absolute truths we could not know them and that the question of truth itself is meaningless. . . . in an Einsteinian view there is no such thing as a truth without a referential system, without a human 'knower.' "[11] And so, as a matter of course, externality fails to remain viable; and ultimately only the internal flux, only the felt reality of characters like Darley and Clea, is real.

Thus it is that Justine can play, in succession, the roles of *femme fatale* and sex goddess, of a rather bourgeois adulteress, of Mata Hari, of an Arab mendicant—without altering in essence. Darley, seeing at last the abundance of personalities the name Justine encompasses, speaks of the

valuable . . . lesson this was, both to art and to life! I had only been attesting, in all I had written, to the power of an image which I had created involuntarily by the *mere act of seeing* Justine. There was no question of true or false. Nymph? Goddess? Vampire? Yes, she was all of these, and none of them. . . . She was there forever, and she had never existed! (*C*, p. 694.)

Similarly, Pursewarden's suicide is unpremeditated and even irrelevant in *Justine*, puzzling and inexplicable in *Balthazar*, the result of a conflict between loyalty to Nessim and his duty in the Foreign Office in *Mountolive*, and in *Clea*, the

11 *Ibid.*, 23–24.

culmination of his incestuous affair with Liza. From time to time other explanations are offered—for example, Pursewarden appears to reach a dead end in art comparable to that he has already reached in love—with the effect that the "real" explanation of the act (like the "real" explanation of the Minotaur in Durrell's *Dark Labyrinth*) ceases to matter, while the act itself gains a mythopoeic significance that renders it perhaps *the* focal event of the *Quartet*. Paradoxically too, Pursewarden becomes a vital character only in death; only "after" his suicide does he speak to Darley and make a strong impression upon him. As Lawrence has indicated, there is the truth of fact and the truth of truth.

In the *Key*, Durrell writes

Under the terms of the new idea [Einstein's principle of indeterminacy] a precise knowledge of the outer world becomes an impossibility. This is because we and the outer world (subject and object) constitute a whole. If we are part of a unity we can no longer objectivize it successfully. (*Key*, p. 30.)

In the universe of relativity,

the picture which each observer makes of the world is in some degree subjective. Even if different observers all take their pictures at the same moment of time, and from the same point in space, these pictures will not be alike—unless the observers happen to be moving at the same speed. (*Key*, p. 28.)

A complex of qualifications which, Durrell might well have added, renders identical observations impossible. " 'There are only as many realities as you care to imagine' writes Pursewarden" (*B*, p. 315).

According to Durrell, "time and the ego are the two determinants of style for the twentieth century; if one grasps the ideas about them one has, I think, the key to much that has happened" (*Key*, p. 117). One would have, indeed, a key to

Durrell's own writings. Regarding time, Durrell's sense of its unevenness and discontinuity resembles Proust's. "There are mountainous, uncomfortable days, up which one takes an infinite time to pass, and days downward sloping, through which one can go at full tilt, singing as one goes."[12] Both writers recognize that velocity is a factor not of clocks and calendars but of the reacting consciousness; and Durrell cites Bergson's " 'indivisible flux of consciousness,' " *la durée*, which is made continuous only by memory and intuition (*Key*, pp. 116–17). Durrell writes:

Time has become a thick opaque medium, welded to space—no longer the quickly flowing river of the Christian hymns, moving from here to there along a marked series of stages. But an always-present yet always recurring thing. . . . In Proust and Joyce you see something like a slow-motion camera at work. Their books do not proceed along a straight line, but in a circular manner, coiling and uncoiling upon themselves, embedded in the stagnant flux and reflux of a medium which is always changing yet always the same. This attitude towards the material of the work has its effect on character also. Characters have a significance almost independent of the actions they engage in: they hang above the time-track which leads from birth to action, and from action to death: and, spreading out time in this manner, contribute a significance to everything about them. An article of clothing worn by a character becomes as significant as anything he does, or any drama he enacts. If there is any movement at all it is circular, cyclic, and significant only because it is repeated. (*Key*, p. 31.)

Durrell has come as close here as anyone to defining what the *Quartet* is doing. As in the stream-of-consciousness novel, external events lose their independent existence both because the flux is internal and because, as in Eliot's *Four Quartets*, all time is eternally present. The *Quartet* too coils and recoils upon itself, continuously circling about unending

12 Proust, *Swann's Way*, 560.

layers of meaning that will not stay still, will not stay in place, never arriving at the still point of the turning world because, except in the heraldic universe of artistic creation, it does not exist. Characters no longer take a David Copperfield journey from Time A to Time B, but often "move" perpendicular to, or askew of, or in direct opposition to, the notion of chronological time. Objectively defined reality no longer determines the essence of personality; rather, as with the principle of indeterminacy, the viewer, by the very act of observation, alters and thereby creates what he observes. Life, as Balthazar tells us, imitates art; when Pursewarden

was deeply immersed in the novel he was writing . . . he found that his ordinary life, in a distorted sort of way, was beginning to follow the curvature of his book. He explained this by saying that any concentration of the will displaces life (Archimedes' bathwater) and gives it bias in motion. Reality, he believed, was always trying to copy the imagination of man, from which it derived. (*B*, p. 286.)

And when Bergson and William James—and the novelists who employ derivative or analogous concepts—emphasize that no cross section of the flux, and certainly not the present, can be isolated, abstracted, rendered unequivocal, then man's imagination, personality itself, becomes similarly unstable and intractable. Freud and Groddeck seek explanations within and beyond the ego for the irrationality (that is, multiplicity) of personality; Lawrence seeks to break up the old notion of the stable ego; and Virginia Woolf's *Orlando* is, among other things, both fantasy and parody of personality, for the title figure "lives" three and a half centuries, both sexes, and all manner of approach to externality. Personality, the manifestation of the flux, becomes as open-ended as the stream of life itself, no-faceted rather than multifaceted. More than thirty-five years ago Joseph Warren Beach wrote:

Modern psychology does not conceive the soul as something which can be adequately rendered in terms of a single dramatic action with a highly simplified issue. . . . The soul . . . is a vast fluid, or even vaporous, mass, wide-spreading far beyond the feeble village lights of our conventional reading of character, deep-sounding into our nervous and animal organization, into childhood, heredity. It runs out and down far beyond thought, beyond memory and consciousness. It is not uniform and homogeneous, but varying and full of a great diversity of tinctures and infusions. There are all sorts of debris and driftwood floating on the surface, and huge water-soaked logs lurking far below. At the bottom is mud, and in the depths are octopuses and starfish and all kinds of undreamed-of monsters. The soul is not one identity but many identities grouped about many centers and often at war with one another, or indifferent and unaware of one another's existence.

For the most part it is no identity at all, but a kind of dreaming welter of sensations and reactions so instantaneous and spontaneous that we never become conscious of them. In many aspects the soul is not individualized as belonging to this or that ego, but is a mere jet of the vitality common to our race or sex or social group. Our consciousness, which is a small part of our soul, does not proceed logically or coherently except at certain times and for certain periods under the pressure of some urgent practical need. For the most part it follows an association of ideas so freakish—though natural—that we cannot chart the progress, running off constantly into what seem irrelevancies as judged by reference to any recognized dominant interest. The soul is supremely indifferent to past and future, near and far. It is a highly specialized faculty of our rational mind that has devised these conventions, these instruments for controlling material things and guiding conduct. Each soul is attached to an individual physical organism; but through the imagination, through the infinite nervous connections between organism and organism, souls have a large capacity for interpenetration.[13]

It is no wonder, then, that Groddeck sought the indetermin-

13 *The Twentieth Century Novel, Studies in Technique*, 332–33.

ate It, that Durrell created and animated his Alexandria, for these mental constructs, vast and complex enough, it was hoped, to emblematize the flux, afford a context, an objective correlative, for the protean nature of reality.

Durrell's Alexandria is of course greatly indebted to Groddeck, whose It concept was vague and poetic enough to encompass all of man's seemingly irrational actions and thoughts, those which cannot be causally connected with the *données* of a given character. Durrell writes:

If reality is somehow extra-causal, then a whole new vista of ideas is opened up—a territory hitherto only colonized by intuition. If the result of every experiment, of every motion of nature, is completely unforeseen and unpredictable—then everything is perpetually brand new, everything is, if you care to think of it like that, a miracle. (*Key*, p. 30.)

(That Durrell does "care to think of it like that" will be clear in a moment, when we consider the significance of the ending of the *Quartet*.) The It—or Alexandria—then becomes a kind of mortar which both fills the gaps and binds the disparate elements that the exigencies of story or emotion demand of the various characters. Thus, when Justine seems irrationally to seek the pain of unhappiness, Darley sees her action not as masochism or devious intrigue—the most obvious explanations—but as the "plotting" of the city whose true child Justine is. When her pursuit of "deeper sexual pleasures" served to warp and enfeeble Clea, Justine "was simply [being] a victim of that Oriental desire to please . . ." (*B*, p. 243). What is modern about Durrell's "modern love" is that, like Meredith's, "No villain need be," for all our villains have become victims—of that extension of themselves called, in this case, Alexandria. Our incessant psychologizing, like Arnauti's, has tended to destroy, at least in fiction, the very concept of personal, willful evil. In *The Alexandria Quartet*, it is meaningless to point a finger of blame at anyone, no matter how seemingly guilty; for whenever we are tempted to condemn, we are reminded, first, that the supposed agent was simply an instrument of the Alexandrian will and, second, that judgment of actions, motivations, consequences must be suspended in any event because the viewpoint of the judger is fragmented, a fractional aspect of a multifaceted, if not infinite, whole.

The notion of place as metaphoric protagonist—or antagonist—is implicit even in Homer's Troy, and emerges as dramatically viable in such works as Shakespeare's Roman plays and Hardy's Wessex novels. Yet Durrell's conscious borrowings from Groddeck's psychological explorations not only invests the pervading presence of his created place with a heightened anthropomorphism, but helps him to envisage characters whose internal makeup as well as actions can be viewed as products of this immediate and intense equivalent of Wordsworthian nature or Hardy's Immanent Will. One critic writes that "the 'spirit of place' is strong in Alexandria: its inhabitants are in its power, and there is no escape."[14] Although it is crucial that ultimately there *is* escape, it is true that Durrell's sense of place, the most impressive sign of his uniqueness, links up at this point with the impressionistic tradition, to which the objective correlative of place makes a significant contribution. For if characters partake of a vast mythical presence, if they appear as poetic aspects of a larger whole—simultaneously independent and interdependent— it is no wonder that they view a fragmented reality and that the vision encompasses realms of meaning broader than narrowly circumscribed facts. For the truth of facts, Alexandria substitutes the Truth of myth and poetry, of art and love.

Yet Alexandria is also a place of death—the original title

[14] John A. Weigel, *Lawrence Durrell*, 97.

of the *Quartet* was *The Book of the Dead.* Like *Panic Spring,* *The Dark Labyrinth, Bitter Lemons,* and *An Irish Faustus,* each of the books of the *Quartet* expends its climactic energy on the violence of literal or symbolic death: the duck hunt and the supposed accidental shooting of Capodistria; the Sadean carnival and the murder of Toto de Brunel; the violent death of Narouz and the great lamentation; the near death of Clea and the loss of her hand in the waters of the dead. Scobie, Melissa, Pursewarden—and, on a lower level of significance, Cohen, Fosca, Leila—all fall victim to the Alexandrian equivalent of *The Black Book's* "English Death." But the notion of death, as has already been suggested, has altered as a consequence of the new views regarding the nature of time and reality. It is no longer stable and unequivocal; unlike those in the premodernist novel, characters are no longer sharply delineated entities with discernible wills and motivations moving from birth to death along a clearly defined road called life. Durrell writes:

Time is the measure of our death-consciousness. There are other organisms, we know, which measure time by a heat-unit. They must have a different idea of death. Then there are those so-called simple cells which multiply by binary fission—they simply divide into two. You might say one dies into two, leaving no corpse behind it as a human being does. Does the caterpillar die to become a moth or would you call it being born? We do not know. In some cases birth and death would seem to be almost interchangeable terms. (*Key,* p. 4.)

And thus it is that Scobie is resurrected as El Scob; Melissa is reincarnated in Clea; and Pursewarden, despite his suicide, becomes increasingly vital throughout the *Quartet.*

By means of understanding *Clea,* one becomes aware that the *Quartet* as a whole is concerned fundamentally with regeneration and maturation, the process by which art and love become viable. The depersonalized individual, fragmented and passive, gradually attains artistic consciousness, an enlarged range of perception, even something akin to the old-fashioned sense of identity. The realization that the old way of life, the world of surface appearance, is dying or dead is the beginning of the regenerative process for the artist seeking to go beyond the impression of reality; and it leads him into the heraldic realm of art as myth making in which the *Quartet* is written and in which Clea begins to paint with a hand that is steel yet alive.

All those offered the opportunity to begin anew at the end of *Clea* have emerged from intense personal crisis; by means of Joycean epiphany, they have achieved a meaningful and viable acceptance of life as it is. The final act—affirmative flight from the confines of Alexandria—reflects the acausal "miracle" which is the re-emergence of personality within those long-dormant subjects of the city's greater presence, as well as the regeneration of the heraldic universe of artistic creation. (Rarely, until the final pages of *Clea*, do we witness any of the *Quartet*'s many artists actually creating.) In the end, these characters do not make the futile attempt to overcome Alexandria—rather, they accept it as a fact of life, one as immutable as a force of nature; but they leave it, as they would a flooded beach or a blazing forest, when they learn that they need not choose suicide. By leaving, Durrell's regenerative coda indicates, they opt for life and therefore for at least the possibility of meaning and value. These things will not come easily, and perhaps not at all. Durrell is too good a realist—in the best sense of the word—to offer pigeonholing and definitive statements regarding the future. Rather, the open-endedness of the *Quartet* (and the final Workpoints) suggests not that all has been arranged but that, the past and the present having accommodated themselves to each other, the future can begin to begin. Simply, Durrell has not affirmed that his characters have triumphed and made great successes of life, but that it is at last possible for them to attempt to do so now that they have rediscovered the old verities of art and love—with the latter a consequence of the former, since, after all, life imitates man's imagination, which has produced it. Nothing is fixed or certain—except that infinite pathways exist where, for one reason or another, there had seemed to be only dead ends. Despite what Clea says, we cannot be certain that Justine and Nessim, Mountolive and Liza, Clea and Darley, will bring peace to each other. But certainly by the novel's end we would deny neither such a possibility nor Clea's right to assert *her* impression of present and future. With "Once upon a time. . ." all avenues are open, and no visionary world of man's imagination remains artificially prevented from being created. At least for the moment—and therefore for all time, since each moment contains all time—the impeding checks have been removed; art and life are at last possible.

To a large degree, the *Key* remains pivotal—those critics who find it pretentious tend to dismiss all of Durrell's work. But their fundamental mistake, as I hope this chapter has made clear, is in confusing eclecticism and dilettantism. Durrell ranges widely in such fields as anthropology, psychology, and science, but it is only "the ninnies of critics" (Tennyson's phrase) who insistently emphasize the obvious—that Durrell is not expert in all these areas. Durrell of course claims no such thing. He writes in the Preface to the *Key*:

In order to clear the approaches to poetry, something like a brief disintoxication course is needed. The problem is, in some sort, how to persuade people to become their own contemporaries. To this end I have tried to set out, not according to rigid pattern but haphazardly, a few of the influences of the age, picking up now a theory from psychoanalysis, now a hypothesis from modern physics. Deficient in true scholarship I have been able to bring to the job only a wide if haphazard reading, and enough practice in writing poetry to have learned to distrust everybody's theories about it: my own most of all. . . . I have thought to present poetry as one dialect of a greater language comprising the whole universe of ideas—a universe perpetually shifting, changing its relations and tenses as verbs do in speech, altering its outlines. (Pp. x–xi.)

Durrell reveals himself as very much a contemporary when he acknowledges the influence upon his thinking of the great minds of modern anthropology, psychology, and science. Clearly, he does not mean that he has become learned in these disciplines but, rather, that literature, "one facet of the prism which we call culture," is inextricably interdependent with them. He adds, "I have always regarded these various fields of thought as interlocking and mutually fertilizing, and have never hesitated to borrow an idea from one to apply in another" (*Key*, p. xii). But then why should he? After all, as Erich Auerbach's *Mimesis* has so ably shown, literature is conditioned by the age of its germination. Durrell does not pretend that he has mastered Einsteinian relativity, only that he recognizes its radical influence upon poetry—and literature in general—an area in which he may indeed claim a special competence. Certainly all of us, and perhaps poets more than most, are altered by modes of thought we do not begin to comprehend and of which we may never even have heard. Durrell's notes to the *Quartet*, his many statements regarding technique, style, and subject matter, the *Key* itself —all demonstrate his intense awareness of precisely this situation; they also reveal that a mind of perhaps surprising versatility and strength is now at work.

Durrell, no towering intellect, nonetheless has read widely and well, and has made uniquely his own and his art's all that he has absorbed. His eclecticism is as far removed from dilettantism as the *Quartet* is from the black-and-white, technically conventional novels of the so-called angry young men. With sensitivity and awareness, Durrell writes:

Poetry today reflects the anxieties and triumphs visible in many different fields of knowledge, philosophy, physics and psychology. . . . a generalized knowledge of the preoccupations of the twentieth century is essential today if we wish to understand why language has been pushed so far out of shape, and used in such odd ways. The revolution in ideas, both about the outer world (physics, cosmology) and about the world of the self (the ego) is clearly reflected in the technique of modern poetry, and can help us to elucidate its shifting apprehensions and attitudes. Dylan Thomas is more easily comprehensible to the critic who has read Jung, than to one who is only anxious to trace his influences in Edith Sitwell and Hopkins. . . . (*Key*, pp. 206–207.)

And he emphasizes that "I am not suggesting that modern poetry is constructed to illustrate the quantum theory, but I do suggest that it unconsciously reproduces something like the space-time continuum in the way that it uses words and phrases: and the way in which its forms are cyclic rather than extended" (*Key*, p. 26). As a consequence of his insights, and despite his various achievements in poetry, drama, and the island books, Durrell's most enduring place, as the early part of this chapter suggests, seems most likely to be in the continuing tradition—which maintains momentum at least in part because of Durrell—of the modern experimental novel. For, like the supreme novelists of this century—Conrad, Proust, Joyce, Lawrence, Faulkner, Mann—Durrell seeks both to create art of lasting significance and to offer new modes of thought, new ways of viewing a world he too has been instrumental in bringing into being.

Appendix: Letter from Lawrence Durrell

18 Oct 1964   Provence

Dear Mr. Friedman;

Thank you for your sympathetic letter, and I wish it were possible to answer it at length; but if you saw my desk you would sympathise with me. This week I have received two huge PHD theses (unsolicited) about the quartet, the proofs of a monograph being published by an American University, plus three long articles in three different tongues and places. And each of the authors wants me to answer a list of questions. I haven't time. Nor really does the 'meaning' of a work of art, either big or small, finally reside in something that can be paraphrased. I like and respect critics and criticism, but the best always seem to have more to do with the insight of the critic and his expression of his own understanding than anything else. The work under review is only the springboard for a new creative enterprise. Would you rather have Coleridge on Shakespeare than Shakespeare? I wouldn't, but nor would I surrender Coleridge. The variety of response to the quartet has been really remarkable, but in what I read about it I seem to find that each one remakes it according to his

own needs and intuitions; and this is consoling. The poor
thing may turn out to be a decent work of art. When I was
a teacher I often had to 'correct' twenty essays on the same
subject, say a play by Racine or Shakespeare. Some were
better than others, but all were different and the difference
cut to the very bone of the mind of the observer; just as my
judgement about better and worse was conditioned by my
own needs, intuitions, desires, etc. Life, you see, is far too
short—at least now at fifty two I find it so, to go on inter-
posing a screen between the life giving objects and one's
own living. So I yawn, pour myself a glass of red wine, and
go out to cut down a dead olive tree, which is what I must do
today instead of helping you. Please forgive (I should only
be hindering after all).

[signed] Sincerely,
Lawrence Durrell

Bibliography

NOTE ON DURRELL BIBLIOGRAPHIES

To date, eight significant Durrell bibliographies have been published—the items marked with asterisks in my Bibliography IB. Of these, the Potter-Whiting *Checklist* and the Thomas "Bibliography" in Fraser are the most important; the former lists, by year and alphabetically within each year, 311 numbered items, including both original and subsequent appearances of each item. It covers the period from 1931, Durrell's first appearance in print, to June 30, 1961, and includes "On Collecting Lawrence Durrell," by Lawrence Clark Powell, an introduction by Robert A. Potter, and a Title Index. The "Bibliography" by Alan G. Thomas claims completeness for "Books, Prefaces and Translations," and also contains an extensive listing of contributions to books and periodicals, as well as of Durrell's work in other media: records, radio, television, film.

The *Checklist*, as Potter acknowledges, builds upon the Thomas-Powell "Some Uncollected Authors," the earliest Durrell bibliography of significance, and the Knerr "Regarding a Checklist," which offers valuable additions and corrections to the Thomas-Powell work. The Stone bibliography, despite its length, is less useful than these others, for it fails to include the titles of periodical publications and is less complete than the *Checklist*.

Under works by Durrell, both Unterecker and Weigel include

only major books, as well as several interviews and recordings Durrell has made; more important, they are the first to include critical works on Durrell (if we except Stone's sketchy "A Selection of Reviews of His Work," which omits authors, titles, and page references). The Weigel bibliography is especially useful, for not only is the critical section fairly extensive (29 items) and annotated (albeit sketchily) but also it includes "Background and Reference Works," which is comparable to my Bibliography III. The more recent Beebe "Checklist" of criticism includes 98 books and essays on Durrell and his writings; the Thomas bibliography is about as extensive and includes some anecdotal annotation.

The present Bibliography has three main units. I, "Durrell's Writings and Bibliographies of Writings," includes in Section A a list of all major Durrell publications, all those in any way alluded to in the text, and others consulted or considered in any way relevant; the list is not exhaustive, but may be used effectively in conjunction with the *Checklist* or the Thomas bibliography. IB lists "Correspondence, Interviews, and Bibliographies" of Durrell. II, "About Durrell and His Writing," includes in Section A all items in Weigel, Unterecker, and Beebe, plus other major discussions and even obviously minor criticism (reviews and the like) which seem of interest. Again, IIB, "Additional Works Containing Specific Mention of Durrell," and III, "Related Sources," are representative rather than exhaustive. The former offers some perspective on the kinds of contexts in which Durrell is being viewed; the latter focuses on Durrell's background: personal, familial, geographic, philosophical, critical, thematic, and the like. This last section, already extensive, could be added to almost indefinitely, but to do so would serve little purpose and would violate an already sorely tried sense of common decency and restraint.

I. DURRELL'S WRITINGS AND BIBLIOGRAPHIES OF WRITINGS

A. *Works by Lawrence Durrell*

1. Books (listed according to date of initial publication)
Quaint Fragment. London, Cecil Press, 1931.

Bibliography

Ten Poems. London, Caduceus Press, 1932. (Dedicated "For Nancy.")

Bromo Bombastes. London, Caduceus Press, 1933.

Transition: Poems. London, Caduceus Press, 1934.

Pied Piper of Lovers. London, Cassell and Co., 1935.

Panic Spring. Published under pseudonym Charles Norden. London, Faber and Faber, 1937.

La Descente du Styx. "Traduit de l'anglais par F. J. Temple et suivi du texte original." Paris, 1964. Published originally in English in *The Booster* (December, 1937–January, 1938), 14–17.

The Black Book. New York, Pocket Books, Inc., 1962 [1938].

A Private Country. London, Faber and Faber, 1943.

Prospero's Cell: A Guide to the Landscape and Manners of the Island of Corcyra. London, Faber and Faber, 1945.

Cities, Plains and People. London, Faber and Faber, 1946.

A Landmark Gone. Privately printed for Lawrence Clark Powell. Los Angeles, Reuben Pearson, 1949 [1946].

The Dark Labyrinth. New York, Dutton, 1964. (First published as *Cefalû*.) London, Editions Poetry, 1947.

Zero and Asylum in the Snow: Two Excursions into Reality. Berkeley, Circle Edition, 1947. "Asylum in the Snow" first published in *Seven*, No. 3 (Winter, 1938), 49–54; "Zero" first published in *Seven*, No. 6 (Fall, 1939).

On Seeming to Presume. London, Faber and Faber, 1948.

Deus Loci. Privately printed. Ischia, Di Mato Vito, 1950.

Sappho: A Play in Verse. London, Faber and Faber, 1950.

A Key to Modern British Poetry. Norman, University of Oklahoma Press, 1952.

Reflections on a Marine Venus: A Companion to the Landscape of Rhodes. New York, Dutton, 1962 [1953].

The Tree of Idleness. London, Faber and Faber, 1955.

Selected Poems. London, Faber and Faber, 1956.

Bitter Lemons. New York, Dutton, 1957. (Originally entitled *Bitter Lemons of Cyprus*.)

Esprit de Corps: Sketches from Diplomatic Life. New York, Dutton, 1961 [1957].

Justine. New York, Pocket Books, Inc., 1957.

White Eagles over Serbia. London, Faber and Faber, 1957.
Balthazar. New York, Pocket Books, Inc., 1958.
Stiff Upper Lip: Life among the Diplomats. New York, Dutton, 1961 [1958].
Mountolive. New York, Pocket Books, Inc., 1959.
Clea. New York, Pocket Books, Inc., 1960.
Collected Poems. New York, Dutton, 1960.
"Acté or The Prisoners of Time," *Show,* Vol. I, No. 3 (December, 1961), 45–55, 95–105. With an introduction by Lawrence Durrell. Published as a book. New York, Dutton, 1966.
The Alexandria Quartet. London, Faber and Faber, 1962.
The Poetry of Lawrence Durrell. New York, Dutton, 1962.
Beccafico. Privately printed. La Licorne, 1963.
An Irish Faustus: A Morality in Nine Scenes. New York, Dutton, 1964.
The Ikons and Other Poems. London, Faber and Faber, 1966.
Sauve qui peut. London, Faber and Faber, 1966.
Nothing is Lost, Sweet Self. Set to music by Wallace Southam. London, Turret Books, 1967.
Tunc. London, Faber and Faber, 1968.
Spirit of Place. New York, Dutton, 1969.

2. INTRODUCTIONS, PREFACES, TRANSLATIONS (listed according to date of publication)
Preface to *Climax in Crete,* by Theodore Stephanides. London, Faber and Faber, 1946.
Translation of *The King of Asine and Other Poems,* by George Seferis. Introduction by Rex Warner. London, John Lehmann, 1948.
Preface to *Below the Tide,* by Penelope Tremayne. London, Hutchinson, 1958.
Preface to *Children of the Albatross,* by Anais Nin. London, Peter Owen, 1959.
Preface to *Christ and Freud,* by Arthur Guirdham. London, Allen and Unwin, 1959.
Introduction to Dylan Thomas' "Letters to Lawrence Durrell," *Two Cities,* No. 4 (May 15, 1960), 1 ff.
Translation of *Pope Joan,* by Emmanuel Royidis. Preface by Lawrence Durrell. New York, Dutton, 1961.

Bibliography

Introduction to *The Book of the It,* by Georg Groddeck. New York, Vintage Books, 1961.

Preface to *The Passionate Epicure,* by Marcel Rouff. Translated by Claude [Durrell?]. London, Faber and Faber, 1961.

Preface to *Sexus,* by Henry Miller. New York, Grove Press, 1962.

Introduction to *The Best of Henry Miller,* ed. Lawrence Durrell. London, Melbourne, Toronto, Heinemann Ltd., 1963.

Foreword to *The Journey's Echo: Selections from Freya Stark.* London, John Murray, 1963.

Preface to *Lear's Corfu: An Anthology Drawn from the Painter's Letters.* Corfu, Corfu Travel, 1965.

Foreword to *The Mind and Art of Henry Miller,* by William A. Gordon. Baton Rouge, Louisiana State University Press, 1967.

3. OTHER CONTRIBUTIONS TO BOOKS (listed according to date of initial publication)

"Unckebunck: A Biography in Little," "Five Soliloquies Upon the Tomb," and "Themes Heraldic (Selections From)," in *Proems* (London, Fortune Press, 1938), 25–43.

"The Happy Rock," in *The Happy Rock: A Book about Henry Miller* (Berkeley, Bern Porter, 1945), 1–6. Partially reprinted in *The Griffin,* Vol. X, No. 9 (August, 1961), 4.

"Anniversary," in *T. S. Eliot: A Symposium,* ed. Richard March and Tambimuttu (London, Editions Poetry, 1948), 88.

"Delos," "This Unimportant Morning," "To Ping-Kû Asleep," and "Eight Aspects of Melissa," in *The New British Poets: An Anthology,* ed. Kenneth Rexroth (Norfolk, Conn., New Directions, 1949), 44–53.

"Studies in Genius: Henry Miller," in *Henry Miller and The Critics,* ed. George Wickes (Carbondale, Southern Illinois University Press, 1963), 86–107. Reprinted from *Horizon,* Vol. XX, No. 115 (July, 1949), 45–61.

"Sarajevo," in *New Poems: 1952,* ed. Clifford Dyment, Roy Fuller, and Montagu Slater (London, Michael Joseph, 1952), 60.

"Clouds of Glory" and "Chanel," in *New Poems: 1953,* ed. Robert Conquest, Michael Hamburger, and Howard Sergeant (London, Michael Joseph, 1953), 75–77.

"The Octagon Room, National Gallery '55," in *New Poems*: 1956, ed. Stephen Spender, Elizabeth Jennings, and Dannie Abse (London, Michael Joseph, 1956), 49–50.

"A Ballad of the Good Lord Nelson" and "Alexandria" in *Poetry Now, an Anthology*, ed. G. S. Fraser (London, Faber and Faber, 1956), 57–60

["The Shades of Dylan Thomas"], in *Dylan Thomas: The Legend and the Poet: A Collection of Biographical and Critical Essays*, ed. E. W. Tedlock (London, Heinemann Ltd., 1961), 34–40. Reprinted from *Encounter*, Vol. IX (December, 1957), 56–59.

"No Clue to Living," in *The Writer's Dilemma*, essays first published in *The Times Literary Supplement* under the heading *"Limits of Control."* With an introduction by Stephen Spender (London, Oxford University Press, 1961), 17–24. Reprinted from *TLS* (May 27, 1960), 339.

"On Henry Miller," in *Writers in Revolt: An Anthology*, ed. Richard Seaver, Terry Southern, and Alexander Trocchi (New York, Frederick Fell, Inc., 1963), 130–45.

"Three Carols," "A Ballad of the Good Lord Nelson," and "Deus Loci," in *The Penguin Book of Contemporary Verse*, ed. and introduction by Kenneth Allot (Harmondsworth, Penguin Books, 1963), 266–74.

Twenty-six poems, in *Penguin Modern Poets 1* (Harmondsworth, Penguin Books, 1963), 13–47.

4. PERIODICAL PUBLICATIONS (*listed according to date of initial publication*)

Booster-Delta, a monthly in French and English founded by the American Country Club of France and edited by Lawrence Durrell, Alfred Perlès, Henry Miller, and William Saroyan (September, 1937–Easter, 1939; seven numbers in all). Durrell's contributions include: "Sportlight" (under pseudonym Charles Norden), *Booster*, Vol. II (September, 1937), 6–11, and (October, 1937), 9–13; "A Lyric for Nikh," *Booster*, Vol. II (September, 1937), 37; "The Black Book (Coda to Nancy)," *Booster*, Vol. II (October, 1937), 19–23; "Down the Styx in an Air-Conditioned

Canoe," *Booster*, Vol. II (December, 1937–January, 1938), 14–17; "Poem to Gerald," *Delta* (April, 1938), 9; "Hamlet, Prince of China," *Delta* (Christmas, 1938), 38–45; "The Sonnet of Hamlet," *Delta* (Easter, 1939), 27–35.

"Studies in Genius VI: Groddeck," *Horizon*, Vol. XVII, No. 102 (June, 1948), 384–403.

Cyprus Review (Nicosia), ed. Lawrence Durrell (October, 1954–December, 1955).

"Liberation Celebration Machine," *Atlantic Monthly*, Vol. CC (September, 1957), 46–48.

"Letter in the Sofa," London *Evening Standard*, November 22, 1957, p. 12. Reprinted in Glasgow *Evening Citizen*, January 17, 1959.

"Cyprus: Personal Reflections," *Nation*, Vol. CLXXXVII (July 19, 1958), 23ff.

"First Steps," *3 Arts Quarterly*, No. 2 (Summer, 1960), 2–4.

"Cavafy," *3 Arts Quarterly*, No. 3 (Autumn, 1960), 20–22.

"I Wish One Could Be More Like the Birds—to Sing Unfaltering, at Peace," *Réalités* (New York), No. 120 (November, 1960), 56ff.

"Mr. Ought and Mrs. Should: An Approach to the Problems of Our Time," *Man About Town*, Vol. II, No. 1 (January, 1961), 42–45.

"The Art of Fiction: Henry Miller," *Paris Review*, No. 28 (1962), 129–59.

"Actis," *Spectator*, Vol. CCVIII (January 19, 1962), 61.

"Vidourle," *TLS*, April 22, 1965, p. 312.

"The Other T. S. Eliot," *Atlantic Monthly*, Vol. CCXV (May, 1965), 60–64.

"One Grey Greek Stone," *TLS*, July 29, 1965, p. 648.

"Prix Blondel," *TLS*, September 30, 1965, p. 877.

"Delphi," *The New Yorker*, Vol. XLI (November 6, 1965), 219.

"Salamis," *The New Yorker*, Vol. XLI (November 20, 1965), 50.

"Acropolis: 200 drachmae" and "Apteros," *Reporter*, Vol. XXXIV (March 10, 1966), 48.

"Paphos," *The New Yorker*, Vol. XLII (March 26, 1966), 57.

"The Little Affair in Paris," *Saturday Evening Post* (June 4, 1966), 64–70.

"Return to Corfu," *Holiday*, Vol. XL (October, 1966), 58–65.

"Taking the Consequences," *Mademoiselle*, Vol. LXIV (December, 1966), 131.

"Blood-count," *Encounter*, Vol. XXVIII (January, 1967), 53.

"Moonlight," *Encounter*, Vol. XXVIII (March, 1967), 19.

B. Correspondence, Interviews, Bibliographies

*Beebe, Maurice. "Criticism of Lawrence Durrell: A Selected Checklist," *Modern Fiction Studies*, Vol. XIII, No. 3 (Autumn, 1967), 417–21.

Durrell, Lawrence. "Correspondence" [letter to Tambimuttu], *Poetry* (London), Vol. I (April, 1939).

———. "Letter to Henry Miller," in Henry Miller, *The Colossus of Maroussi*. Harmondsworth, Penguin Books, 1950. First published 1941.

———. "Correspondence" [letter to Tambimuttu], *Poetry* (London-New York), No. 1 (March–April, 1956), 34–35.

———. "The Kneller Tape (Hamburg)," in Harry T. Moore (ed.), *The World of Lawrence Durrell* (Carbondale, Southern Illinois University Press, 1962), 161–68.

———. "Letters from Lawrence Durrell" (to Jean Fanchette), in Moore (ed.), *The World of Lawrence Durrell*, 222–39. Reprinted in *Two Cities* (Paris), No. 9 (Autumn, 1964), 9–22.

"Durrell Interviewed," *Books and Bookman* (London), Vol. V (February, 1960), 9.

Durrell, Lawrence, Alfred Perlès, and Henry Miller. *Art and Outrage: A Correspondence about Henry Miller*. New York, Dutton, 1961.

Durrell, Lawrence, and Henry Miller. "An Exchange of Letters," *Paris Review*, Vol. VIII, No. 29 (Winter–Spring, 1963), 133–59.

———. *A Private Correspondence*, ed. George Wickes. New York, Dutton, 1963.

"Ein Abend mit Lawrence Durrell," *Die Zeit* (Hamburg), November 27, 1959.

Holloway, David. "Why Mr. Durrell Can't Afford to Write Poetry," *News Chronicle* (London), September 9, 1959.

Bibliography

Juin, Hubert. "Paroles avec Lawrence Durrell," *Les Lettres Français*, December 17, 1959.

*Knerr, Anthony. "Regarding a Checklist of Lawrence Durrell," *Papers of the Bibliographical Society of America*, Vol. LV (1961), 142–52.

"Lawrence Durrell Vous Parle," *Réalités* (Paris), No. 178(November, 1960), 105.

Mitchell, Julian, and Gene Andrewski. "The Art of Fiction, XXIII: Lawrence Durrell," *Paris Review*, No. 22 (Autumn–Winter, 1959–60), 33–61. Reprinted in *Writers at Work: "The Paris Review" Interviews (Second Series)*, ed. George Plimpton (New York, Viking Press, 1963), 257–82.

Mullins, Edwin. "Lawrence Durrell Answers a Few Questions," *Two Cities* (Paris), Vol. I, No. 1 (April 15, 1959), 25–28. Reprinted in Moore (ed.), *The World of Lawrence Durrell*, 156–60.

*Potter, Robert A., and Brooke Whiting. *Lawrence Durrell: A Checklist*. Los Angeles, Library of the University of California at Los Angeles, 1961.

*Stone, Bernard. "Bibliography," in Alfred Perlès' *My Friend Lawrence Durrell: An Intimate Memoir on the Author of "The Alexandria Quartet"* (Middlesex, Scorpion Press, 1961), 47–62.

*Thomas, Alan G. "Recollections of a Durrell Collector" and "Bibliography," in *Lawrence Durrell: A Study*, by G. S. Fraser (London, Faber and Faber, 1968), 192–250.

*Thomas, Alan G., and Lawrence Clark Powell. "Some Uncollected Authors, XXIII: Lawrence Durrell. Recollections of a Durrell Collector," *Book Collector*, Vol. IX (1960), 56–63.

*Unterecker, John. "Bibliography," in *Lawrence Durrell*, Columbia Essays on Modern Writers, No. 6 (New York and London, Columbia University Press, 1964), 46–48.

*Weigel, John A. "Bibliography," in *Lawrence Durrell* (New York, Twayne Publishers, 1965), 163–70.

Young, Kenneth. "A Dialogue with Durrell," *Encounter*, Vol. XIII, No. 6 (December, 1959), 61–68.

II. ABOUT DURRELL AND HIS WRITING

A. *Criticism of Lawrence Durrell*

Albérès, R. M. "Lawrence Durrell ou le roman pentagonal," *Revue de Paris*, Vol. LXXII (June, 1965), 102–12.

Arban, Dominique. "Lawrence Durrell," *Preuves*, No. 109 (March, 1960), 86–94.

Arthos, John. "Lawrence Durrell's Gnosticism," *Personalist*, Vol. XLIII (1962), 360–73.

Baldanza, Frank. "Lawrence Durrell's 'Word Continuum,'" *Critique*, Vol. IV, No. 2 (Spring–Summer, 1961), 3–17.

Bergonzi, Bernard. "Stale Incense," *New York Review*, Vol. XI, No. 1 (July 11, 1968), 37–39.

Bork, Alfred M. "Durrell and Relativity," *Centennial Review of Arts and Sciences* (Michigan State), Vol. VII, No. 2 (Spring, 1963), 191–203.

Bosquet, Alain. "Lawrence Durrell ou l'azur ironique," *Nouvelle Revue Française*, Vol. XIV (June, 1966), 1116–23.

Bowen, J. "One Man's Meat: The Idea of Individual Responsibility," *TLS* (August 7, 1959), *xii–xiii*.

Brown, Sharon Lee. "*The Black Book*: A Search for Method," *Modern Fiction Studies*, Vol. XIII, No. 3 (Autumn, 1967), 319–28.

———. "Lawrence Durrell and Relativity," *DA*, Vol. XXVI (1966), 7310.

Burns, J. Christopher. "Durrell's Heraldic Universe," *Modern Fiction Studies*, Vol. XIII, No. 3 (Autumn, 1967), 375–88.

"Carnal Jigsaw," *Time*, Vol. LXXV (April 4, 1960), 94.

Carruth, Hayden. "Inversion of the Accepted," *Saturday Review*, Vol. XLIV (January 7, 1961), 28.

Cate, Curtis. "Lawrence Durrell," *Atlantic Monthly*, Vol. CCVIII (December, 1961), 63–69.

Cole, Douglas. "Faust and Anti-Faust in Modern Drama," *Drama Studies*, Vol. V (1966), 39–52.

Coleman, John. "Mr. Durrell's Dimensions," *Spectator*, Vol. CCIV (February 19, 1960), 256–57.

Corke, Hilary. "Lawrence Durrell," *Literary Half-Yearly*, Vol. II (January, 1961), 43–49.

———. "Mr. Durrell and Brother Criticus," *Encounter* Vol. XIV (May, 1960), 65–70.

Cortland, Peter. "Durrell's Sentimentalism," *English Record*, Vol. XIV, No. 4 (April, 1964), 15–19.

Crowder, Richard. "Durrell, *Libido*, and *Eros*," *Ball State Teachers College Forum*, Vol. III, No. 2 (Winter, 1962–63), 34–39.

Dare, Captain H. "The Quest for Durrell's Scobie," *Modern Fiction Studies*, Vol. X, No. 4 (Winter, 1964–65), 379–83.

DeMott, Benjamin. "Grading the Emanglons," *Hudson Review*, Vol. XIII (Autumn, 1960), 457–64.

Dennis, Nigel. "New Four-Star King of Novelists," *Life*, Vol. XLIX (November 21, 1960), 96–109.

Enright, D. J. "Alexandrian Night's Entertainment: Lawrence Durrell's *Quartet*," *International Literary Annual* (London), Vol. III (1961), 30–39.

Eskin, Stanley G. "Durrell's Themes in *The Alexandria Quartet*," *Texas Quarterly*, Vol. V, No. 4 (Winter, 1962), 43–60.

Flint, R. W. "A Major Novelist," *Commentary*, Vol. XXVII (April, 1959), 353–56.

Fraiberg, Louis. "Durrell's Dissonant Quartet," in Charles Shapiro (ed.), *Contemporary British Novelists* (Carbondale, Southern Illinois University Press, 1965), 16–35.

Fraser, G. S. *Lawrence Durrell: A Study*. London, Faber and Faber, 1968.

Friar, Kimon. "In the Shadow of the Parthenon," *Saturday Review*, Vol. XLIII (November 12, 1960), 35.

Friedman, Alan Warren. "A 'Key' to Lawrence Durrell," *Wisconsin Studies in Contemporary Literature*, Vol. VIII, No. 1 (Winter, 1967), 31–42.

———. "Place and Durrell's Island Books," *Modern Fiction Studies*, Vol. XIII, No. 3 (Autumn, 1967), 329–41.

Gaster, B. "Lawrence Durrell," *Contemporary Review*, Vol. CCV (July, 1964), 375–79.

Gerard, Albert. "Durrell: Un grand talent de basse époque," *Revue générale belge* (October, 1962), 15–29.

Glicksberg, Charles I. "*The Alexandria Quartet*," in *The Self in*

Modern Literature (University Park, Pennsylvania State University Press, 1963), 89–94.

————. "The Fictional World of Lawrence Durrell," *Bucknell Review*, Vol. XI, No. 2 (March, 1963), 118–33.

Godshalk, William Leigh. "Some Sources of Durrell's *Alexandria Quartet*," *Modern Fiction Studies*, Vol. XIII, No. 3 (Autumn, 1967), 361–74.

Goldberg, Gerald Jay. "The Search for the Artist in Some Recent British Fiction," *South Atlantic Quarterly*, Vol. LXII, No. 3 (Summer, 1963), 387–401.

Gordon, Ambrose, Jr. "Time, Space and Eros: *The Alexandria Quartet* Rehearsed," in William O. S. Sutherland (ed.), *Six Contemporary Novels: Six Introductory Essays in Modern Fiction* (Austin, University of Texas Press, 1962), 6–21.

Gossman, Ann. "Some Characters in Search of a Mirror," *Critique*, Vol. VIII, No. 3 (Spring–Summer, 1966), 79–84.

Hagopian, John V. "Lawrence Durrell: 'The Halcyon Summer,' " in John V. Hagopian and Martin Dolch (eds.), *Insight II: Analyses of Modern British Literature* (Frankfurt, Hirschgraben-Verlag, 1965), 94–104.

————. "The Resolution of *The Alexandria Quartet*," *Critique*, Vol. VII, No. 1 (Spring, 1964), 97–106.

Hamard, Jean-Paul. "L'espace et le temps dans les romans de Lawrence Durrell," *Critique* (Paris), No. 156 (May, 1960), 387–413.

————. "Lawrence Durrell, rénovateur assagi," *Critique* (Paris), No. 163 (December, 1960), 1025–33.

Hawkins, Joanna Lynn. "A Study of the Relationship of Point of View to the Structure of *The Alexandria Quartet*," DA, Vol. XXVI (1965), 3338–39.

Hawkins, Tiger Tim. *Eve: The Common Muse of Henry Miller and Lawrence Durrell*. San Francisco, Ahab Press, 1963.

Highet, Gilbert. "The Alexandrians of Lawrence Durrell," *Horizon*, Vol. II (March, 1960), 113–18.

Howard, Ron. "The Plays of Lawrence Durrell," *Balcony: The Sydney Review* (University of Sydney), No. 5 (1966), 43–47.

Bibliography

Howarth, Herbert. "Lawrence Durrell and Some Early Masters," *Books Abroad,* Vol. XXXVII, No. 1 (Winter, 1963), 5–11.

———. "A Segment of Durrell's *Quartet,*" *University of Toronto Quarterly,* Vol. XXXII (April, 1963), 282–93.

Howlett, J. "Balthazar of Lawrence Durrell," *Les lettres nouvelles,* Vol. II (1959), 19–20.

Hutchens, Eleanor H. "The Heraldic Universe in *The Alexandria Quartet,*" *College English,* Vol. XXIV (October, 1962), 56–61.

Karl, Frederick R. "Lawrence Durrell: Physical and Metaphysical Love," *The Contemporary English Novel* (New York, Farrar, Straus and Cudahy, 1962), 40–61.

Kazin, Alfred. "Lawrence Durrell's Rosy-finger'd Egypt," *Contemporaries* (Boston, Little, Brown, 1959), 199–202.

Kelly, John C. "Lawrence Durrell: *The Alexandria Quartet,*" *Studies* (Irish Quarterly Review), Vol. LII (Spring, 1963), 52–68.

———. "Lawrence Durrell's Style," *Studies* (Irish Quarterly Review), Vol. LII (Summer, 1963), 199–204.

Kermode, Frank. "Durrell and Others," *Puzzles and Epiphanies* (New York, Chilmark Press, 1962), 214–27.

———. "Fourth Dimension," *Review of English Literature,* Vol. I, No. 2 (April, 1960), 73–77.

Kruppa, Joseph E. "Durrell's *Alexandria Quartet* and the 'Implosion' of the Modern Consciousness," *Modern Fiction Studies,* Vol. XIII, No. 3 (Autumn, 1967), 401–16.

Lemon, Lee T. "*The Alexandria Quartet*: Form and Fiction," *Wisconsin Studies in Contemporary Literature,* Vol. IV, No. 3 (Autumn, 1963), 327–38.

Leslie, Ann. "This Infuriating Man—Lawrence Durrell," *Irish Digest,* Vol. LXXXII, No. 4 (February, 1965), 67–70.

Levidova, I. "A 'Four-Decker' in Stagnant Waters," *Anglo-Soviet Journal,* Vol. XXIII (Summer, 1962), 39–41.

Levitt, Morton P. "Art and Correspondences: Durrell, Miller, and *The Alexandria Quartet,*" *Modern Fiction Studies,* Vol. XIII, No. 3 (Autumn, 1967), 299–318.

Littlejohn, David. "Lawrence Durrell: The Novelist as Entertainer," *Motive,* Vol. XXIII (November, 1962), 14–16.

Lawrence Durrell and *The Alexandria Quartet*

——. "The Permanence of Durrell," *Colorado Quarterly*, Vol. XIV, No. 1 (Summer, 1965), 63–71.

Lund, Mary Graham. "The Alexandrian Projection," *Antioch Review*, Vol. XXI, No. 2 (Summer, 1961), 193–204.

——. "The Big Rock Crystal Mountain," *Four Quarters*, Vol. XI, No. 4 (May, 1962), 15–18.

——. "Durrell: Soft Focus on Crime," *Prairie Schooner*, Vol. XXXV, No. 4 (Winter, 1961–62), 339–44.

——. "Eight Aspects of Melissa," *Forum*, Vol. III, No. 9 (1962), 18–22.

——. "Submerge for Reality: The New Novel Form of Lawrence Durrell," *Southwest Review*, Vol. XLIV, No. 3 (Summer, 1959), 229–35.

Mandel, S. "In Search of the Senses," *Saturday Review*, Vol. XL (September 21, 1957), 39–40.

Manzalaoui, Mahmoud. "Curate's Egg; An Alexandrian Opinion of Durrell's *Quartet*," *Etudes Anglaises*, Vol. XV (1962), 248–60.

Merrick, G. "Will Lawrence Durrell Spoil America?" *New Republic*, Vol. CXXXVIII (May 26, 1958), 20–21.

Michot, Paulette. "Lawrence Durrell's *Alexandria Quartet*," *Revue des langues vivantes*, Vol. XXVI, No. 5 (1960), 361–67.

Miller, Henry. "A Boost for *The Black Book*," *Booster*, Vol. II (October, 1937), 18.

Moore, Harry T. (ed.). *The World of Lawrence Durrell*. Carbondale, Southern Illinois University Press, 1962. Includes Richard Aldington: "A Note on Lawrence Durrell"; Carl Bode: "A Guide to Alexandria"; Victor Brombert: "Lawrence Durrell and His French Reputation"; Hayden Carruth: "Nougat for the Old Bitch"; W. D. G. Cox: "Another Letter to Lawrence Durrell"; Bonamy Dobrée: "Durrell's Alexandrian Series"; George P. Elliott: "The Other Side of the Story"; Martin Green: "Lawrence Durrell: A Minority Report"; "The Kneller Tape (Hamburg)"; "Lawrence Durrell Answers a Few Questions"; "'Letters from Lawrence Durrell (to Jean Fanchette)'"; Lander MacClintock: "Durrell's Plays"; Cecily Mackworth:

"Lawrence Durrell and the New Romanticism"; Henry Miller: "The Durrell of *The Black Book* Days"; Harry T. Moore: "Durrell's *Black Book*"; Derek Stanford: "Lawrence Durrell: An Early View of His Poetry"; George Steiner: "Lawrence Durrell: The Baroque Novel"; Gerald Sykes: "One Vote for the Sun"; Lionel Trilling: "The *Quartet*: Two Reviews"; G. E. Wotton: "A Letter to Lawrence Durrell."

Morcos, Mona Louis. "Elements of the Autobiographical in *The Alexandria Quartet*," *Modern Fiction Studies*, Vol. XIII, No. 3 (Autumn, 1967), 343–59.

Morgan, Thomas B. "The Autumnal Arrival of Lawrence Durrell," *Esquire* (September, 1960), 108–11.

O'Brien, R. A. "Time, Space, and Language in Lawrence Durrell," *Waterloo Review*, Vol. VI (Winter, 1961), 16–24.

"On the Volcano," *Time*, Vol. LXXVI (July 18, 1960), 78ff.

Perlès, Alfred. *My Friend Lawrence Durrell; An Intimate Memoir on the Author of "The Alexandria Quartet."* Middlesex, Scorpion Press, 1961.

"Portrait," *Time*, Vol. LXXII (August 25, 1958), 80.

Proser, Matthew N. "Darley's Dilemma: The Problem of Structure in Durrell's *Alexandria Quartet*," *Critique*, Vol. IV, No. 2 (Spring–Summer, 1961), 18–28.

Read, Phyllis J. "The Illusion of Personality: Cyclical Time in Durrell's *Alexandria Quartet*," *Modern Fiction Studies*, Vol. XIII, No. 3 (Autumn, 1967), 389–99.

Rexroth, Kenneth. "The Artifice of Convincing Immodesty," *Griffin*, Vol. IX, No. 9 (September, 1960), 3–9.

———. "The Footsteps of Horace," *Nation*, Vol. CLXXXIV (May 18, 1957), 444.

———. "Lawrence Durrell," in *Assays* (New York, New Directions, 1962), 118–30.

———. "What Is Wrong with Durrell?" *Nation*, Vol. CXC (June 4, 1960), 493–94.

Robinson, W. R. "Intellect and Imagination in *The Alexandria Quartet*," *Shenandoah*, Vol. XVIII, No. 4 (Summer, 1967), 55–68.

Ross, Alan. "The Poetry of Mnemotechny," in Tambimuttu (ed.),

Poetry London, X (London, Nicholson and Watson, 1944), 236–38.

Scholes, Robert. "Return to Alexandria: Lawrence Durrell and Western Narrative Tradition," *Virginia Quarterly Review*, Vol. XL, No. 3 (Summer, 1964), 411–20. Reprinted (in slightly altered form) in Robert Scholes, *The Fabulators* (New York, Oxford University Press, 1967), 17–31.

Shainheit, Howard L. "Who Wrote *Mountolive?* An Investigation of the Relativity-aesthetic of Lawrence Durrell's *The Alexandria Quartet*," unpublished honors thesis, University of Massachusetts, May, 1963.

Silverstein, Norman, and Arthur L. Lewis. "Durrell's 'Song for Zarathustra,'" *Explicator*, Vol. XXI (1962), Item 10.

Stock, R. "Loneliness in the Isles of Greece," *Poetry*, Vol. XCI (March, 1958), 396–99.

Sullivan, Nancy. "Lawrence Durrell's Epitaph for the Novel," *Personalist*, Vol. XLIV (1963), 79–88.

Sykes, Gerald. "Electra Brought Him Black Roses," *Reporter*, Vol. XVIII (April 3, 1958), 46–47.

"Theater Abroad: Goethe Go Home," *Time*, Vol. LXXXIII (January 3, 1964), 56.

"Theater Abroad: Marine Justine," *Time*, Vol. LXXVIII (September 8, 1964), 74ff.

Two Cities (Paris), Vol. I, No. 1 (April 15, 1959), 3–28. Contains *Hommage à Durrell*, which includes: Richard Aldington: "A Note on Lawrence Durrell"; "Durrell Answers a Few Questions"; Henry Miller: "The Durrell of *The Black Book* Days"; Alfred Perlès: "Enter Jupiter Jr."; Edwin Mullins: "On Mountolive"; Frédéric J. Temple, "*Construire un Mur de Pierre Sèche*."

Unterecker, John. *Lawrence Durrell*. Columbia Essays on Modern Writers, No. 6. New York and London, Columbia University Press, 1964.

———. "The Protean World of Lawrence Durrell," in Richard Kostelanetz (ed.), *On Contemporary Literature* (New York, Avon, 1964), 322–29.

Vallette, J. "*Justine, Balthazar*, et Lawrence Durrell," *Mercure de France*, Vol. CCCXXXIV (November, 1958), 536–40.

Bibliography

Weatherhead, A. K. "Romantic Anachronism in *The Alexandria Quartet*," *Modern Fiction Studies*, Vol. XI, No. 2 (Summer, 1964), 128–36.

Weigel, John A. *Lawrence Durrell*. New York, Twayne Publishers, Inc., 1965.

Weyergans, Franz. "*Clea* de Lawrence Durrell," *Revue Nouvelle* (July, 1960), 94–98.

B. *Selected Additional Works Containing Specific Mention of Lawrence Durrell*

Allen, Walter. *The Modern Novel in Britain and the United States*. New York, Dutton, 1965.

Bien, Peter. *Constantine Cavafy*. Columbia Essays on Modern Writers, No. 5. New York and London, Columbia University Press, 1964.

Booth, Wayne C. *The Rhetoric of Fiction*. Chicago and London, University of Chicago Press, 1961.

Burgess, Anthony. *The Novel Now: A Guide to Contemporary Fiction*. New York, Norton, 1968.

Church, Margaret. *Time and Reality: Studies in Contemporary Fiction*. Chapel Hill, University of North Carolina Press, 1963.

Currey, R. N. *Poets of the 1939–45 War*. London, Longmans, Green, 1960.

Daiches, David. *The Present Age in British Literature*. Bloomington, Indiana University Press, 1958.

Durrell, Gerald. *Birds, Beasts, and Relatives*. New York, Viking Press, 1969.

———. *My Family and Other Animals*. New York, Viking Press, 1963.

Fiedler, Leslie A. *Waiting for the End: The Crisis in American Culture and a Portrait of 20th Century American Literature*. New York, Dell Publishing Co., 1964.

Fitzgibbon, Constantine. *The Life of Dylan Thomas*. Boston, Little, Brown, 1965.

Ford, George H. *Double Measure: A Study of the Novels and Stories of D. H. Lawrence*. New York, Holt, Rinehart and Winston, 1965.

Fraser, G. S. *The Modern Writer and His World*. London, Derek Verschoyle, Ltd., 1953.

———. "Recent Verse: London and Cairo," in Tambimuttu (ed.), *Poetry London*, X (London, Nicholson and Watson, 1944), 215–19.

Friedman, Alan. *The Turn of the Novel*. New York, Oxford University Press, 1966.

Friedman, Alan Warren. "The Pitching of Love's Mansion in the *Tropics* of Henry Miller," in Thomas Whitbread (ed.), *Seven Contemporary Authors* (Austin and London, University of Texas Press, 1966), 23–48.

Gindin, J. J. "Some Current Fads," in *Postwar British Fiction: New Accents and Attitudes* (Berkeley and Los Angeles, University of California Press, 1962), 207–25.

Glicksberg, Charles Irving. *Literature and Religion: A Study in Conflict*. Dallas, Southern Methodist University Press, 1960.

———. *The Tragic Vision in Twentieth-Century Literature*. Carbondale, Southern Illinois University Press, 1963.

Gordon, Ambrose, Jr. *The Invisible Tent: The War Novels of Ford Madox Ford*. Austin, University of Texas Press, 1964.

Hartt, Julian N. *The Lost Image of Man*. Baton Rouge, Louisiana State University Press, 1963.

Hassan, Ihab. *The Literature of Silence: Henry Miller and Samuel Beckett*. New York, Knopf, 1967.

Littlejohn, David. "The Anti-Realists," *Daedalus*, Vol. XCII, No. 2 (Spring, 1963), 250–64.

Miller, Henry. *The Books in My Life*. London, Peter Owen, Ltd., 1952.

———. *The Cosmological Eye*. Norfolk, Conn., New Directions, 1939.

———. *Remember to Remember*. Norfolk, Conn., New Directions, 1947.

Miller, Karl. "Poet's Novels," *Listener*, Vol. LXI (1959), 1099–1100.

Millgate, Michael. "Contemporary English Fiction: Some Observations," *Venture*, Vol. II, No. 3/4 (September–December, 1961), 214–20.

Moore, Harry T. "Richard Aldington in His Last Years," *Texas Quarterly*, Vol. VI, No. 3 (Autumn, 1963), 60–74.

Perlès, Alfred. *My Friend Henry Miller: An Intimate Biography.* New York, John Day Co., 1956.

Powell, Lawrence Clark. *Books in My Baggage.* Cleveland and New York, World Publishing Co., 1960.

Pritchett, V. S. *The Working Novelist.* London, Chatto and Windus, 1965.

Rippier, Joseph S. *Some Postwar British Novelists.* Frankfurt, Verlag Moritz Diesterweg, 1965.

Scott-James, F. A. *Fifty Years of English Literature: 1900–1950.* London, Longmans, Green, 1951.

Stevenson, Lionel. *Yesterday and After.* New York, Barnes and Noble, 1968.

Tindall, William York. *Forces in Modern British Literature, 1885–1946.* New York, Knopf, 1947.

———. *Forces in Modern British Literature, 1885–1956.* New York, Random House, 1956.

Wakin, Edward. *A Lonely Minority: The Modern Story of Egypt's Copts.* New York, William Morrow, 1963.

West, Paul. *The Modern Novel.* New York, Hillary House, 1965.

Wickes, George. *Masters of Modern British Fiction.* New York, Macmillan Co., 1963.

Widmer, Kingsley. *Henry Miller.* New York, Twayne Publishers, Inc., 1963.

III. RELATED SOURCES

Abrams, M. H. *The Mirror and The Lamp: Romantic Theory and The Critical Tradition.* New York, W. W. Norton, 1958.

Allen, Walter. *The English Novel.* Harmondsworth, Penguin Books, 1954.

Auerbach, Erich. *Mimesis: The Representation of Reality in Western Literature.* New York, Anchor Books, 1957.

Beach, Joseph Warren. *The Twentieth Century Novel: Studies in Technique.* New York and London, The Century Co., 1932.

Beauvoir, Simone de. *Must We Burn de Sade?* London, Peter Nevill, 1953.

Beckett, Samuel. *Proust.* New York, Grove Press, 1931.

Bentley, Eric. "Yeats as a Playwright," *Kenyon Review*, Vol. X, No. 2 (Spring, 1948), 196–208. Reprinted in James Hall and Martin Steinmann (eds.), *The Permanence of Yeats* (New York, Collier Books, 1950), 213–23.

Bergson, Henri. *Time and Free Will*. New York, Harper Torchbooks, 1960.

Bowra, C. M. *The Creative Experiment*. London, Macmillan, 1949.

Brooks, Cleanth. *The Well Wrought Urn: Studies in the Structure of Poetry*. New York, Harvest Books, 1947.

Brown, Ivor. "Sappho of Lesbos," in *Dark Ladies* (London, Collins, 1957), 91–159.

Browning, Robert. *The Ring and The Book*. New York, W. W. Norton, 1961.

Cassell, Richard A. *Ford Madox Ford, A Study of His Novels*. Baltimore, Johns Hopkins University Press, 1961.

Cavafy, C. P. *The Complete Poems of Cavafy*, translated by Rae Dalven. New York, Harcourt, Brace and World, Inc., 1961.

———. *The Poems of C. P. Cavafy*, translated by John Mavrogordato. London, Hogarth Press, 1951.

Conrad, Joseph. *Lord Jim*. New York, Holt, Rinehart and Winston, 1963.

Douglas, Norman. *South Wind*. New York, Modern Library, 1925.

Durrell, Gerald. *The Bafut Beagles*. New York, Ballantine, 1954.

———. *The Drunken Forest*. Harmondsworth, Penguin Books, 1956.

———. *Encounters with Animals*. Harmondsworth, Penguin Books, 1964.

———. *Menagerie Manor*. London, Rupert Hart-Davis, 1964.

———. *The Overloaded Ark*. New York, Viking Press, 1953.

———. *Rosy is My Relative*. London, Collins, 1968.

———. *Three Singles to Adventure*. Harmondsworth, Penguin Books, 1964.

———. *Two in the Bush*. New York, Viking Press, 1966.

———. *The Whispering Land*. Harmondsworth, Penguin Books, 1964.

————. *A Zoo in My Luggage.* Harmondsworth, Penguin Books, 1964.

Edel, Leon. *The Psychological Novel, 1900–1950.* London, Rupert Hart-Davis, 1961.

Einstein, Albert. *Essays in Science.* New York, Philosophical Library, 1934.

————. *Ideas and Opinions.* New York, Crown Publishers, 1954.

Eliot, T. S. *Four Quartets.* London, Faber and Faber, 1959.

Ford, Ford Madox. *The Good Soldier.* New York, Vintage Books, 1955.

————. *Joseph Conrad: A Personal Remembrance.* London, Duckworth and Co., 1924.

————. *The March of Literature from Confucius' Day to Our Own.* New York, Dial Press, 1938.

Forster, E. M. *Alexandria: A History and A Guide.* New York, Anchor Books, 1961.

————. *Aspects of the Novel.* Harmondsworth, Penguin Books, 1964.

————. *Pharos and Pharillon.* New York, Knopf, 1962.

————. "The Poetry of C. P. Cavafy," *Athene: The American Magazine of Hellenic Thought,* Vol. IV (June, 1943), 52–53, 69.

Freud, Sigmund. *The Interpretation of Dreams.* New York, Modern Library, 1950.

Frye, Northrop. *Anatomy Of Criticism.* New York, Atheneum, 1967.

Giedion, Siegfried. *Space, Time, and Architecture.* Cambridge, Mass., Harvard University Press, 1954.

Gorer, Geoffrey. *The Marquis de Sade: A Short Account of His Life and Work.* New York, Peter Owen, 1934.

Guerard, Albert J. *Conrad the Novelist.* Cambridge, Mass., Harvard University Press, 1958.

Hall, Manly P. *Questions and Answers: Fundamentals of the Occult Sciences.* Los Angeles, Philosophers Press, 1937.

Holmes, Elizabeth. *Henry Vaughan and the Hermetic Philosophy.* Oxford, Blackwell, 1932.

Houghton (Oldfield), Claude. *I Am Jonathan Scrivener.* New York, Simon and Schuster, 1930.

Humphrey, Robert. *Stream of Consciousness in the Modern Novel*. Berkeley and Los Angeles, University of California Press, 1955.

James, Henry. *The Art of the Novel: Critical Prefaces*. New York, Scribner's, 1962.

James, William. *The Varieties of Religious Experience*. Garden City, N. Y., Doubleday, n.d.

Keeley, Edmund, and Philip Sherrard. *Six Poets of Modern Greece*. London, Thames and Hudson, 1960.

Kumar, Shiv K. *Bergson and the Stream of Consciousness Novel*. New York, New York University Press, 1963.

Leavis, F. R. *New Bearings in English Poetry*. Ann Arbor, University of Michigan Press, 1960.

Lely, Gilbert. *The Marquis de Sade: A Biography*. New York, Grove Press, 1962.

Lewis, Wyndham. *Time and Western Man*. Boston, Beacon Press, 1957.

Lid, Richard W. *Ford Maddox Ford: The Essence of His Art*. Berkeley and Los Angeles, University of California Press, 1964.

Lind, Frank. *How to Understand the Tarot*. London, Bazaar, Exchange and Mart, Ltd., n.d.

Lubbock, Percy. *The Craft of Fiction*. New York, Compass Books, 1962.

Maurois, André. *Proust: A Biography*. New York, Meridian Books, 1960.

Mendilow, A. A. *Time and the Novel*. London, Peter Nevill, 1952.

Meyerhoff, Hans. *Time in Literature*. Berkeley and Los Angeles, University of California Press, 1960.

Miller, Henry. *Black Spring*. New York, Grove Press, 1963.

———. *A Devil in Paradise*. New York, Signet Books, 1956.

———. *The Intimate Henry Miller*. New York, Signet Books, 1959.

———. *Nexus*. New York, Grove Press, 1965.

———. *Plexus*. New York, Grove Press, 1965.

———. *Sexus*. New York, Grove Press, 1962.

———. *Sunday after the War*. Norfolk, Conn., New Directions, 1944.

Bibliography

————. *Tropic of Cancer*. Paris, Obelisk Press, 1934.

————. *Tropic of Capricorn*. New York, Grove Press, 1961.

Nelson, Benjamin (ed.). *Freud and the Twentieth Century*. Cleveland and New York, Meridian Books, 1963.

O'Connor, William Van. *Forms of Modern Fiction: Essays Collected in Honor of Joseph Warren Beach*. Minneapolis, University of Minnesota Press, 1948.

Ouspensky, P. D. *The Symbolism of the Tarot: Philosophy of Occultism in Pictures and Numbers*. St. Petersburg, Trood Printing and Publishing Co., 1913.

Plato. *The Myths of Plato*. Edited by G. R. Levy. Carbondale, Southern Illinois University Press, 1960.

Poulet, Georges. *Studies in Human Time*. New York, Harper, 1959.

Pratt, William, ed. *The Imagist Poem*. New York, Dutton, 1963.

Praz, Mario. *The Romantic Agony*. New York, Meridian Books, 1956.

Proust, Marcel. *Swann's Way*. New York, Modern Library, 1956.

Rickword, Edgell. "Notes for a Study of Sade," *Calendar of Modern Letters*, Vol. II, No. 12 (February, 1926), 421–31.

Russell, Bertrand. *The ABC of Relativity*. New York, Mentor Books, 1959.

Sade, Marquis de. *Cahiers personnels (1803–1804)*. Paris, 1953.

————. *Justine or The Misfortunes of Virtue*. Paris, Editions du Courrier Graphique, n.d.

————. *Selected Writings of de Sade*. New York, Lancer Books, 1953.

Suzuki, Daisetz T. *The Essentials of Zen Buddhism*. New York, Dutton, 1962.

Waite, Arthur Edward. *The Pictorial Key to the Tarot*. New Hyde Park, N.Y., University Books, 1959.

Wilson, Edmund. *Axel's Castle: A Study of the Imaginative Literature of 1870–1930*. London, Fontana Library, 1961.

————. "The Vogue of the Marquis de Sade," in *Eight Essays* (New York, Doubleday, 1954), 167–80.

Worrell, William H. *A Short Account of the Copts*. Ann Arbor, University of Michigan Press, 1945.

Young, Kenneth. *Ford Madox Ford*. London, Longmans, Green, 1956.

Index

Index

Archimedes: 180
Athens: *see under* Greece
Auden, W. H.: 26
Auerbach, Erich (*Mimesis*): 187
Augustus: 34

Bacchus: 9–10
Balthazar: 72, 85, 87–110, 131, 136, 177–78, 182; love in, 75, 89; and *Justine*, 87–91, 97, 102, 105–107, 110; climax of, 89, 102, 105–107, 140n., 184; and *Justine* vs. *Mountolive*, 111–12, 129–30, 132, 134–35, 163; narrative voice in, 129–30, 176; and *Justine* and *Mountolive* vs. *Clea*, 136–37; "Note" to, 141, 161; *see also Alexandria Quartet, Clea, Justine, and Mountolive*
Beach, Joseph Warren: 180–81
Bergson, Henri: 174, 179, 180
Bitter Lemons: 48, 51–61, 184; "Bitter Lemons" (poem), 52; narrative technique in, 52; Enosis in, 53–56
———, characters in: Joanides, 55; Paul, 55; Panos, 58–59
Black Book, The: 3, 4–6, 50, 83, 184; "English Death" in, 4–5, 66, 184; climax of, 40
———, characters in: Lawrence Lucifer, 4, 5; Horace "Death" Gregory, 5, 66
Blake, William: 125, 176
Bode, Carl: 166
Booth, Wayne C., *The Rhetoric of Fiction*: 119, 128n.
Botticelli, Sandro: 158
Browning, Robert, *The Ring and the Book*: 104, 169–70
Byzantium: 8

Cairo: *see under* Egypt
Carroll, Lewis, *Alice's Adventures in Wonderland*: 93
Cary, Joyce: 175–76
Cavafy, Constantine P.: 71

Cefalû: *see Dark Labyrinth*
Cities, Plains and People (poems): 11, 18–25; "Pressmarked Urgent," 18; "Two Poems in Basic English," 18–19; "Delos," 19; "The Pilot," 19; "This Unimportant Morning," 19; "Water Music," 19; "Cities, Plains and People," 20–21; "Six Landscape Painters of Greece," 21–22; "Eight Aspects of Melissa," 22–24; "Conon in Alexandria," 24–25
Clea: 81, 82, 85, 97, 136–65, 177–78; as sequel, 64; affirmation in, 82, 121, 164–65, 184–86; ending of, 84, 113, 141–43, 160–65, 184–86; vs. *Justine, Balthazar*, and *Mountolive*, 136–37; role in *Quartet* of, 136–37, 184–86; death in, 137–38, 151; uses of the past in, 137–39; regeneration in, 138–53, 156–58, 164, 184–85; symbolism in, 142, 148–49; narrative voice in, 176; *see also Alexandria Quartet, Balthazar, Justine, and Mountolive*
Cleopatra: 36
Conrad, Joseph: 171, 175–76, 188; *Lord Jim*, 104, 111, 129, 172–74; *Youth*, 170
Copts: 114, 116, 119, 123, 132, 147
Corfu: *see under* Greece
Crete: *see under* Greece
Cyprus: 48, 51–61 *passim*

Dark Labyrinth, The (Cefalû): 3–4, 50, 178, 184; climax of, 40
Darwin, Charles Robert: 167
DeMott, Benjamin: 133
De Sade, D.A.F.: *see* Sade
Descartes, René: 70
"Deus Loci" (in *The Tree of Idleness*): 8, 9–11
Dickens, Charles, *Great Expectations*: 128
Dobrée, Bonamy: 70, 74
Dorset: *see under* England

217

Index

Lawrence Durrell and *The Alexandria Quartet*

Index

Sterne, Laurence, *Tristram Shandy*: 107

Stevens, Wallace: 23

Tennyson, Alfred: 186; "Ulysses," 167

"Themes Heraldic" (in *Proems*): 8–9

Thomas, Dylan: 188

Tibet: 6, 20

Trilling, Lionel: 76, 143

Tunc: 11, 22, 122n.; climax of, 40

Unterecker, John: 39–40

Vergil, *The Aeneid*: 40

White Eagles over Serbia: 3

Wilson, Edmund: 170

Woolf, Virginia: 170, 174–75; *Orlando*, 180

Wordsworth, William: 183

Yeats, William Butler: 8

Yugoslavia: 3, 52

Zero and Asylum in the Snow: 6–7, 66

The paper on which this book is printed bears the watermark of the University of Oklahoma Press and has an effective life of at least three hundred years.